SHOE INNOVATIONS
A VISUAL CELEBRATION OF 60 STYLES

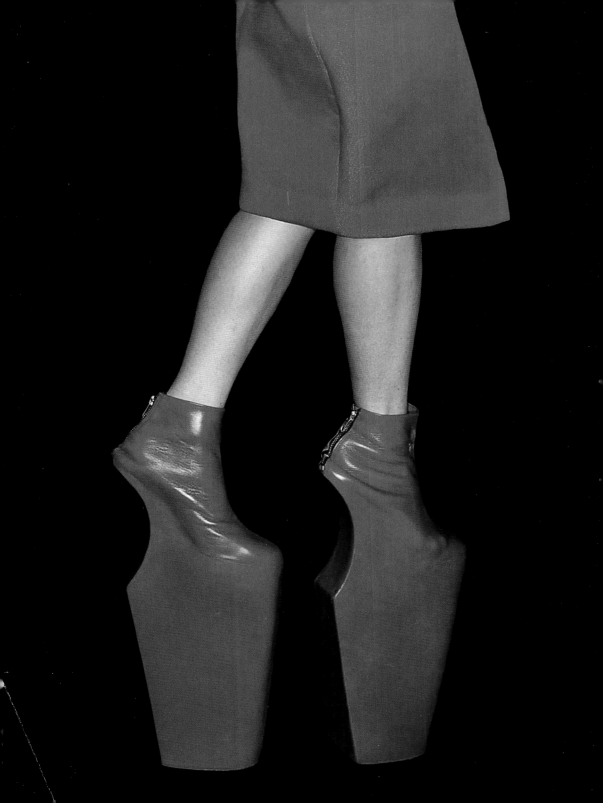

SHOE INNOVATIONS
A VISUAL CELEBRATION OF 60 STYLES

Caroline Cox

FIREFLY BOOKS

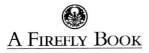

A FIREFLY BOOK

Published by Firefly Books Ltd. 2012

First printing

Publisher Cataloging-in-Publication Data (U.S.)

Cox, Caroline.
    Shoe innovations : a visual celebration of 60 styles / Caroline Cox.
[256] p. : col. photos. ; cm.
Includes index.
Summary: Shoe design and production from the prehistoric
sandal through 21st-century forms, including the origins and social
significance of the sixty iconic shoes,
ISBN-13: 978-1-77085-034-7 (pbk.)
1. Shoes — History. 2. Shoes – Social aspect. I. Title.
391.413 dc23 GT2130.C69 2012

Library and Archives Canada Cataloguing in Publication

Cox, Caroline
    Shoe innovations : a visual celebration of 60 styles / Caroline Cox.
Includes index.
ISBN 978-1-77085-034-7
    1. Shoes. 2. Shoes —History. 3. Shoes—Design—History.
4. Shoes—Pictorial works. I. Title.
GT2130.C695 2012   391.4'1309   C2012-901818-X

Published in the United States by
Firefly Books (U.S.) Inc.
P.O. Box 1338, Ellicott Station
Buffalo, New York 14205

Published in Canada by
Firefly Books Ltd.
66 Leek Crescent
Richmond Hill, Ontario L4B 1H1

Printed in China

This book was designed and produced by
Quintessence, 230 City Road, London EC1V 2TT

Senior Editor: Ruth Patrick
Senior Designer: Nicole Kuderer
Picture Researcher: Olivia Young
Production Manager: Anna Pauletti
Editorial Director: Jane Laing
Publisher: Mark Fletcher

CONTENTS

Introduction	8	Spats	104	Floating Heel	188
		Slipper	106	Ankle Strap	190
Pre-16th Century	16	Cuban Heel	112	Biker Boot	194
Sandal	18	Valenki	116	Slingback	196
Moccasin	22	Galosh	120	Loafer	200
Mule	26			Ankle Boot	202
Gladiator	30	19th Century	122	Weejun	208
Flip-flop	36	Wellington	124	Peep-toe	210
Tabi	40	Ugg	128	Desert Boot	214
Buckle	42	Mary Jane	132	Brothel Creeper	216
Winklepicker	44	Stacked Heel	136	Stiletto	222
Clog	46	Tennis Shoe	138	Springolator Mule	228
Espadrille	52	Chelsea Boot	140	Kitten Heel	230
Thigh-high Boot	56	Button Boot	144	Exercise Sandal	232
Platform	62	Pump	148	Pilgrim Pump	238
Wedge	70	Cowboy Boot	152	Kinky Boot	242
		Spectator	158	Go-go Boot	246
16–18th Centuries	76	Fetish Shoe	162	Moon Boot	248
Riding Boot	78			Cone Heel	250
Jackboot	82	20th Century	166		
Brogue	84	Saddle Shoe	168	Index	252
Slap Sole	88	Tango Shoe	170		
Oxford	90	Dr. Marten	172	Picture Credits	256
Louis Heel	94	Pirate Boot	178		
Ballet Flat	98	Sneaker	180	Acknowledgments	256

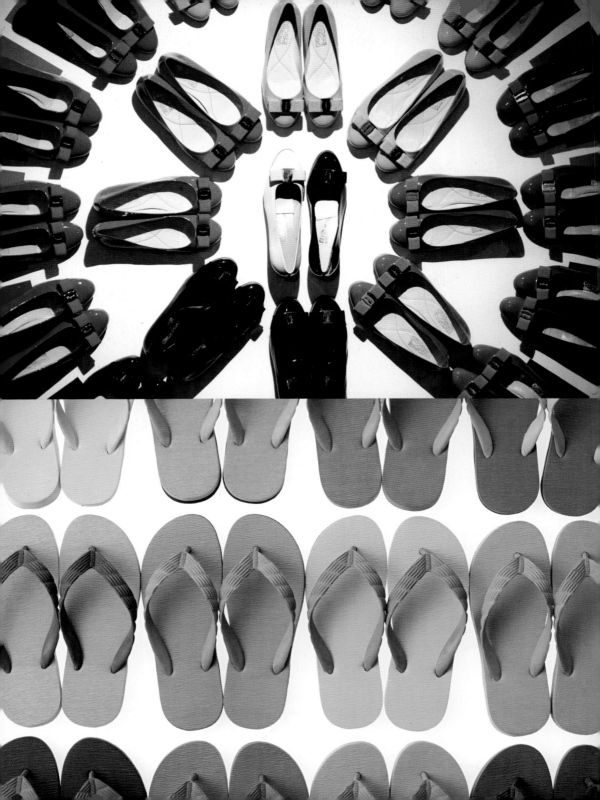

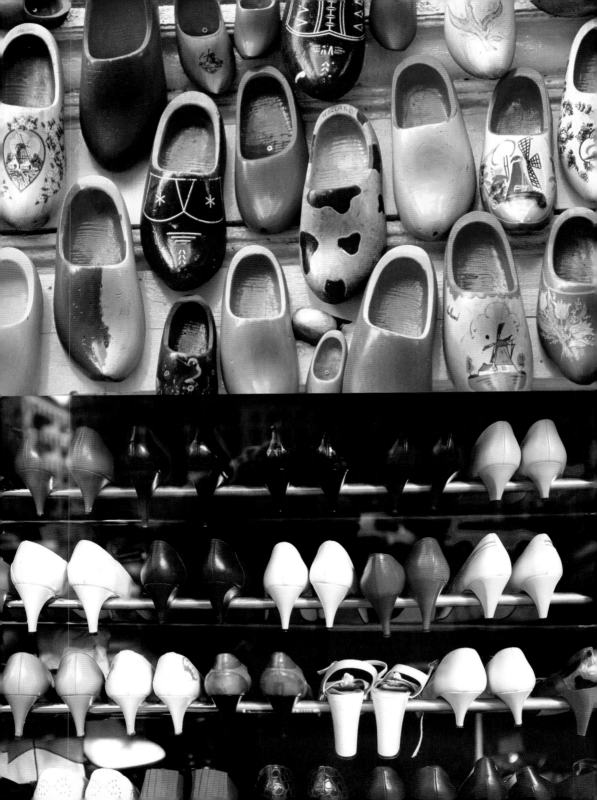

INTRODUCTION

"As we are not in a period of real innovation, you have to be... different while... being the same. The new way is to combine elements from the past with new proportions."

Pierre Hardy

Maverick shoe designer Pierre Hardy, inventor of the infamous Lego heels for Balenciaga, is clear in the above statement: shoes, like any form of fashion, have to adapt to survive. Take the platform, a shoe with an elevated sole originally derived from the medieval chopine or patten. In its first form, the platform was a raised wedge affixed to the foot by leather or cloth bands and it kept the wearer's feet from the filth of the city streets. As it was second only to the Chinese bound foot in rendering the owner immobile, one would have thought that the platform might have been lost in the mists of time. Not so, for in the 1930s, the platform had a full-on Hollywood makeover when designers André Perugia, Roger Vivier, David Evins, and Salvatore Ferragamo attached a platform sole to the high-heeled pump, giving it a sexy lift. The new platform-soled shoe was an absolute innovation; it added height but made the shoe much easier to walk in, and Ferragamo's platforms were the most glamorous of the decade with their exuberant arches and multilayered rainbow-colored soles. Fast forward to the 2010s via 1970s glam, and the so-called "power platform" by Christian Louboutin, marked out by the red-lacquered flash of its sole, heralded yet another renaissance of this once-ancient style.

The crepe sole of a blue-suede brothel creeper, the pastel-pink glass beading of a Roger Vivier mule, and the wet-look plastic of a go-go boot are all snapshots from an album of fashion innovation that also includes the 1920s tango shoe in golden kidskin, a shoe that conjures up a lipsticked flapper in the dance halls of Harlem; or a pair of sky-blue cone-heeled Maud Frizons that clamored

right:

Ferragamo's workshop
Salvatore Ferragamo in his Florence workshop in 1956 with some of the lasts used to make shoes for his distinguished clients.

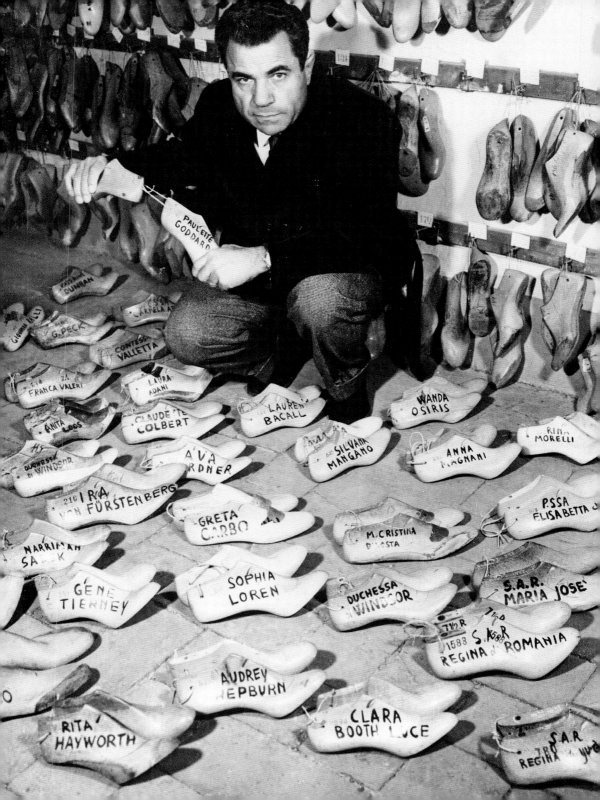

for attention in the executive boardrooms of the power-hungry 1980s. Significant shoes such as these are so marketable that they remain ripe for creative remodeling, either completely mashed up with a postmodernist's eye, or simply copied. There will always be anomalies though—Pietro Yanturni's slippers covered with the tiny quills of 500 Japanese hummingbirds may have been worn by the pampered great mistresses of the Belle Epoque, but because they bear no relationship to the lifestyle of today's modern woman (and are prohibitively expensive) the style has failed to make a reappearance. The shoes that do survive have been the ones that can be innovated.

Many of the best-known forms like the sandal or clog have a long history, and others had a more recent birth, such as the 1950s stiletto heel. Heels existed before the 1950s, of course; the first

"Give a girl the right shoes and she can conquer the world."

Bette Midler

were created in the sixteenth century as functional stirrup holders on men's riding boots, but as anthropologist Margaret Visser astutely points out, "their first purpose was to raise the owners, enable them to pose impressively, and stretch their legs so that their calf muscles bulged impressively out." By the eighteenth century, heels were worn at court by women too, literally raising both sexes from the "common herd" and providing what historian Quentin Bell called, "the most effectual guarantee of social standing." In the twentieth century, the standard convention is that only women wear high heels and they seem to have been so successfully subsumed into feminine culture that men only wear them when in drag. However, male high heels exist in the macho forms of the Cuban-heeled boot and the cowboy boot. This was a boot developed to cater to the needs of the *vaquero*, a working rider who lived on the back of his horse, and the boot had a slim toe to slip easily into the stirrup and a low undercut heel to keep it there, plus an arch with a steel shank to rest on the stirrup's bar. Heavy leather protected the feet from the venomous bite of the rattlesnake, cacti spikes, and the chafing of the saddle, and the high sides protected the pants from being torn by mesquite thorns. The wide boot top and slick leather sole of the cowboy boot—two of its most ubiquitous features—were developed originally for safety, since they allowed the cowboy to pull his foot quickly out of the boot or his boot out of the stirrup if he was thrown from his horse. Today, many styles of shoe heel have been developed, including the Cuban, Louis, platform, kitten, and stiletto, and these are comprehensively analyzed on the following pages.

The power of the shoe runs throughout popular culture and is made manifest in a myriad of ways. Although they were almost the same height, Prince Charles stood one step above his fiancée Lady Diana Spencer for their engagement photos to maintain the illusion of the tall, dark, handsome (and dominant) male. After the split, a defiant and no longer deferential Diana cut a striking and streamlined silhouette in killer-heeled Jimmy Choos. The relationship between femininity, capitalism, and consumer spending is also embodied in the shoe, most notably with shoe-obsessive Imelda Marcos, First Lady of the Philippines. Her ever-expanding shoe collection traced her rise from petty bourgeois officialdom to her position as wife of President Ferdinand E. Marcos. Imelda forcefully shopped the world from the Via Condotti in Rome, where she bought her Ferragamos, to Bloomingdales in New York. On her flight to exile, the First Lady reputedly left behind 3,000 pairs of shoes, all size 11 (UK 8.5) in

"I did not have three thousand pairs of shoes, I had one thousand and sixty."

Imelda Marcos

custom-made racking. American congressman Stephen Solarz was heard to remark, "Compared to her, Marie Antoinette was a bag lady." Today singer Cheryl Cole admits to having 2,000 pairs of shoes, saying, "I've always, always loved shoes but over the past few years I've definitely developed a proper fetish. I hoard them all over the house, in cupboards in the kitchen, in the bathroom, every room. There is a big chance when you open the fridge in my house there will be a pair of shoes at the bottom."

Why do shoes inspire such devotion? Sigmund Freud described how a fetish object could result from a male child recognizing his mother's lack of phallus, and fearing the possibility of a similar castration needs a substitute for pleasurable comfort.

One of the earliest examples of a footwear fetish appears in the work of writer Rétif de la Bretonne (1734–1806), who invests his lover Colette's shoe with her own corporeal presence: "Dragged away from the stormiest, completely adoring passion for Colette, I imagined seeing and feeling her in body and spirit by caressing the shoes she had worn just a moment ago with my hands. I pressed my lips on one of the jewels while the other substituted as woman during a frenzied fit... this bizarre mad pleasure seemed to—how should I say?—seemed to lead me straight to Colette herself."

"You want to fall in love with a shoe, go ahead. A shoe can't love you back, but, on the other hand, a shoe can't hurt you too deeply either. And there are so many nice-looking shoes."

Allan Sherman

Shoes were originally produced entirely by hand by the local cobbler and were expensive items designed to last a lifetime. By the mid-nineteenth century, shoes were beginning to be sold through drapers, where women went to study the new fashionable styles from Paris and buy material and trimmings in which to have their own copies of the most *de rigueur* gowns made. Gradually specialist shoe stores began to emerge: Lilley & Skinner of London in 1842; Florsheim of Chicago in 1904. With industrialization came a more mechanized shoe industry—shoes were cheaper and more readily available, and thus became agents of change, thrown out for the latest version because they were old-fashioned rather than no longer fit for purpose. By the twentieth century, a parade of new styles had been invented that said much about the social position of the women who wore them. Take the ballet flat of the 1960s designed by Robert Capezio and worn by Audrey Hepburn—it seemed to presage the youth invasion of fashion, making Marilyn Monroe's marabou mules and Sophia Loren's spigot stiletto heels seem vulgar and overblown. When Brigitte Bardot was seen in the flat, it seemed just the right height for the 1960s.

In the late twentieth century, the gladiator has emerged; a 2,000-year-old sandal that has found its way from the Coliseum to the runway (with a name that's pretty ironic, considering most Roman gladiators would have fought with bare feet when standing in the sand of the combat arena). Its recent incarnation dates from when the fashion brand Prada showed knife-pleated gladiator skirts on the catwalk in 2001, the exact same year when Alexander McQueen—a designer who used some of the fiercest of shoes in his catwalk shows, including the "Armadillo"—launched an Amazonian T-strap sandal with laces that reached the knee. After being worn by Kate Moss in New York and Glastonbury in 2003, the gladiator sandal, or gladiator flat as it was sometimes known, began to appear in cities all over the world, reaching the peak of its popularity in 2008–09.

In the last two decades, the monikers of shoe designers have become public knowledge and have entered everyday vocabulary thanks to endorsements such as Sarah Jessica Parker in *Sex and the City*, who in one episode bemoans her

"Creativity often consists of merely turning up what is already there. Did you know that right and left shoes were thought up only a little more than a century ago?"

Bernice Fitz-Gibbon

lost "Choo-choos," a.k.a. Jimmy Choo heels. Gina, a family firm that dates back to the 1950s, makes bejeweled evening sandals that regularly sashay down red carpets; Terry de Havilland, the rock 'n' roll cobbler, has been engineering ingenious platforms out of patchwork python since the 1960s. Other names have joined them to become major players on the international footwear scene including Sergio Rossi, Cesare Paciotti, Christian Louboutin, and Nicholas Kirkwood. The latter's innovative, architectural designs in laser-cut suede and leather featured in this book show how he has helped innovate many iconic shoe shapes today.

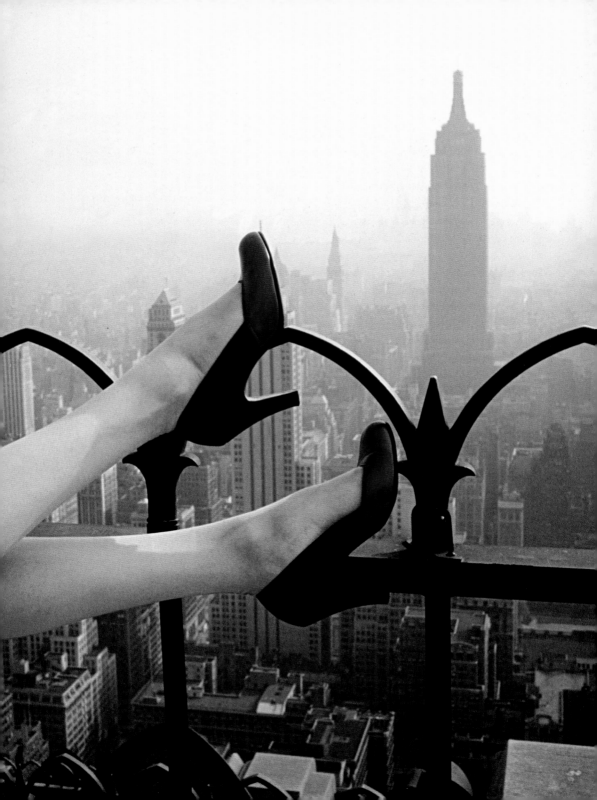

This book then, is the story of shoe design, charting the history of the sixty most iconic shoe styles from their origins through the range of innovative shapes they have assumed during the decades. It traces the chronology of shoe fashion through the twentieth and twenty-first centuries, and places the featured benchmark shoe designs in their cultural context by highlighting the pioneering work of key designers such as Paris' Roger Vivier and celebrity relationships such as Vivienne Westwood and Kate Moss, who in the early 2000s was rarely seen out of her stack-heeled Westwood pirate boots, and in the 2010s made Hunter Wellingtons cool. The text and accompanying images will show how shoes, once an afterthought in a fashionable ensemble, have become a key point of the wardrobe since the early twentieth century, and an important generator of revenue for fashion houses and modern brands. It is clear we have a

"A pair of new shoes might not cure a broken heart or soothe a tension headache but they will relieve the symptoms and chase away the blues."

Fashion writer Holly Brubach

cultural obsession with shoes: they reflect our lifestyles, aspirations, and function as a social marker of the person we hope to project to others; they act as sexual lures; provide the practical necessity of protecting our feet; and, quite simply, some days just make us feel better when we slip them on. For as Carrie Bradshaw said in *Sex and the City* (a series full of veritable shoe pornography), "It's really hard to walk in a single woman's shoes—that's why you sometimes need really special shoes to make the walk a lot more fun."

Caroline Cox

left:
New Look pumps
The 1950s was a time of post-war optimism and fashion innovation, perfectly encapsulated in this Manhattan rooftop shot.

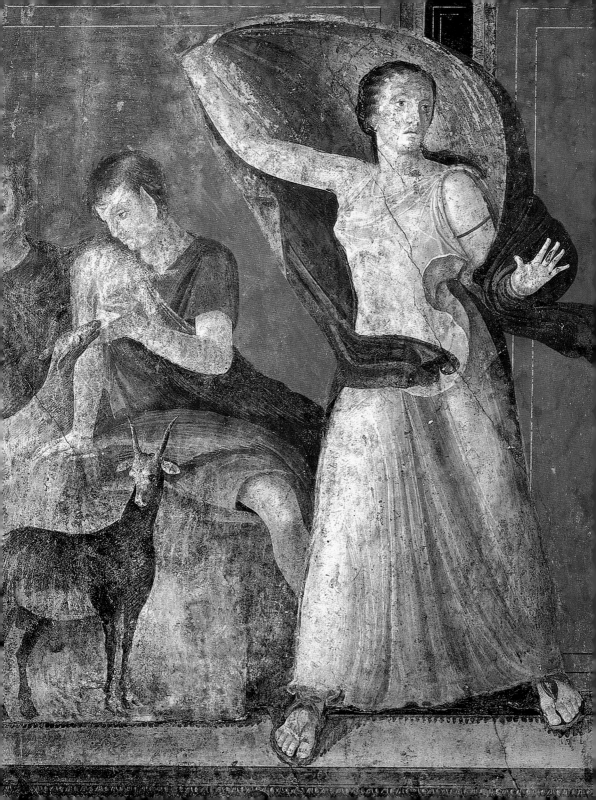

Pre-16th CENTURY

Many modern shoes have their origins in this period such as the sandal, one of the earliest types of footwear, and the winklepicker, a pointed-toe shoe derived from the infamous and heavily criticized medieval poulaine. Shoes such as the wedge—a once purely practical form of footwear that lifted the wearer's feet from the mud churned up in the city streets—have evolved into objects that through their design development display our fashion credentials and modern lust for labels.

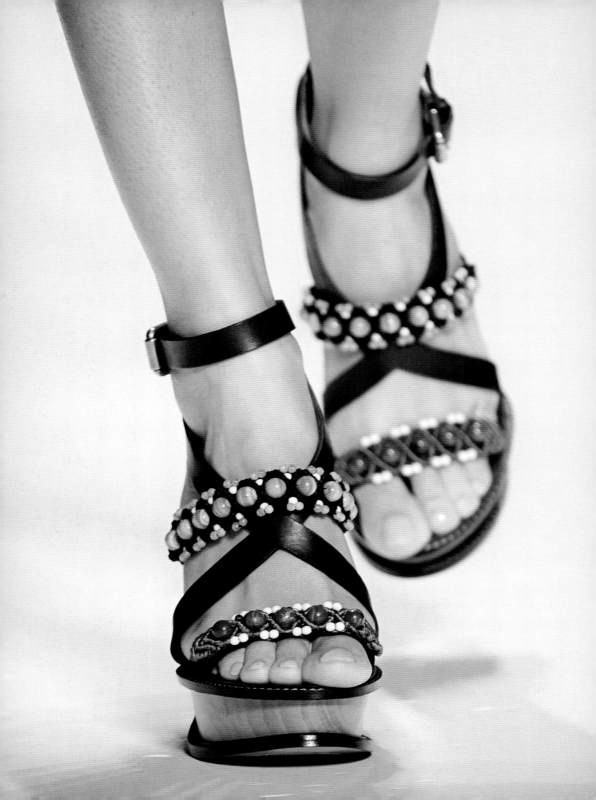

SANDAL

"And the angel said unto him, 'Gird thyself, and bind on thy sandals.' And so he did."

King James Bible (Cambridge Ed.), Acts 12:8

The sandal was the very first form of footwear to grace human feet, and from this all other shoe styles have evolved. The first use of the term "sandal" described a fully fashioned sole held onto the foot by means of simple leather, rush stalks, or woven papyrus straps, but by the 1930s, a sandal was any type of heeled or flat shoe that exposed the upper part of the foot. Sandals date back to the Ice Age and many civilizations have their own versions of this shoe, such as the braided *zori* in Japan and the *paduka* sandal in India, but the style originates mainly from civilizations based in hot climates, such as Ancient Egypt and the Mediterranean.

In Ancient Egypt, wearing leather, woven straw, or palm sandals indicated a person's social status, distinguishing the barefoot slave from the pharaoh who employed his own sandal bearer for important ceremonies. In Ancient Greece, both men and women wore sandals and styles that ranged from the heavy and practical to the lighter and decorative with intricately cut patterns and gilded leather straps. Roman sandals were virtually identical in their unisex design, with soles of cork and leather straps or laces. Soldiers wore *caliga*, a form of sandal with a leather sole that had nails tapped into it. The nailheads were arranged to create a pattern on the ground that identified the legion each soldier belonged to—an effect also used by courtesans, whose soles spelled out "follow me" in the sand. Thus, almost from the very beginning, sandals trod a tightrope between function and seduction—they were a necessity to protect feet, but the display of the naked foot created a frisson of the erotic. Art historian Quentin Bell explained this well when he wrote in 1947, "If we wrap an object in some kind of envelope, so that the eyes may infer rather than see the object that is enclosed, the inferred or imagined form is likely to be more perfect that it would appear if it

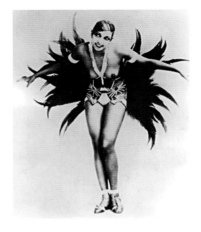

above:

Josephine Baker

This American stage performer stunned 1920s Paris with her dare-to-bare costumes and cutaway sandals.

left:

Etro Spring/Summer 2011

These robust platform sandals lasso an almost nude foot with a series of leather and embellished straps.

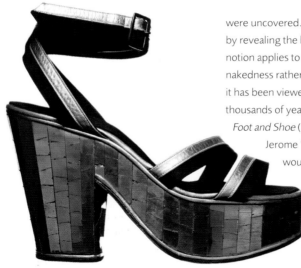

Platform sandal (1936)
Designed for Carmen Miranda by
Salvatore Ferragamo. The heel and
platform are laminated with gilded glass.

were uncovered. [Dress] heightens the sexual imagination partly by revealing the body but partly by judicious discretion." The same notion applies to the sandal; it eroticizes the foot by alluding to its nakedness rather than fully baring it—this may account for the way it has been viewed in some cultures during its metamorphosis over thousands of years. William A. Rossi, author of *The Sex Life of the Foot and Shoe* (1977), describes how during the Christian era, St. Jerome "solemnly counseled women to wear shoes that would cover the whole foot and thus subdue the carnal inclinations lurking in men's eyes." In the third century, St. Clement of Alexandria commanded women not to bare their toes in public, condemning "the mischievous device of sandals that evokes temptations."

The fashionable rather than functional sandal disappeared until the 1920s, when it reappeared as a form of beach fashion with the launch of the French Riviera as a fashionable destination. By the 1930s, designer André Perugia was responsible for moving the sandal from beach to dance floor, after creating a range of high-heeled sandals for eveningwear. One of his most renowned designs was a pair of gray leather Louis-heeled peep-toe sandals for celebrated dancer Josephine Baker in 1928 based on her trademark turban.

The term "sandal" was now habitually used to describe a shoe in which the foot was visible and the straps were conspicuous. It was in this era that the seductive nature of the shoe began to be most apparent, particularly when in the hands of David Evins, footwear designer to the stars. Evins' most famous design is the tubular, strapped, multicolored, pavé wedge sandal worn by Claudette Colbert in the film *Cleopatra* (1934); other customers included the Duchess of Windsor, Judy Garland, Elizabeth Taylor, and Grace Kelly.

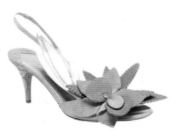

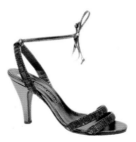

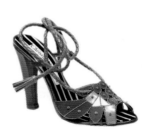

From the 1930s through the mid-1950s, Italian shoemaker Salvatore Ferragamo was responsible for creating some of the most extravagantly experimental sandals. Designs included the "Kimo" of 1951, a sandal with an interchangeable gold, red, or black satin ankle sock and high-cut interlaced straps made of burnt-gold soft leather, and the "Vitrea" of 1952–54, a gold soft leather slingback sandal with a tapered wooden high heel and a vinyl peep-toe strap decorated with pearls, pink glass, and topaz beads. His sandals could have brass-cage silhouetted stiletto heels and the most minimal of black leather straps or be platform-soled, ankle-strapped neo-Roman versions covered in an intricate laminate of gilded glass.

The strappy sandal maintained its popularity throughout the 1950s with T-bars and slingbacks giving the feet a "nude" appearance that matched the femininity of eveningwear inspired by the New Look. By the end of the 1960s, the practical sandal revealed itself once more as a response to the hippie culture that began to influence mainstream fashion. Young people in America and Europe began to advocate a return to a more "natural" look after the fashion excesses of the space-age 1960s, and the flat earthbound sandal made a reappearance. The Birkenstock sandal was launched in 1964 and was perfectly poised to cater to this new market with its contoured foot bed made out of layered cork and strong thread—it soon became a badge of the environmentalist, particularly due to its sustainable sole. In the 2000s, the humble Birkenstock underwent a rebranding exercise and a series of limited editions were seen on the feet of celebrities such as Gwyneth Paltrow and Jennifer Aniston. After being revived during the heady days of 1970s disco by Andrea Pfister and Kurt Geiger, the high-heeled strappy sandal remains a popular evening and summer shoe, from Manolo Blahnik's gold leather "Sizzle Sandal" of the 1990s through to Jimmy Choo's red satin thong sandal of 2003.

below from left to right:

Slingback sandal
Pink suede "Amanda" sandal with leather corsage by Givenchy (2003).

Ankle-tie sandal
Fashioned by Andrea Pfister in bronze leather with beaded toe straps (1990).

Flamboyant sandal
By Christian Lacroix in purple satin silk and multicolored calf leather (2008).

Minimalist sandal
Black velvet silk sandal with fixed strass chain by Vera Wang (1997).

Platform sandal
A typically maverick constructivist design by Pierre Hardy covered in multicolored suede (2010).

Butterfly sandal
Yves Saint-Laurent's patent leather sandal uses a motif to give a symbolic flight to the feet (1983).

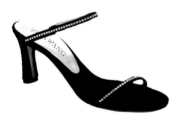
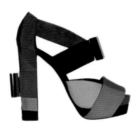
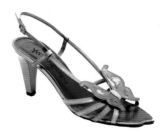

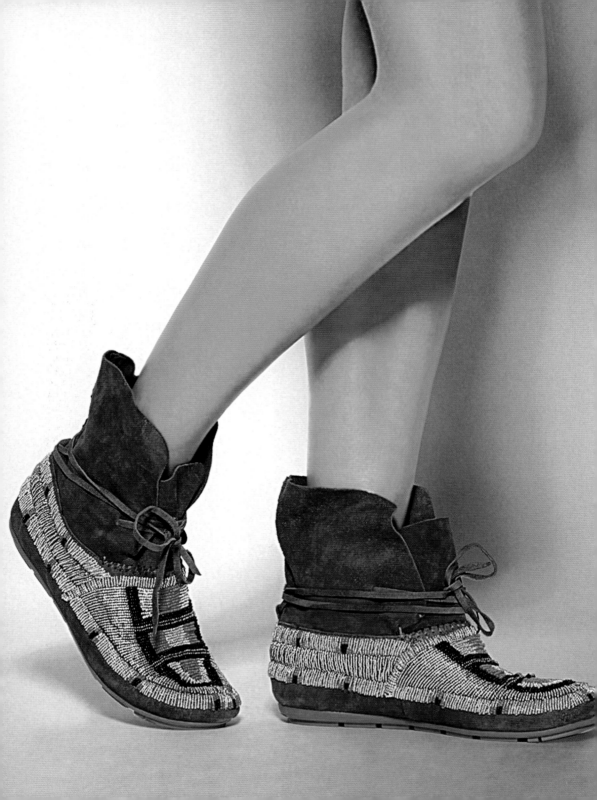

MOCCASIN

"Don't judge any man until you have walked two moons in his moccasins."

Traditional Native American proverb

A moccasin is a lightweight tanned deerskin or soft leather shoe with the sole and sides made of one piece of leather stitched in at the top with sinew. The shoe is essentially a slip-on "bag" for the foot and is derived from the traditional footwear of Native Americans. The most popular version has a U-shaped apron or "plug" that gathers in the top edges of the vamp (part of the upper) with the stitching positioned higher up the foot, originally to prevent waterlogging.

Native American moccasins were designed to be sturdy enough to protect the feet yet supple enough to allow the wearer to feel the ground through the sole. Thus a simple slip-on shoe became the closest thing to being barefoot and displayed the Native Americans' respectful relationship with nature—the idea that one should glide silently through one's surroundings, leaving without a trace.

The moccasin was an intensely personal shoe because over time the leather shaped itself to the contours of the owner's feet. Everyday moccasins were plain and made from tanned buffalo, elk, moose, and deer hides; decorative ones were worn for special occasions. Moccasins were traditionally patterned with dyed porcupine quills and after contact with European traders, beadwork was introduced, stitched in geometric patterns such as bars, stripes, and chevrons, and having personal, spiritual, or ceremonial significance. Any applied decoration was designed to face the owner of the shoe rather than the viewer. The decoration served as a reminder of a person's place in nature, and during ceremonies, the most important members of the tribe wore moccasins with beaded soles that could be appreciated by those sitting opposite them.

Moccasins may appear to differ little across Native American territories but that is because the changes are so subtle and are only visible to the trained eye. Tribes were said to be able to recognize

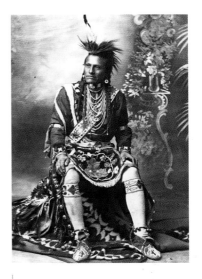

above:

Native American moccasin
Original deerskin moccasins of 1897 worn in Idaho as both protective and distinctive tribal footwear.

left:

"Maddie" moccasin (2010)
A hi-top variant designed by Nicole Richie under her House of Harlow 1960 label in beaded suede.

each other from the faintest of footprints that depicted the tiniest differences in stitching, detailing, and the finishing of the heel. Certain features were significant, though. For example, tribes that lived in more mountainous terrain used rawhide to harden the sole, while tribes in colder climates added rabbit linings for extra warmth. Ankle-wrappings gave stability over rough ground and were the forerunner of the moccasin boot.

In the 1750s, a French soldier described in detail how moccasins were made: "On their feet they wear a covering made of deerskin, scraped, rubbed, and smoked, which by this process, becomes as supple as tanned sheepskin. The women prepare the skin, and make the shoes for the men and for themselves. These shoes, or 'mockassins,' are gathered at the toe and are sewn above and behind with a raised flap on either side. This is turned down over the cord below the ankle (that) ties on the shoes."

The moccasin was adopted by traders and European settlers, including women who used them as house slippers or overshoes. By the twentieth century, moccasins were a popular souvenir and Minnetonka, a company established in 1946 in Minnesota, became the biggest manufacturer for the tourist market. The breakthrough into mainstream culture came with the adoption of the shoe by hippies in the late 1960s. They created a look that was motivated by identification with cultures that had been decimated by North American capitalism, and Native American culture became an important influence on this band of peaceful protesters. Beading and fringing elements entered into fashion—singers Sonny and Cher wore Native American-inspired outfits by Hollywood tailor Nudie and the moccasin was adopted as the hippies' shoe of choice. The Minnetonka "Thunderbird," a hand-stitched moccasin in hide or deerskin with soft soles, was a bestseller in the late 1960s.

The cultural associations with the peace and love movement have stuck; today one can buy a Minnetonka "Woodstock" boot, and at the height of the fashion for boho-chic—a new version of hippie deluxe spearheaded by UK designer Matthew Williamson in the early 2000s—Kate Moss was seen wandering the fields of the Glastonbury festival in a pair of "Tramper" boots with a rubber crepe sole for increased durability. Nicole Richie—another advocate of the boho trend, a.k.a. "cocktail

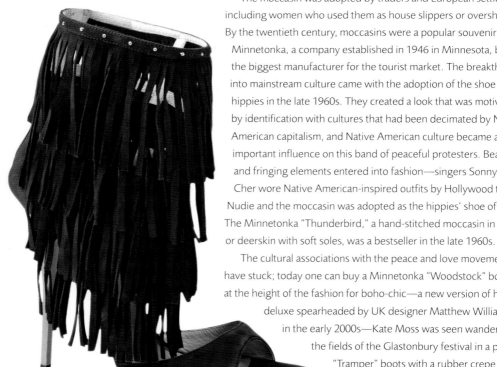

below:
"Raquel" moccasin (2012)
Based on actor Raquel Welch's footwear in *One Million Years B.C.* (1966), this fringed design by Jimmy Choo adds a stiletto heel.

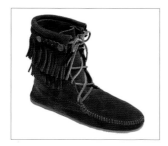
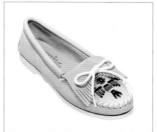
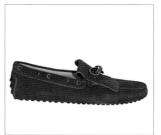
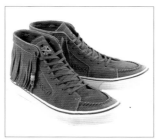

grunge" in the United States—offered a modern suede lace-up
moccasin boot with gold and pearl metal studs and the "Maddie"
beaded moccasin under her label House of Harlow 1960.

The comfort of the moccasin has caused it to be a shape for
informal shoes, such as slippers, and in 1979 the driving shoe, after
the company JP Tod's was founded by Italian designer Diego Della
Valle. His unisex "Gommini" moccasin of 1988, so named because
the sole and heel is embedded with 133 rubber studs or "pebbles"
for extra grip, comes in over one hundred different colors and has
been a global success, particularly because he cleverly managed to
combine the concept of comfort with Italian luxury.

Today, Italian firm Attilo Giusti Leombruni, founded in 1958,
creates hand-sewn soft lambskin moccasins with leather soles, and
American label Eastman, founded in 1955, is known for its chunky
classic slip-on shape. The moccasin shape has also entered sports
shoes in the form of the New Balance "A20 Moccasin Basketball"
shoe and Vans "SK8-Hi Fringe Pack Mashes Moccasin Sneakers,"
an unlikely hybrid of laid-back hippie chic and urban sports. In 2012,
the moccasin was removed from the preserve of the comfortable by
Jimmy Choo's "Raquel" moccasin, so called because it was based on
the prehistoric footwear worn by Raquel Welch in *One Million Years
B.C.* (1966)—only the fringing remained.

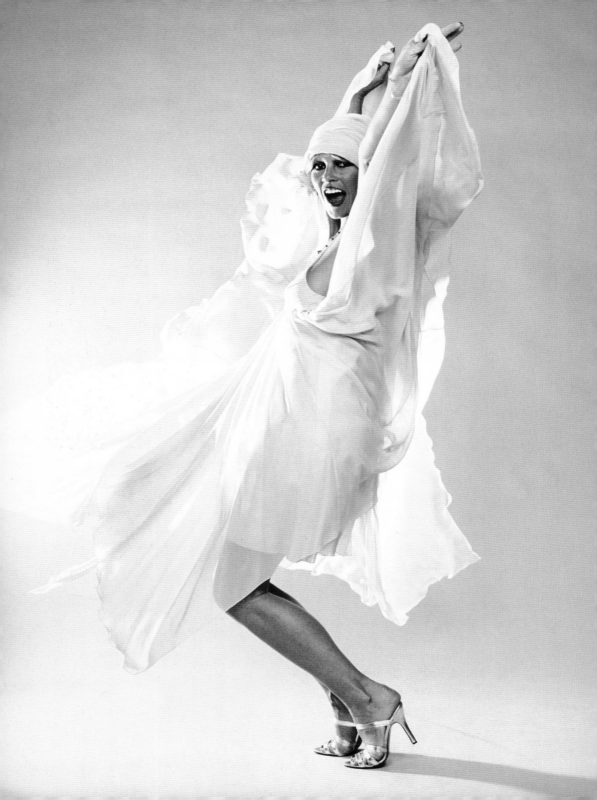

MULE

"They are not shoes. They are a political conspiracy."

Patt Morrison, *Los Angeles Times*, February 21, 1992

A mule is a backless, heeled shoe that has come to symbolize the va-va-voom of vintage Hollywood, such as the marabou or stork-feather mule worn by blonde bombshell Jean Harlow in 1930s Hollywood. The mule, in fact, dates back to the Roman *calceus mulleus*, a ceremonial shoe in red leather worn by aristocrats. The open back of the mule declared that the owner lived a life of leisure rather than physicality, since the shoe had little practical use; it also suggested that the wearer could afford more than one pair of shoes in a time when shoes were an expensive commodity. Thus the mule became the shoe for the privileged and a favorite of the European courts, rising in popularity during the seventeenth century when embroidered silk or brocade versions with long square toes were worn as an indoor shoe.

In the eighteenth century, mules were known as "pantable" from the French *pantoufle*, meaning "slipper," and were worn by both men and women. France had become the center of fashion, with fine craftsmen setting up in Paris to cater to the court of Versailles. Sumptuous dress was the order of the day with aristocrats competing with one another by dressing to impress. Madame de Pompadour, the mistress of Louis XV, created lavish boudoirs in the royal palaces where she reclined on a day bed listening for the sound of the king's tread on the stairs that directly connected his bedroom to her lair. In this intimate room de Pompadour changed from her formal court dress into *dishabille*, also known as *négligée*, a casually wrapped look derived from seventeenth-century portraiture consisting of multilayers of loose, delicately colored fabric described by contemporary writer Horace Walpole as "fantastic nightgowns fastened with a pin." This "sweet disorder in the dress" was key to

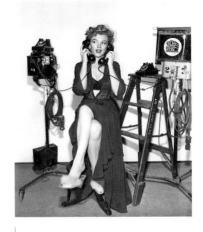

above:

Marilyn Monroe in mules
By the 1950s, the combination of lingerie and mules became the uniform of seduction both on and off screen.

left:

Brigitte Bardot (1976)
Bardot wears the 1970s incarnation of the mule; high stiletto heels, strappy, and disco-bright silver leather.

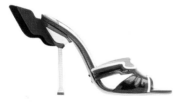

creating sexual tension and initiating seduction before the invention of lingerie; sensuality was conveyed through the outline of a thigh swathed in muslin, the hint of décolletage, or the dangling of a velvet mule from the toe of a dainty foot.

In Fragonard's infamous painting *The Swing* (1766), ripe with sexual symbolism, the pink silk high-heeled mule is an important prop in the narrative. The painting was commissioned by Baron Saint-Julien, treasurer of the Church in France, and shows a secret tryst between a woman and her lover. As she is pushed on a swing by her husband, she spies her man hiding in the garden and, by coquettishly kicking off her mule toward him, allows him a glimpse up her skirts. The mule had evolved into a sexy female shoe and stayed that way into the twentieth century.

above:

Needle heel

John Galliano refines the heel down to a sharpened point and combines it with an Art Nouveau-inspired upper.

In the Edwardian era, it accompanied the new lingerie designs that were entering women's fashion when attitudes toward sex (as long as it was performed within the sanctity of marriage) relaxed. Lingerie was a form of dress implicitly designed for sensual pleasure and writer Emile Zola observed how lingerie displays in the Paris stores looked "as though a group of pretty girls had undressed, layer by layer, down to the satin nudity of their skin." By 1902, one female fashion journalist felt brave enough to state, "Lovely lingerie does not belong only to the fast... dainty undergarments are not necessarily a sign of depravity. The most virtuous of us are now allowed to possess pretty undergarments without being looked upon as suspicious characters." The mule played part of this erogenous *mise-en-scène*; a shoe that evoked the heavily scented Rococo boudoir of the eighteenth century. Edwardian mules had thin leather soles, a Louis heel, and beaded vamps.

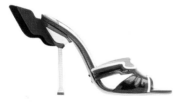

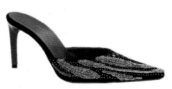

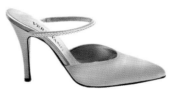

By the 1930s, the mule was a Hollywood staple whenever there was a boudoir scene with Jean Harlow in it. She was the epitome of movie-star glamor with her public appearances and publicity photos emphasizing her sexuality. The ban on the naked body demanded by the Hays Code was cleverly sidestepped by having Harlow in a white satin peignoir and her foot appearing half naked from a rhinestone-encrusted high-heeled mule that, as with de Pompadour, dangled seductively from her foot. André Perugia understood the nuances well when in the same decade he designed an overtly erotic pair of mules for the French showgirl Mistinguett, whose legendary legs were said to be insured for $1 million USD. Her mules were fit for a femme fatale, with green suede heels, gold-speckled suede vamps in a deceptive leather finish that mimicked snakeskin, and ocelot fur edging.

The 1950s were dominated by the "Springolator Mule" developed by Beth Levine and reintroduced by Terry de Havilland in the 1970s. In 1992 the mule made a comeback, the most beautiful designed by Manolo Blahnik, who believes the mule is "as good today as it was for Madame de Pompadour slipping from her bed." But not all women have been enchanted by this vintage Hollywood style. Writer Patt Morrison said, "They are not shoes. They are a political conspiracy. They are not much good for anything outside of the boudoir. Mules seem suspiciously like the Western world's version of foot binding, useless footgear for anyone who does more than loll around in bias-cut satin waiting for Her Man to come home. So you buy one pair with big rhinestones. Suddenly it's too hard to double-clutch to drive to work, too hard to make it up the escalator to your office. So you start staying home. End of contact with the outside world, end of career, end of life as a grown-up."

In 2012, Prada launched a new mule, the "Rocket Mule," seemingly propelled by the faux flames at the back.

below from left to right:

Prada "Rocket Mule"
Prada's 2012 mule gives a formerly seductive shoe a tougher edge.

Embellished mule
The luxurious sequins on Lacroix's mule refer to its boudoir origins.

Wedding mule (1997)
A bridal mule by Vera Wang in her trademark white silk and pearls.

Logo mule
Classic Chanel mule in beige satin with the double-C logo.

Stack heel mule
The "Indigo," an innovative chunky version of a traditionally delicate style by Christian Louboutin.

Go west
Vivienne Westwood channels the 1950s starlet with her nude-leather bow-fronted mule.

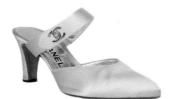

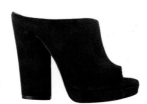

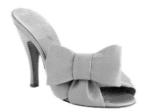

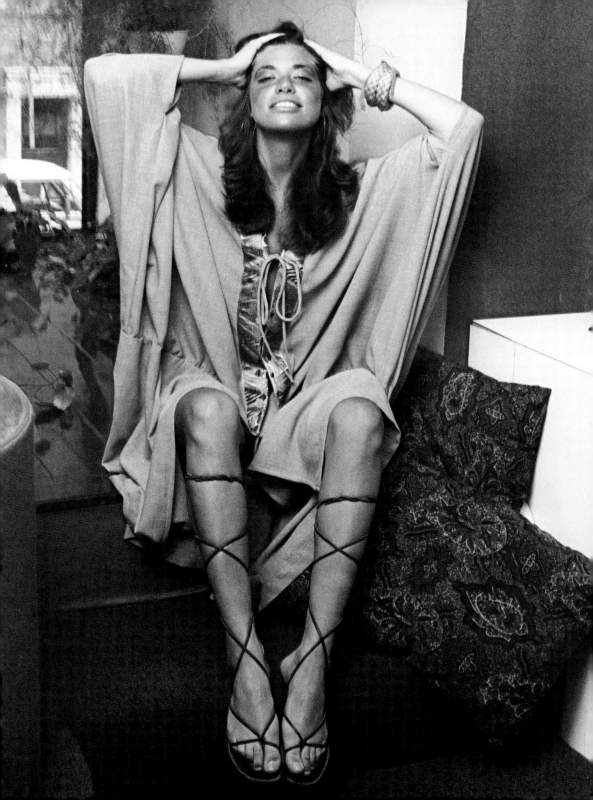

GLADIATOR

"I see before me the gladiator lie: / He leans upon his hand; his manly brow / Consents to death, but conquers agony...."

Lord Byron, "The Gladiator"

The gladiator is a 2,000-year-old sandal that has wandered from the Coliseum to the runway, with a name that's pretty ironic considering most Roman gladiators would have fought with bare feet when standing in the sand of the combat arena. The gladiator was the toughest of warriors who, after being picked from the ranks of slaves, criminals, and prisoners of war, underwent a punishing training regime before being forced to fight in the great amphitheaters of Rome. His feats of strength in man-to-man combat or bloody battles against wild beasts made the gladiator among the most well-known celebrities of the day, although few lived long enough to enjoy the fruits of their physical endeavors and few names survive today. Gladiators really only wore a form of Roman leather sandal studded with hobnails in battle reenactments when they were playing the part of soldiers. The leather came from cattle or deer and was expertly tanned to make a tough leather sole with straps to attach it to the foot that could tie, if needed, up to the knee. Sandals were commonly worn with a metal leg guard or armor that protected the shins and could rise as far as the thigh.

In the twentieth and twenty-first centuries, whenever the biblical "sword and sandals" epic movie has become popular, a version of the gladiator sandal has swept into fashion again. In the late 1950s and early 1960s, after a flurry of biblically inspired films were made including *The Robe* (1953), *Ben Hur* (1959), and *Spartacus* (1960), the Nero or Caesar haircut entered men's fashion vocabulary and women wore the gladiator beach sandal, a strappy affair in leather that laced up the leg.

What made a gladiator sandal stand out from the crowd of summer footwear was a strap that ran along the top of the foot and connected to a series of straps that branched off the sides, creating

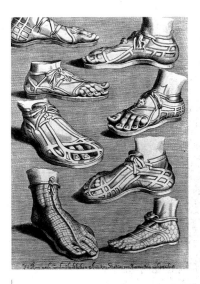

above:

Roman sandals

The gladiator sandal has its origins in the sandal designs worn during the Roman Empire.

left:

1970s gladiators

Singer Carly Simon in a hippie deluxe outfit of kaftan and lace-up gladiator sandals.

Runway gladiators (2012)

In the 2000s, the gladiator sandal became a modern classic with many designers, such as Michael Kors, creating their own versions.

Theatrical gladiators

Rupert Sanderson was commissioned to design this one-off dramatic shoe for the opera *Aida* in 2011.

a webbing on the front of the foot. Embellishment could then be added in the form of additional straps or laces that ran around the ankle or up the leg in some styles. Flat gladiator sandals with the most fashion credibility were made by K. Jacques of Saint-Tropez. This small workshop run by shoemaker Jacques Keklikian opened in 1933, when the Riviera's most exclusive destination was a small fishing village, and catered to the local fishermen who wanted sandals that could stand the wear and tear of the beach. Keklikian made hand-stitched leather sandals that gained their glamor when Brigitte Bardot was spotted in a pair, and their fame, like her adopted home, grew throughout the 1960s. After Keklikian's son Jacques went to Rome, their trademark gladiator strapped sandal was launched and became synonymous with Riviera chic when worn with a white T-shirt and Capri-cut jeans. The K. Jacques "Darius" gladiator sandal in gold leather with half-inch heel remains a worldwide bestseller today.

In 2000, the hugely successful film *Gladiator* starring über-macho actor Russell Crowe premiered, the first ancient epic to be made since the 1960s and the stimulus for an epidemic in gladiator-style footwear (although throughout most of the film the actor wore closed-toe boots). In 2001, Prada paraded knife-pleated gladiator skirts on the catwalk, and a fierce-looking T-strap sandal with laces that reached the knee was launched by Alexander McQueen in the same year. After being worn by Kate Moss in New York and Glastonbury in 2003, the gladiator sandal, or flat as it was sometimes known, began to appear in trendy neighborhoods all over the world, reaching the peak of its popularity in 2008–09—in one year, New Look sold 100,000 pairs in the UK alone.

There was a strange incongruity at work with the shoe—it emanated from the most ferocious of masculine arenas yet was adopted by women who wore it with Boho maxi dresses or bodycon minis, and many morphed into almost tribal or Native American shoe shapes with the addition of fringing and multicolored beads. Fashion designer Savannah Miller mused on the popularity of the sandal's severe good looks in 2009: "I think women are feeling like we need to be tough. There's a survival thing going on. The fighting spirit

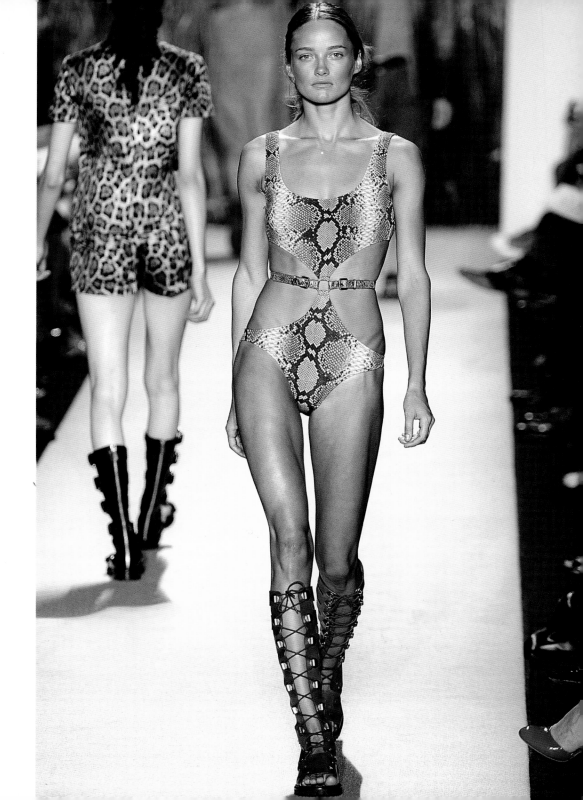

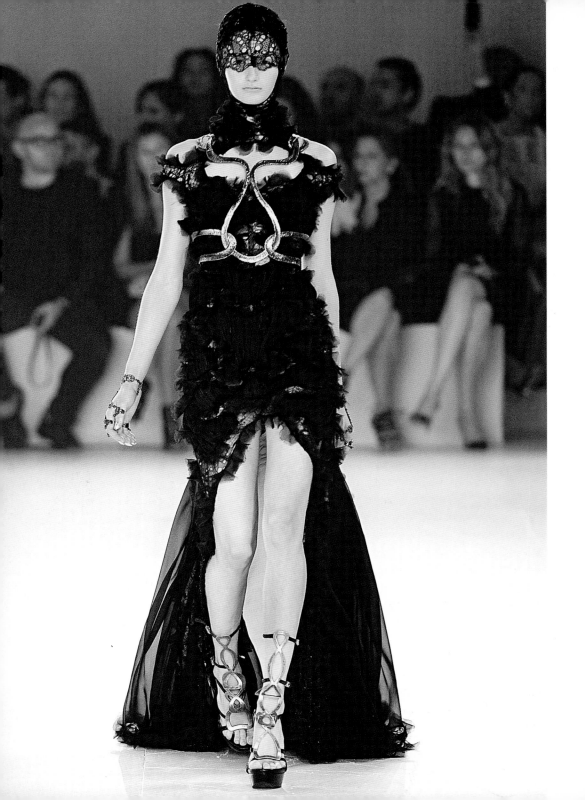

has been brought out in all of us. Women will always need silk and prettiness and sensuality, but at the moment we will definitely also need a shell of a jacket or a killer shoe."

Balenciaga was there to supply it with its bizarre knee-high cages of 2010/11, but the gladiator could take many forms from Givenchy's delicate embellished metallic to the Dior "Extreme Gladiators" as worn by Sarah Jessica Parker with a green prom dress in *Sex and the City: The Movie* (2008). These were a new form of gladiator—the gladiator heel—and fashion designer Cynthia Rowley debuted nude platform gladiators with a faux armor plate that stretched over the foot and up the ankle, describing her design as "sort of orthopedic Spartan shoes," and explained her inspiration as *300* (2006), a film of the Battle of Thermopylae (480 BCE). Stuart Weitzman, Balmain, Azzedine Alaia, and Marc Jacobs sold both buckled gladiator sandals and heels—and soon much cheaper versions could be found in most main street stores such as Forever 21 and Top Shop.

The shoe began to morph into an accessory that owed more to punk and fetishism than Rome, with accents such as studs, chains, and a whole host of buckles—the most extreme gladiators of all were made by Balenciaga, gladiator boots that covered the leg in intricate leather disk-work and braids as worn by pop star Rihanna to much comment. Perhaps most oddly though, when targeted at men in 2010 by Louis Vuitton, Dries van Noten, Bottega Veneta, and Dolce & Gabbana, this testosterone-heavy shoe never really caught on. One fashion critic, Lawrence Garwood, said, "I would consider wearing gladiators if I lived somewhere hot, already had a tan and was among friends who wouldn't laugh." The problem was in the proportions: When affixed to more muscular (and hairy) masculine legs, the look was just too biblical. J. Artola's "Domain Gladiator Sandal" was an attempt to break the mold—with its thick leather straps and heavy topstitching—but it was still a little too *Ben Hur*. Dior Homme's version of 2011 took a more witty approach, playing with the fashion faux pas of the sock-wearing sandal-shod man. This black calf-leather gladiator had a removable cotton lace-up sock.

left:
Alexander McQueen
McQueen is the designer most associated with the rise of the gladiator sandal in the 2000s.

below:
Dominatrix
A multistrap version of the gladiator sandal in black leather by Vivienne Westwood (Spring/Summer 2009).

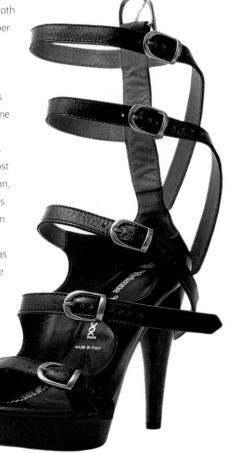

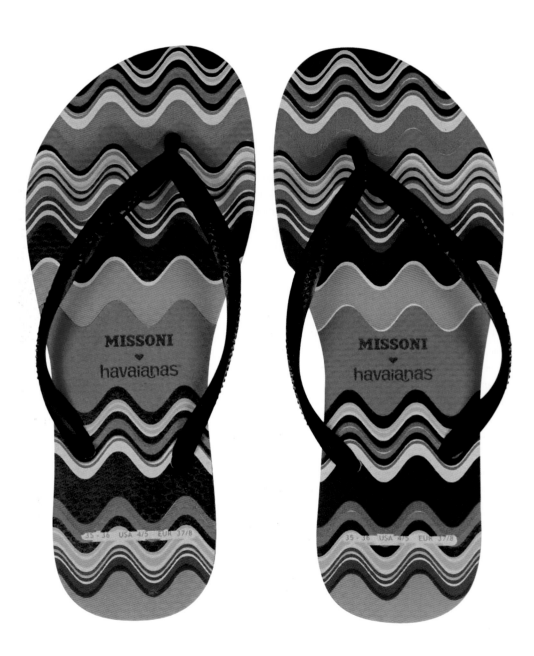

FLIP-FLOP

"The guy who owns the mansion wears them, and the guy that cleans his swimming pool wears them too."

Fernando Tigre, former president of Havaianas

In the 1960s, a simple cheap rubber sandal with a Y-shaped toe strap was named the flip-flop because of the sound it made on the ground when worn. It went on to become the bestselling shoe in the world. However, the shape has been in existence for over 6,000 years, and flip-flops appear in most cultures under different names and using different toes to anchor the foot to the sandal. Japan has the *zori*, for instance, a sandal made of fabric straps with rice straw soles that dates from the Heian period (794–1185) and formed part of traditional dress; in Ancient Egypt they were made from papyrus; in Texas the flip-flop is also known as the clam-digger; Australians have thongs, whereas New Zealanders wear jandals. Ancient Greeks secured the flip-flop by the big toe; Romans, the second; Mesopotamians, the third.

In the 1930s, rubber-soled flip-flops were manufactured for the first time in Kobe, Japan, and after the Second World War many entrepreneurs helped in the country's economic recovery by making the shoe. Mitsubishi was one of the first exporters of flip-flops on a grand scale. Another rubber version was manufactured by John Cowie in Hong Kong and imported in New Zealand by Morris Yock under the name "jandals," or Japanese sandals. They began to catch on after being manufactured in the bright bubble-gum color palette of the post-war years, since they perfectly encapsulated the burgeoning Californian lifestyle of outdoor living, barbecues, and beach culture. Every beachfront store sold cheap rubber flip-flops and a version called "foam zori" were targeted at American housewives to be worn at home by day. At the end of the 1950s, flip-flops had taken over as the alternative to bare feet for billions of people in temperate climates because they were such an affordable form of footwear.

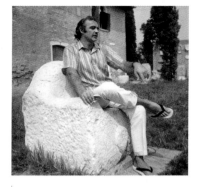

above:

Sean Connery in Venice
By the 1970s, the rubber flip-flop was a unisex holiday shoe that had a certain cosmopolitan chic.

left:

Fashion forward flip-flop
Luxury fashion brand Missoni teamed up with Havaianas and applied their distinctive zigzag to the flip-flop.

In Western culture, by the 1970s, flip-flops were placed squarely on the beach, which was where they stayed until the dress-down culture of the 1990s began to take hold. Before long, flip-flops found their way into the city, taking over from trainers in the office on dress-down Fridays. The Brazilian manufacturer Havaianas (established 1962) helped elevate the humble rubber flip-flop worn by the dockworkers of São Paulo into a high-fashion accessory worn by supermodel Gisele. The inspiration for their flip-flop came from the Japanese *zori*, acknowledged in the textured rice-patterned footbed of the Havaianas. In 2004, the company produced a special-edition diamond-studded flip-flop with an 18-karat gold finish in partnership with jeweler H. Stern.

Beloved by beach bums and surfers alike, Rainbow flip-flops have been in production in Laguna Beach, California, since 1974. The company was set up by Jay R. Longley to produce unisex flip-flops in hemp, leather, and rubber. He describes: "It began over thirty-five years ago, it was another beautiful day at the beach... And then I saw another broken sandal littering the very beach I was enjoying. It gave me an idea, why not make a better sandal, one that would last a long time and be comfortable?" From making fifteen pairs per day by hand, the company has relocated its production to a factory in China employing 3,000 workers. Rainbow flip-flops are made up of layers of sponge rubber that are glued together, with "memory" so they mold to the wearer's feet. Reef, another surfie brand, was founded in the 1980s by Fernando and Santiago Aguerre, two brothers from Argentina who had sold surf-related gear since the 1970s. After relocating to La Jolla, California, they began manufacturing footwear including the ubiquitous Reef "Fanning" with its integrated bottle opener, and the water-resistant "Smoothy" flip-flops.

As iconic as jeans, flip-flops have conquered the world, whether high-end Rainbows or cheap Korean imports; as Fernando Tigre, the former president of Havaianas pointed out, "The guy who owns the mansion wears them, and the guy that cleans his swimming pool wears them too." Variations include the FitFlop exercise sandal, the sports flip-flop that combines an athletic shoe's sole with a flip-flop strap, and the kitten heel flip-flop, a shoe that ultimately denies its own functionality, launched by design duo Kari Sigerson and Miranda Morrison of label Sigerson Morrison in 2003 after four years in development. This was the first rubber flip-flop to be mounted

below:

Brigitte Bardot on set
Bardot was one star who popularized the flip-flop in the 1960s when spotted wearing them in Saint-Tropez.

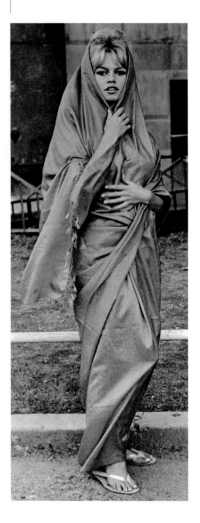

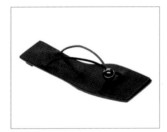

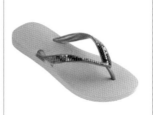

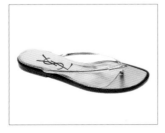

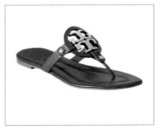

clockwise from top left:

Stealth wealth

The "Clint" flip-flop in sleek black leather by Yves Saint Laurent.

Beach chic

The iconic Brazilian Havaianas with its distinctive rubber sole and toe strap.

Designer brand

Tory Burch adds a low stack heel and ornate gold-tone medallion.

Smart casual

The "Capri" flip-flop by Yves Saint Laurent in gold lamé karung, metal, and crystal.

on a heel, quite a design challenge because of initial problems with stability. The final flip-flop was made with a dual-injection TPU sole and PVC strap made in a single mold. After the launch and attendant publicity, the demand was huge and Morrison described how "we shipped three hundred pairs to our New York shop and they were gone in two-and-a-half-hours. There was a queue forming around the store, and women were bursting into tears when we told them we had run out of supplies." The SwitchFlop by designer Lindsay Philips, marketed with the slogan "Change Your Look, Not Your Sole," has a range of toe straps that can be swapped to coordinate with each outfit including leather and shell flowers, beaded buttons, and animal-print patterns.

Recently there has been a backlash though; journalist Oliver Pritchett argued in favor of an official flip-flop season in 2011 with a definite start-date, which, if ignored, would constitute a social faux pas; Rebecca Armstrong wrote of "the catalog of horrors below the ankle that would make even the bravest chiropodist flinch" on the feet of the average flip-flop wearer in summer; but most worryingly, in 2009, the environmental group Eco-Waste Coalition warned that some flip-flops contain toxic chemicals that are bad for both health and the environment. The problem is phthalate, used as a softening agent in polyvinyl chloride (PVC) plastic, an endocrine disruptor associated with developmental and reproductive disorders.

TABI

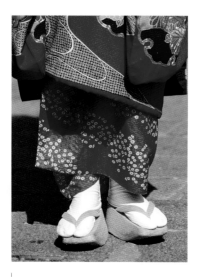

above:

Traditional tabi

A trainee *geisha*, or *gaiko*, wears the split-toe shoe-sock, or tabi, designed to accommodate the shaft of the sandal.

Tabi—the ruling classes of early-modern Japan—operated a strict social hierarchy with the warrior at the top and the merchant classes, including shoemakers, following far behind. Status was enforced through the sartorial in much the same way as sumptuary laws operated in Europe. Within Japanese culture, footwear was considered impure; it housed the feet and touched the dirt of the ground and shoemakers were considered part of the lowest class as a result. Buddhist belief also caused many to frown upon the profession because it included the use of leather and the death of a living animal.

Tabi are split-toe shoe-socks dating from this period and were formed from tanned leather and worn with straw sandals by the warrior class. The separation between the big toe and the others was created to accommodate the shaft of the sandal and the tabi was slip-on, fastening at the back so that no seams interfered with the comfort of the flat sole. With the introduction of *tatami* flooring in Japanese domestic spaces, cotton tabi became popular—they were considered more hygienic than the original leather and kept the mats clean.

In 1906, Shojiro Ishibashi took over the family clothing business in Kurume, Fukuoka Prefecture, and began producing tabi. He sensed a gap in the market and, in 1923, designed the "Jika-Tabi," a work shoe comprised of a tabi with a rubber sole that can still be seen worn on construction sites in Japan today. The shoe was so popular that it gave Ishibashi the capital to start his new business, Bridgestone, now a global tire manufacturer.

The tabi has occasionally made its way into fashion; in 1951, Salvatore Ferragamo created the gold leather "Kimo" sandal with a satin sock insert inspired by the tabi, and in his very first show, in 1989, Belgian deconstructivist designer Martin Margiela incorporated the split toe into his shoe and boot design. The models were covered in red paint before they took to the runway and left distinctive red boot prints on the white cotton floor. Tabi boots have now become one of Margiela's most iconic designs and over the last two decades have been produced in a variety of different materials, including leather covered with his trademark white paint. The intention is to create a *tabula rasa*, a design that shows the march of time, for as the tabi boots are worn the paint slowly cracks off, highlighting the process of aging. As each individual wears the boots differently, each pair of tabi boots develops its own personal patina.

The tabi has also found its way into sports shoe design; in the 1980s, it appeared at the height of the martial-arts craze as the ninja shoe worn by practitioners of Bujinkan; in 1995, the Nike "Air Rift" was launched with a tabi split toe inspired by the barefoot Kenyan runners of the Rift Valley. Journalist Cayte Williams described it as "a cloven-hoofed trainer with a sandal front... guaranteed to make you look like a children's TV presenter circa 1978, with their black/green and purple/yellow color combos. They are made from canvas, cost £150, and babies point and laugh at them in the street."

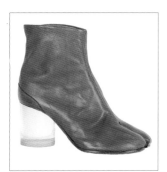

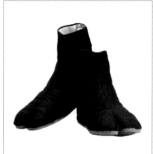

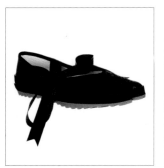

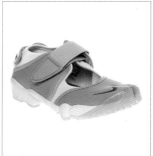

clockwise from top left:

Martin Margiela
One of the few designers to tackle the tabi. This leather design with Plexiglas heel is from Spring/Summer 2012.

Fighting tabi
A boot worn by the practitioners of the Japanese martial art Bujinkan.

Trainer tabi
The "Air Rift" launched by Nike in 1995, with distinctive split-tabi toe.

Street tabi
A casual split-toe tabi with rubber sole and ribbon tie derived from this ancient form of Japanese footwear.

BUCKLE

The shoe buckle is both ornamental and practical whether fashioned from celluloid, pinchbeck, silver, or gold and has two parts: the chape and the ring. The chape and its prongs fasten the strap when it is onward the shoe; the ring is attached to the top of the chape and can be decorated. Functioning buckles were worn from the medieval period on, but by the mid-seventeenth century they also became a form of decoration as the man's exposed lower leg and ankle took on the fashion focus.

During the reign of Louis XV, buckles were ostentatious and covered the front of the shoe. Buckles were status symbols,

> "This day I began to put on buckles to my shoes."
>
> Samuel Pepys, 1660

precious items that could be removed—unlike their modern counterparts—and played an important part in decorating the shoe when there was little change in shoe shape. They could dress up a shabby shoe, as depicted in the novel *Pamela* (1741)—when the father of the bride's shoes are not up to scratch for the wedding ceremony, the groom "was then pleased to give him the silver buckles out of his own shoes."

As young male hipsters began to flash vulgar buckles to show their sense of style, advice began to be given to young men on the etiquette of this shoe accessory. In *The Man of Manners: Or Plebian Polish'd* the author wrote, "We must proportion them to our Shape, our Condition, and our Age: The glittering Buckle upon the gouty Foot must be avoided."

By the 1790s, buckles were replaced by "the effeminate shoe string" as the lace was contemptuously called, only to reappear around the 1900s. Romanticized eighteenth-century

below:

Anglomania
Vivienne Westwood's "Ultragirl Flat" with buckle updates the classic 1960s "Pilgrim Pump" by Roger Vivier.

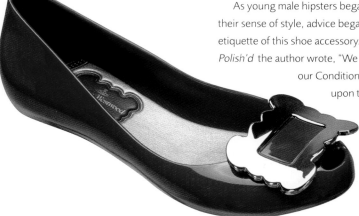

references entered fashion, such as the Louis heel and the large Cromwellian or Puritan-inspired buckle, and lasted well into the 1920s, many made from etched steel.

Buckles also had a functional purpose and gradually took over from buttons as a device to secure the bar straps of Mary Janes (see page 132), tango shoes, and strappy sandals. Their design featured the geometric simplicity of the Art Deco aesthetic, a fashionable expression of Cubism that had gained mainstream popularity after Paris' Exposition des Arts Décoratifs, held to much acclaim in 1924. This exhibition showed the wares of many of France's premier luxury designers and their haute modernism found its way into buckle design as miniature Cubist fantasies were played out in marcasite, rhinestone, and brightly colored enamel.

In the 1930s, women's cutaway sandals exposed more and more of the foot and discreet buckles were sewn into the strap so as not to detract from the nude effect. Buckles did not become oversized again until the 1960s with the success of Roger Vivier's "Pilgrim Pump" and the revival of the Mary Jane, and continued to reappear when shoes assumed exaggerated silhouettes, such as the platform in the 1970s (see page 62).

Big buckles also came to the fore in designs that cited eighteenth-century references, such as in the work of avant-garde shoe designer John Fluevog, who also revived the Louis heel and those designed to accompany Vivienne Westwood's eighteenth-century-inspired runway collections, such as the oversized mirror Plexiglas buckles in the Fall/Winter 1989 Voyage to Cythera collection. Westwood's multi-buckled pirate boot is still in production today. Buckles are now out of favor as the trainer continues to dominate, found less in fashion but in functional shoes such as Birkenstocks, ·Dr. Scholl's, and clogs or, as in the 1930s, as invisible fastenings for evening shoes. The ornate, status-symbol buckle has yet to make a comeback.

above:

Roger Vivier
A designer who consistently used buckles as a decorative device throughout his career. Today the label continues with this design feature.

WINKLEPICKER

The extended toe of the winklepicker is reminiscent of the poulaine, an extraordinary typo of shoe that rose and fell in popularity in Europe from the twelfth to the sixteenth century. Thought to have been inspired by Middle Eastern footwear brought to Europe during the Crusades, the poulaine, named after the "polena" or ship's prow, had a toe that could be up to three times as long as the foot—so long that the myth still abounds that it had to be fixed to the leg with cord to aid movement. It was at its most extreme length in the fourteenth century when the rise of rich merchants prompted changes in fashionable dress as the aristocracy attempted to keep their previously unassailable place at the forefront of fashion.

Dress displayed wealth and leisure, and was at the height of extravagance at this time in the French and Burgundian courts. Women wore trailing skirts with long sleeves that covered the hands, and horned and steepled headdresses; men wore extravagantly long poulaine with toes stuffed with horsehair so they retained their shape. The poulaine is perhaps the most obvious example of shoes denoting social status, in that it was impossible to do any physical work, let alone walk very far, while wearing them. The obvious

right:
Retro-inspired
A modern winklepicker by The Old Curiosity Shop in black ponyskin with brogue detailing.

below:
Salvatore Ferragamo movie design
The winklepicker is thought to have been inspired by the curled-up toes of Middle Eastern footwear.

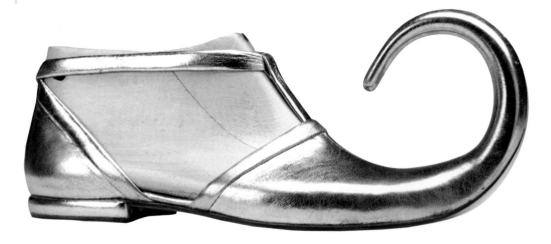

sexual symbolism of the shoes was denounced from the pulpit; even the Pope went so far as to declare them "lewd" in 1468.

The winklepicker inspired similar condemnation in the 1950s when the pointed-toed shoe rose again, first as a symbol of subcultural protest on the streets of Harlem and New York, and then as a mainstream teenage fashion. The 1950s version of the poulaine was dubbed the "winklepicker" for the sharp pin used by vacationers to pry winkles from their shells on day trips to the seaside. It entered men's fashion as an elegant shoe or boot with a stacked heel that worked well with the tapered trousers worn at the time by Teddy Boys, then mods and finally punks in the 1970s, with the most overtly stylized being produced by Stan's of Battersea, a shoe outlet described by Pathé news in 1960 as "a mecca today for members of the Beat generation."

The winklepicker reached its sartorial height in women's shoe design in the late 1950s up to 1963 when it was accompanied

> "I really hate incredibly long shoes, where the last is very pointy, almost like Aladdin."
>
> Christian Louboutin

by the stiletto heel that was approaching the zenith of its most extreme height. As the heels of the shoes became higher, so the toes became more exaggeratedly pointed and the untenable shape of the shoe created ergonomics that were totally off-kilter with the feet. All the pressure of the body weight was directed onto the toes squeezed into the shoe's tapered shape—the wearer suffered acute discomfort with the attendant possibility of painful hammer toes and bunions if winklepickers were worn all the time. This was increasingly the case as young women loved this extreme shoe and wore it day and night. By 1963, the winklepicker was replaced by the chisel toe, only to resurface in mainstream fashion in the 1990s with the renaissance of the stiletto heel. It remains a staple and is still a sexy shoe style.

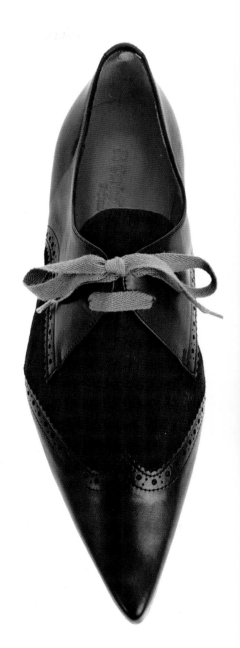

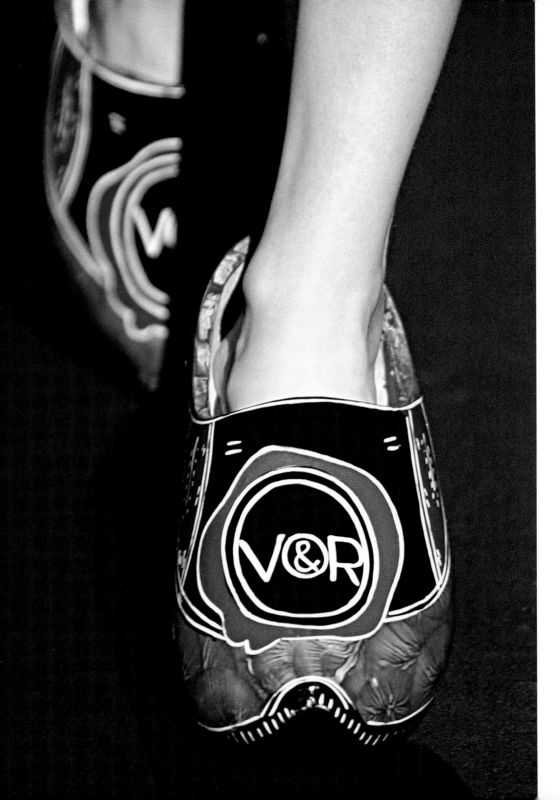

CLOG

"I hate the concept of the clog! It's fake,
it's ugly, and it's not even comfortable!"
Christian Louboutin

A unisex durable work shoe derived from the medieval Dutch
klompen and the French *sabot*, both closed wooden shoes that kept
the foot dry and safe from both farming implements and fish hooks.
The oldest surviving clog was discovered in Amsterdam and dates
from around 1230, entirely appropriate as clogs have become
a national, if stereotypical, symbol of Holland alongside windmills
and Edam cheese. Clogs were originally made by hand and each
pair had to be cut and cured from the wood of the same tree at the
same time to prevent uneven shrinkage. A saw was used to rough
out the shape followed by chisels to hollow out and create the
internal space. Today the machine has taken over and most clog soles
are industrially produced.

The clog was a popular shoe all over Northern Europe. When few
could afford enough leather to cover the entire foot, it was a cheap
alternative, better than being barefoot, and a clog could withstand
water and last a lifetime. Wood, whether it be beech, birch,
sycamore, or alder, was readily available—the only downside was the
clog's rigidity, which could prove uncomfortable when walking over
long distances, thus the shoes tended to be worn with thick socks
and handfuls of straw stuffed down each side.

By the nineteenth century, the industrialization of Britain moved
the clog from the country to the city where it was seen on the feet
of factory workers in the north of England. Manufacturing centers
such as Lancashire, famed for its cotton mills and collieries, also
spawned a new form of working-class entertainment: solo-step clog
dancing. Inspired by the clatter and movement of machinery in the
mills, dancers beat out a rhythm on the cobbled streets, performing
a series of intricate tapping steps. This urban entertainment made
its way into music halls with performers such as Dan Leno drawing

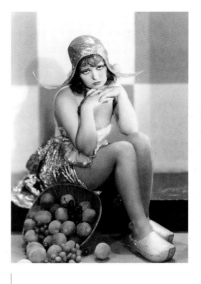

above:
Clara Bow
The clog has become a stereotypical
feature of Dutch-girl style.

left:
A new take (Fall/Winter 2007)
Functional footwear appears on
the catwalk when designers such
as Viktor & Rolf want to play with
notions of glamor.

admiring crowds in 1883 after being crowned Clog Dancing Champion of the World.

By the 1920s, a more sophisticated version of clog dancing took over: tap; a form far more suited to the syncopated sounds of jazz and without the associations with poverty. Clog wearing declined until the 1940s, when leather shortages meant this practical form of footwear made a reappearance. Fashion magazines including *Vogue* attempted to push the clog as not only the most patriotic form of footwear, but also an up-to-the-minute fashion statement; however, the majority of women were not impressed with the utilitarian shoe and stuck to the slightly more glamorous wedge (see page 70).

From this point on, the clog began a series of revivals, magically appearing in times of austerity and recession as a symbol of seriousness, disappearing again when times were good. The 1970s saw the clog take a starring role at the exact same time as the optimism of the 1960s had disappeared, snuffed out in a drug-addled haze of self-destruction. An economic downturn loomed and a resolute protest led by writer Germaine Greer ensued after her dazzling feminist tract *The Female Eunuch* was published in 1971, a strident polemic against patriarchy and its relationship with capitalism. Greer saw the fashion system as one of many cultural institutions that suppressed women by promoting ideals of beauty that were impossible to live up to and specifically condemned impractical footwear that "alters the torsion of the muscles of the thighs and pelvis and throws the spine into an angle which is still in some circles considered essential to allure." What could the radical feminist wear without becoming a fashion victim or sex object and still look relatively stylish? Clump forward the clog, the shoe that became a fashion statement at last, ironically due to the sartorial demands of an anti-fashion movement.

Traditional Swedish brands became astonishingly popular, including Sandgrens and Troentorp—companies that had been producing high-quality clogs since the early twentieth century— and Ugglebo, founded in 1965. President of Ugglebo Dave Giese calls the 1970s the era of "clog mania. Absolutely no-one could produce enough clogs for all the people infected by a need for the latest clog styles and colors. This applied not only to Sweden but all over the world. Retailers had to have every pair that they could

right:

Chanel (Spring/Summer 2010)
Chanel reintroduced the chunky platform clog that had formerly reigned supreme in the 1970s.

below:

1970s leopard-print clogs
The 1970s were the era of "clog mania," with the shoes being worn by both women and men.

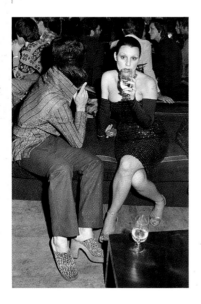

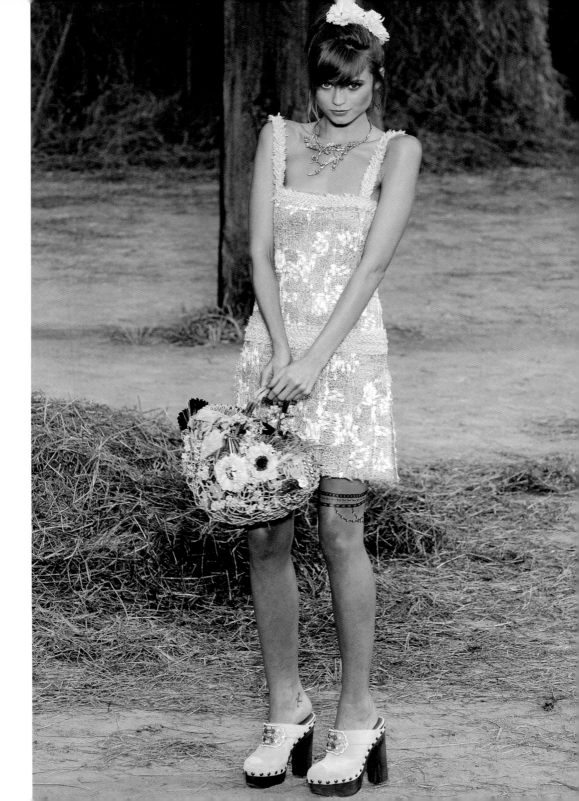

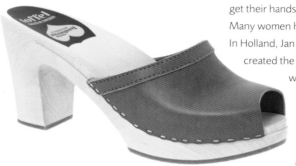

above:

Eco-clog (Spring/Summer 2011)
Hasbeen, the Swedish label, has been synonymous with handmade clogs with natural-grain leather uppers since the 1970s.

get their hands on in order to satisfy the public's insatiable demand. Many women had ten to twelve different pairs in their wardrobe." In Holland, Jan Jansen reimagined the traditional Dutch clog and created the "Woody," a clog with a brightly colored leather upper with scalloped edging and scooped-out peepholes on the sides. It was a global success story, selling 100,000 pairs, and other footwear designers such as Bruno Magli began to experiment with the traditional clog shape. It was not long before all thoughts of function disappeared and the clog was sexed up for the fashion rather than feminist market. Heels got chunkier and platforms more towering until by 1978 Candie's "Slide Clogs," as worn by Olivia Newton John in *Grease*, were one of the biggest selling lines in America.

In the early 1980s, the demand for clogs disappeared, but more recently, the clog is staging a comeback as the economy takes a turn for the worse. Pierre Hardy's wooden platform clogs sold out immediately when launched in Gap in 2010 and brands such as Chanel, Miu Miu, Marni, Jimmy Choo, and Ralph Lauren have launched clog designs. They have achieved eco-chic in the hands of Los Angeles-based designer Calleen Cordero who launched in 1999 with the aim of reintroducing artisan footwear to the United States. Her wooden footwear is manufactured by hand from sustainable alder and vegetable-tanned leather customized with brass and nickel studs, and in clog terms is the total antithesis of the Croc. This innovative clog, a veritable shoe phenomenon, is loved and loathed by many with equal enthusiasm.

The Colorado-based Croc company was founded in 2002 by three men, George Boedecker Jr, Lyndon V. Hanson, and Scott Seamans, in order to market, manufacture, and distribute a lightweight clog–sandal hybrid with straps, in a range of solid, bright

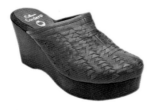

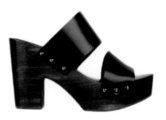

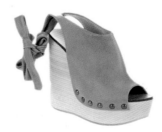

colors and made out of Croslite, a molded plastic resin developed by the Canadian company Foam Creations. The Croc brought a childlike whimsy into functional footwear that had enormous appeal but the shoe had comfort, ventilation, and circulatory benefits for the feet, too. The trio soon realized they had a hit on their hands, so bought out Foam Creations in 2004 and thus the exclusive rights to Croslite.

The Croc was a massive global success; its chunky "Beach" model with drainage holes came in over twenty different colors and celebrity wearers included Al Pacino, Jack Nicholson, Jared Leto, Kate Middleton—even President George W. Bush was spotted wearing a gray pair. The vibrant colors drew the eye when the shoe was displayed on vertical racks in stores and the childlike image continued with the happy-faced crocodile logo. In 2005, production went from a standing start to over 1,000,000 shoes per month, reaching a revenue of $847 million USD by 2007. Yet a word of caution was uttered in that same year by Robert Frick of Kiplinger's *Personal Finance* magazine: "If ever something looked like a walking, breathing fad, it's Crocs." He went on to say, "Sales growth won't have to decelerate much to cause investors to flee. If Croc's classic shoes suddenly go the way of other footwear fads (think Heelys or Earth Shoes), shares could plummet. If ever there was a stock to unload at the first sign of trouble, it's a creature of fashion like Crocs."

Frick's words were prophetic, for in 2009 sales seemed to stall and the company cut 2,000 jobs. In May 2010 *Time* magazine listed Crocs as one of "The 50 Worst Inventions," saying "It doesn't matter how popular they are, they're pretty ugly." By 2011 however, Crocs began to stage a comeback as they launched "Crocassins," or moccasins made out of their trademark Croslite, as well as flip-flops, boots, and trainers. Significantly, in many underdeveloped countries, the cheap Croc has supplanted the less-protective flip-flop.

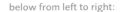
below from left to right:

Wedge clog
Calleen Cordero attaches a high wedge to her waxed leather "Gaucho."

Platform clog
Kurt Geiger adds studded black leather to give the clog a fetish feel.

Tie-up clog
Chloe injects modern glamor with a high wedge and ties.

Clog boot
Hasbeen attaches a wooden clog sole to a black leather ankle boot upper.

Mule clog
Chloë Sevigny designed this sky-high, black-leather clog mule for Opening Ceremony (2010).

Cuffed clog
Carvela cuff the "Alpine" clog ankle boot with faux fur for winter warmth.

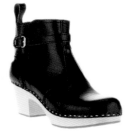
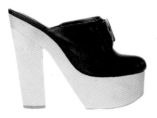
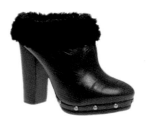

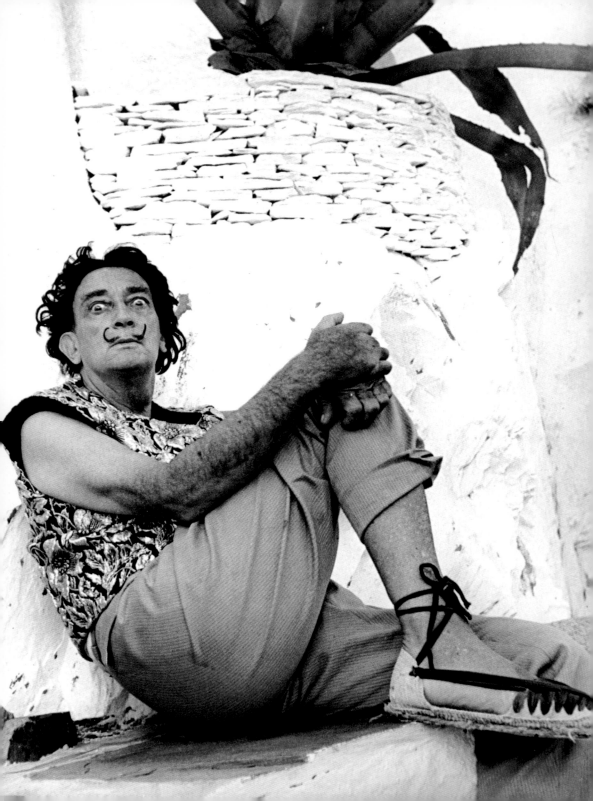

ESPADRILLE

"Ah, the espadrille wedge: the sandal that never goes out of style."

Hannah Rockwell, *The Times*, 9 June, 2010

A traditional unisex *paysan* shoe from Catalonia, Spain, that takes the form of a jute rope-soled sandal, with the sole covered in pitch for protection and a canvas upper that is seamed to the sole at the sides; some versions have cotton ties to hold the shoe more securely on the foot when walking over rough ground. The name *espadrille* is derived from *esparto*, the robust Mediterranean grass used in the production of rope. This unassuming shoe has been manufactured in small-scale cottage industries in the Mediterranean since the fourteenth century, although more recently Bangladesh has taken over as the center for the large-scale production of rope soles that are then imported into Europe where the canvas uppers are added. The twines of the jute are braided by machine and then formed into the shape of the sole by hand. The sole is heat pressed and vertically stitched into place and vulcanized underneath to give a waterproof finish.

Specialist espadrille makers still exist in Spain, however, such as Antigua Casa Crespo of Madrid established in 1863, and Epart who have been operating from Balans since 1886. In France the center of espadrille production is Mauleon, a small town nestled in the foothills of the Pyrenees and makes 75 percent of all traditional espadrilles sold in the country. Every year on August 15, the town holds an espadrille festival to celebrate its heritage and events include the famous espadrille-throwing contest.

This utilitarian shoe crossed over into beachwear in the inter-war period; Pinet, the prestigious French firm, made deluxe examples in 1929 that could be spotted on the fashionable beaches of the Côte d'Azur and the traditional version hit the headlines in menswear when spotted on the feet of none other than John F. Kennedy in 1938. In the 1980s, actor Don Johnson from the show *Miami Vice*,

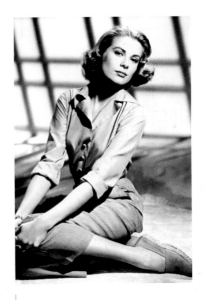

above:

Grace Kelly

Kelly was an expert in understated elegance, here combining tailored pants with espadrilles.

left:

Salvador Dalí

Surrealist artist Dalí draws on his Spanish origins by sporting the traditional unisex *paysan* shoe.

Simon Le Bon of Duran Duran, and George Michael and Andrew Ridgeley of Wham! sported rolled-up chinos and espadrilles, conflating the humble rope-soled shoe with a mix of sun, sea, and designer threads that chimed with the rise of the Yuppie, a young, urban professional who was prospering under the economic policies of Margaret Thatcher in the UK and Ronald Reagan in the United States.

The female espadrille underwent more innovation, making a successful appearance as a fashionable evening shoe when the hippie deluxe or "rich peasant" look was at its height in the early 1970s. Yves Saint Laurent elevated hippie to haute couture by appropriating its ethnic references and recasting them as high fashion for the very rich. The shoes that complemented this look resulted from a chance meeting at a shoe exhibition in 1972 in Paris. Here, Saint Laurent came across espadrille makers Lorenzo and Isabel Castaner, whose family firm had been producing traditional espadrilles since 1927. The designer asked them to sex up the vernacular shoe with primary-colored canvas uppers, high wedges, and overlong cotton ties that were then sold under his YSL label.

In London the espadrille was appearing on the catwalks too as a result of the collaboration between English fashion designer Ossie Clark and shoe star Manolo Blahnik, to accompany Clark's Spring/Summer runway show in 1972. Blahnik was at the start of his career as a shoe designer, chock-full of ideas but with little technical expertise. For the show staged at the Royal Court Theatre he created a modern take on the espadrille, a teetering high-heeled and open-toed creation, later named "Ossie" after the designer, with uppers of overlapping green suede and ties that wrapped around the ankle complete with dangling fake red cherries. Unfortunately the rubber heels had no structural or spinal support and made the models feel as if they were "walking on quicksand" as they buckled under their weight but the deliciousness of the design was to give Blahnik his big breakthrough. Looking back, Blahnik said, "'I thought it was going to end my career. The models were walking in a very strange way. Luckily, people thought it was the new way of walking."

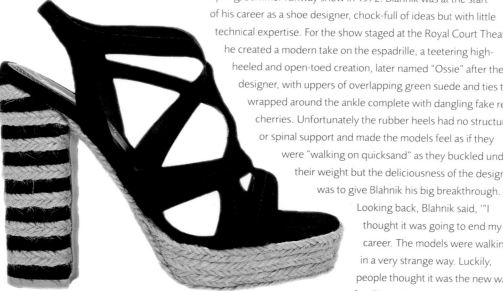

below:

"Gipsy Chyc" espadrilles
Yves Saint Laurent adds a high rubber sole and a *trompe l'œil* stacked straw heel.

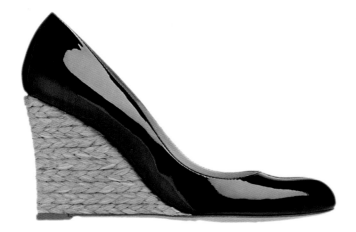

"Kate" espadrille
The "Greta" espadrille wedge by
L.K Bennett hit the headlines in
2011 when worn by Kate Middleton,
inspiring the name change to "Kate."

The espadrille entered the American market through French-born designer André Assous, who spotted a market there for an all-natural, environmentally friendly shoe. He gave the shape a high woven platform and lengthened the original cotton braid so as to lace farther up the ankle. Many manufacturers copied the idea, and by the mid-1970s it was almost unrecognizable from its traditional origins, as the rope sole became a key feature of platform shoes. As the platform rose higher it had to be lighter, so faux straw soles were made in plastic by injection molding—some as high as five inches—topped with plastic uppers in DayGlo shades of color.

Today, the high-end label Castañer produces avant-garde espadrilles for designer brands such as Hermès, Louis Vuitton, and Christian Louboutin, as well as Coach and Kate Spade. Assous is a global company with an annual turnover of $5–10 million USD. The espadrille is now standard issue for summer all over the world and styles range from the affordable jute-soled original through to the most high-end of designer brands, such as the Louboutin "Delfin," the "3.1" leather espadrille by Phillip Lim, the nautical-stripe version by Tory Burch, and Lanvin's design of 2011, which combined the espadrille with ballet flat to make a rose-satin espadrille flat with grosgrain ankle straps. Kate Middleton, the Duchess of Cambridge, also popularized the espadrille by being seen in a pair of black patent L.K. Bennett "Greta" wedge-soled espadrilles before and after her wedding in 2011.

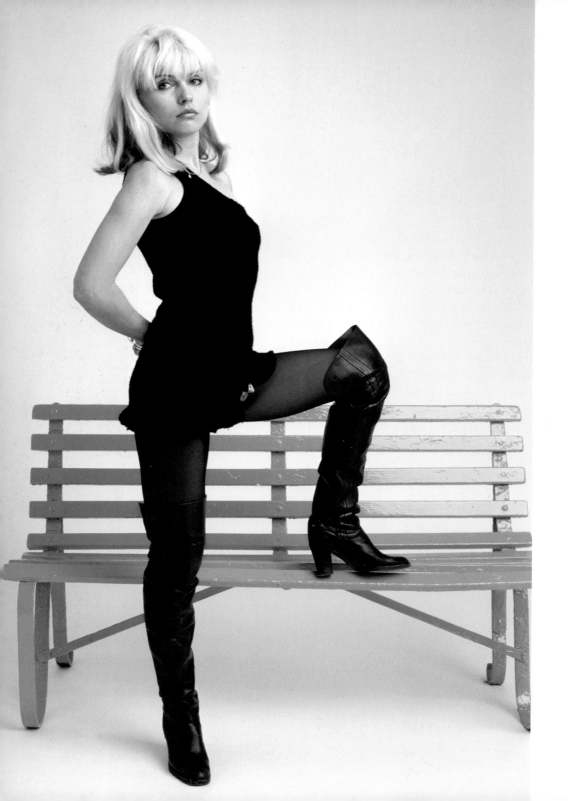

THIGH-HIGH BOOT

"Yeah well if you want me in a tin-foil miniskirt and thigh-high boots, I'm gonna need dinner first."

Gunnery Chief Ashley Williams in *Mass Effect* video game, 2007

In the 1960s, as the mini crept up to the top of the thigh to become the micro, the highest of boots arrived to cover up the expanse of leg on display and give it a powerful sense of strength. In an era of increasing sexual liberation for women, the thigh-high boots, also known as *cuissarde*, were still shocking—especially because before then, they had been seen only in fetish magazines. Thigh-high boots accentuated the lower half of the female body. A woman had to be daring to wear such a provocative boot. In 1967, sex-symbol Brigitte Bardot sat astride a Harley Davidson in the music video for "Je T'Aime Moi Non Plus," a song by her then-boyfriend Serge Gainsbourg. In the video, a tousled blonde Bardot wore a black leather miniskirt and a pair of shiny black thigh-high boots by Roger Vivier, causing millions of men to take notice.

It was a natural step for an experimental footwear designer such as Vivier to play with this shape for women; in 1963 he had been first to create a tantalizing pair of crocodile thigh-high boots with a low heel and softly pointed toe for Yves Saint Laurent. Ballet dancer Rudolph Nureyev pulled on a pair of Vivier croc thigh-highs on his entry into Europe from behind the Iron Curtain, a clear symbol of the Western decadence that had been taboo during his youth.

The shape was picked up by other French couturiers throughout the decade, including Emanuel Ungaro, who collaborated with Vivier; Pierre Cardin's 1968 shiny patent leather thigh-highs had a sexy space-age appeal when combined with monochromatic jersey shifts and matching elbow-length patent leather gloves. Jane Fonda sported another sexually charged version of the boots in the role of Barbarella in the 1968 movie of the same name. Her white leather space-fetish thigh-highs by Italian costume designer Giulio

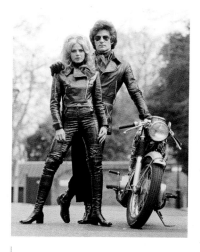

above:

Leather girl

Actress Britt Ekland in black leather thigh-high boots with then-boyfriend Patrick Lichfield (*c.*1970).

left:

Debbie Harry in thigh-highs

The singer poses provocatively in a mini and thigh-high boots at the height of punk, in 1977.

Coltellacci were held up by leather straps that reached all the way up to the shoulders.

The air of sexuality and strength that emanated from these boots was unsurprising, since they had evolved from the Napoleonic military uniform of the elite Grand Armée heavy cavalry of the fifteenth century and successors to medieval knights. Soldiers of Napoleon's army were legendary; heavy men astride huge horses armed with a straight-bladed sword held above their heads like a spear. The correspondingly heavy leather boot, like the original jackboot (see page 82), protected the length of the legs while fighting. Thus, thigh-high boots conveyed a very potent masculinity, conjuring up images of soldiers and swashbuckling musketeers, therefore disturbing when adopted by women such as Joan of Arc—the first woman to wear these boots in battle. At her trial in 1431, the only charge to which she was prepared to plead guilty was the offence of wearing men's military boots both on and off the battlefield.

The sexuality of the boot was picked up by the fetish industry in the 1950s, particularly in the work of Irving Klaw, a.k.a. King of the Pin-ups, whose model Cocoa Brown specialized in thigh-high boots that laced up the back, much like a corset. By 1976, the fetish style was embraced by female punk rockers after fashion designer Vivienne Westwood took the styling of sado-masochism and elevated it to avant-garde fashion with her Bondage Collection,

right:
Bardot on a Harley
This iconic image of Brigitte Bardot in 1967 introduced thigh-high boots to a new generation.

far right:
Leg allure (2008)
The boot leads the eye up the leg, exposing little skin save a flash of thigh, as in this Temperley design.

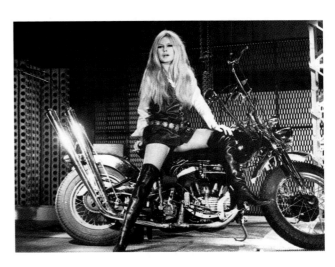

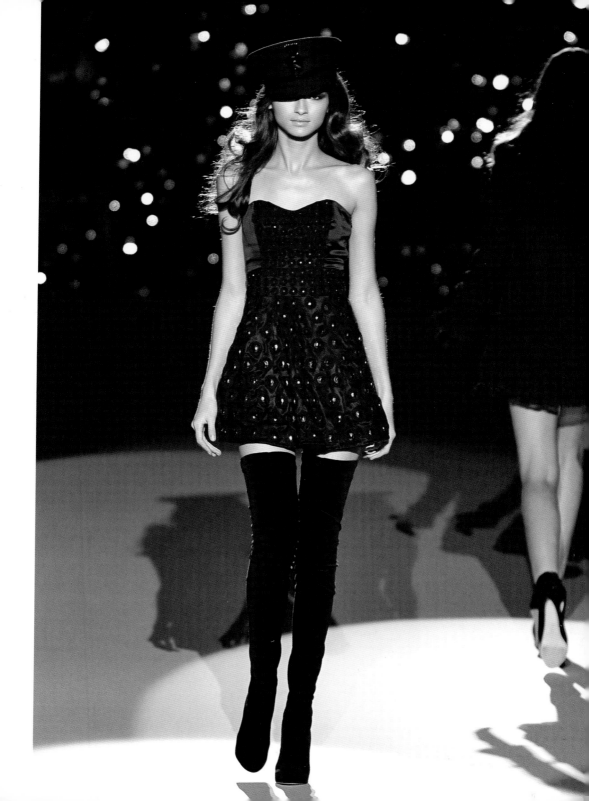

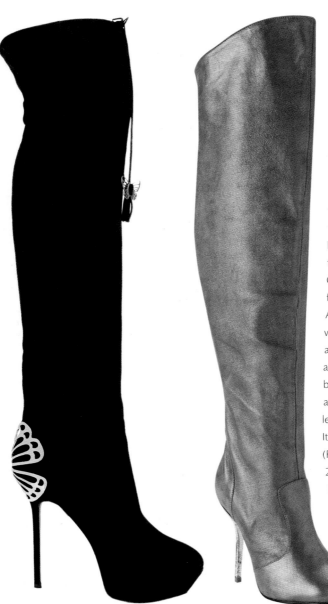

which was released that year. Westwood's shop, Sex, on London's Kings Road became a mecca for this new tribe of rebels who were served by assistant Jordan wearing a rubber miniskirt and thigh-high PVC boots as a form of shock-chic following Westwood's edict that "Sex is the thing that bugs English people more than anything else so that's where I attack." Punk icons Siouxsie Sioux of Siouxsie and the Banshees and Debbie Harry of Blondie both wore the boots, as did pop star and New Romantic Adam Ant, but by the end of the 1980s the boot moved back to the legs of the principal boys of the pantomine circuit and the usual fetish enthusiasts.

It took the film *Pretty Woman* (1990) to catapult the thigh-high boot back into fashion again. Julia Roberts played an escort wearing a stretch cut-out mini dress and black patent thigh-highs who eventually wins the heart of a billionaire played by Richard Gere. The boots soon became a way for female celebrities to display hyper-sexuality. At the height of WAG-mania, for instance, when the extravagant fashions of the wives and girlfriends of highly paid athletes became an influence on mainstream fashion, thigh-high boots were worn by Victoria Beckham with a T-shirt and skinny jeans, designed in black leather with winklepicker toes by flamboyant Italian fashion designer Roberto Cavalli (Fall/Winter 2001) and Chanel (Fall/Winter 2005). Stella McCartney designed pairs in perforated faux leather in 2009 and singer Madonna wore blue satin rabbits' ears with her Louis Vuitton leather and exaggerated Louis heel thigh-high boots at the annual Costume Institute Gala held at New York's Met that same year.

Lately, thigh-highs have made a comeback on the runway as fetishism has infiltrated fashion once more; many houses such as Hermès and Louis Vuitton employ the services of the firm Jean-Gaborit, which makes the finest leather thigh-highs for both male and female consumers involved in high fashion, historical reenactment, and fetish fantasy. The boot now symbolizes extreme sexual confidence; Rihanna sings of S&M in boots that reach well past the thigh. Design critic Stephen Bayley says this style "disguises and advertises at the same time: the curious eye is irresistibly drawn to places more complicated than the knee. Any look-at-me gesture has an erotic character."

Thigh-high boots suit the flamboyant femininity that's such a feature of the 2010s, as evocative of the era as hair extensions and acrylic nails.

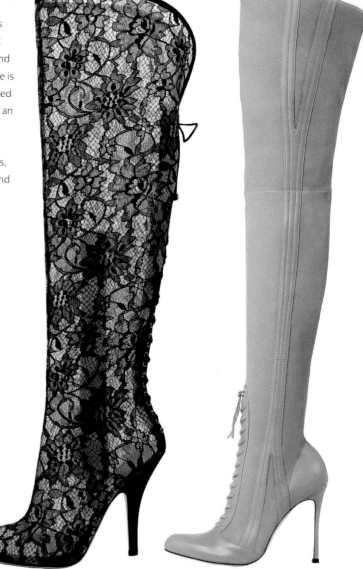

from left to right:
Sergio Rossi (Fall/Winter 2011)
A high platform counterbalances the extreme heel on this boot.
Westwood (Fall/Winter 2011)
Silver leather stiletto thigh-high with trademark molded toe detail.
Sebastian
Black lace thigh-high with corset lacing at back takes the boot to the boudoir.
Gianuto Rossi (Fall/Winter 2011)
A premium thigh-high made of luxurious karung snakeskin.

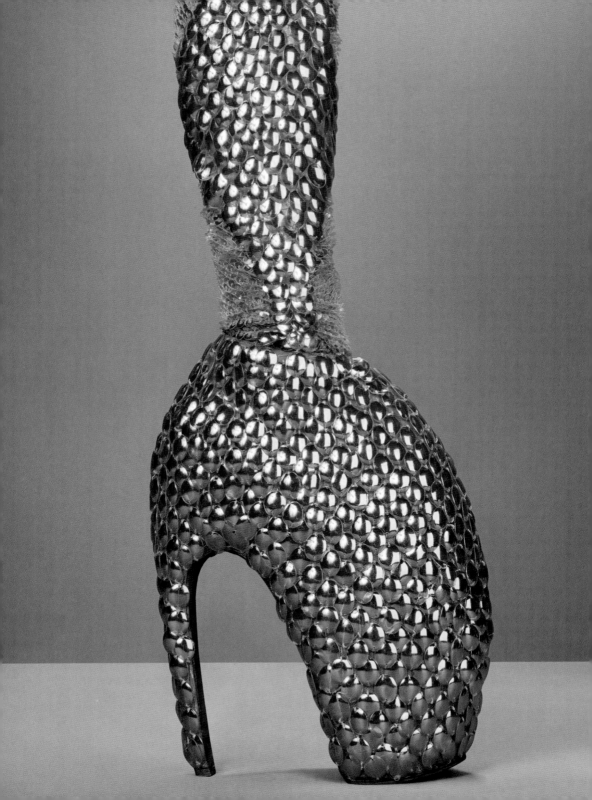

PLATFORM

"I love girls being taller and taller and taller, particularly tall girls wearing platforms. That is heaven for me!"

Terry de Havilland

The elevated sole of the platform is derived from the chopine or patten, a raised wedge sole held on the foot by leather or cloth bands, designed to keep the feet from the dirt of the streets in medieval Europe. In the 1930s, designers André Perugia, Roger Vivier, David Evins, and Salvatore Ferragamo attached a platform sole to the female shoe and instantly added Hollywood magic to a practical style. The platform sole broke all the rules of women's footwear design; it may have been high but it looked heavy. Female feet were supposed to look light and delicate; now they looked clumpy.

The new thick elevated sole, like many inter-war shoe styles, made its first appearance in beach sandals, and from the mid-1930s, the front part of the platform was hinged and interlocked to make the wooden sole flexible and easier to walk in. Perugia injected a much-needed touch of glamor into the style; one pair designed in 1938 for the French film star Arletty was made of gold kidskin with straps that led to a strap that buckled around the ankle, and the cork platform sole was also covered in gold leather. Salvatore Ferragamo's platforms were the most extravagant of the decade with exaggerated arches and multilayered soles; his pair designed for singing sensation Judy Garland in 1938 had uppers crafted of gold kidskin, and cork platforms covered in a rainbow of luxurious *chamois* (sheepskin). For the next ten years the designer experimented with a range of platforms in pressed and rounded layers of leather, wood, and cork, sculpted, painted, and decorated with mosaic mirrors or flashing jewels.

French shoe designer Roger Vivier was another early innovator of the platform and he designed shoes with an elevated sole from the early 1930s. He had discovered a pair of antique Chinese lotus foot slippers at the *Marché des Puces* in Paris and described how "... a close study of those Chinese slippers resulted in my invention

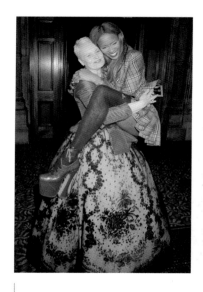

above:
"Super Elevated Ghillie" (1993)
Naomi Campbell drapes a platform-booted leg over designer Vivienne Westwood at London Fashion Week.

left:
Avant-garde Armadillos (2011)
Alexander McQueen's extreme platform shoe design morphed the human foot into a reptilian fantasy.

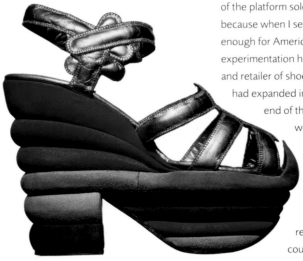

of the platform sole; but my happiness quickly turned to tears
because when I sent it to New York I was told it was not nearly dainty
enough for American women to wear." The rejection of Vivier's
experimentation had come from Herman Delman, a manufacturer
and retailer of shoes whose business had been set up in 1919 and
had expanded into ready-to-wear in the 1930s. Ironically, by the
end of the decade, despite his initial concerns that the shoe
wouldn't sell, Delman's factory was making 2,500
platforms per week, many piped with gold and
silver and painted aluminum to shine in the dark.
The fashion for the platform sole in America
had been helped, in part, by the popularity
of film star Carmen Miranda who in 1946 was
reportedly the highest-paid entertainer in the
country, earning $200,000 USD that year (over
$2 million USD today). She was five feet three inches tall
and supplemented her height on stage and the screen with huge
platforms designed by Ted Saval. By 1941, platform soles were the
height of fashion; Joseph Salon's "Teeter" platforms were advertised
in women's magazines and had reached five inches in height by the
end of the Second World War; Palter de Liso, a New York-based
shoe company (est. 1919) made jewel-colored suede ankle-strap
platforms edged in gold kidskin. However, the platform's reign was
not to last and the style was completely overtaken by the stiletto heel
in the 1950s, disappearing off the radar for over twenty years, only
to resurface in an even more grandiose form in the 1970s.

In 1971 *The Sunday Times* wrote of "monster boots with vast
club-like wedges" and glam rock stars including David Bowie,
Sweet, and Elton John were seen onstage in outlandish platforms
of cartoon proportions in a camp appropriation of female footwear
fashion. Glam rock platforms were worn to create an imposing,
theatrical, and androgynous stage presence, utilized in a swaggering,
macho way later in the decade by rock band KISS. The platform
was the main feature of the shoe, with layers marked out in strips
of metallic or primary-colored leather to draw attention to its height
(and mark out its difference from an orthopedic shoe to which they
were continually compared in the press). This extreme, attention-
grabbing shoe was the highest ever worn by men, and when it went
mainstream, was accompanied by high-waisted flared trousers and

a shirt open to the navel—a boon to those of short stature including Elton John, who confessed that it was the reason he wore them.

Platforms were an incredible hit in America, appearing in 1970s fashion magazines and advertising, and remaining popular into the 1980s in both disco culture and mainstream fashion, manufactured by firms such as Candies, Master John of Toronto, and Cherokee of California. The platform was also associated with "superfly" fashion based on the film of the same name, *SuperFly* (1972) starring Ron O'Neill as Youngblood Priest, a cocaine dealer fighting his way out of the murky underworld of New York to a bestselling soundtrack by Curtis Mayfield. The hyper-masculine style of dress displayed by the pimps in the film included tight shirts and high-waisted flared pants, flashy jewelry anticipating the "bling" of the 2000s, and exaggerated platforms. Isaac Hayes—the man responsible for the soundtrack of *Shaft* (1971), another controversial "blaxploitation" movie—owned twenty-seven pairs of skin-tight thigh-high platform boots. Writer Tom Wolfe evocatively described the look in his essay "Funky Chic" (1973): "All the young aces and dudes are out there lollygagging around the front of the Monterey Club, wearing their two-tone patent Pyramids with the five-inch heels that swell out at the bottom to match the Pierre Chareau Art Deco plaid bell-bottom baggies they have on with the three-inch deep elephant cuffs tapering up toward the 'spray-can' fit in the seat." Wolfe's description of the shoe also suggests another variation of the Spectator (see page 158), a shoe that had an important place in African-American culture since the 1920s.

The existence of acrylic-heeled platforms with a live goldfish swimming inside has been hotly debated over the years; in 1972 the *Montreal Gazette* featured a photograph of shoe salesman Bill Shillan holding the "El Padrino" or "Godfather Shoe" created by Ron Scott of Gentlemen's Jodphur (est. 1971), an American shoemaker and retailer famed for his outlandish platform designs. The "El Padrino" had an upper emblazoned with the stars and stripes and a four-inch Plexiglas heel that, when displayed in the store's window, doubled as a fishbowl that could be looked after through a vent in the insole. The report ended, "Think there's something

below:

Dominatrix

A fetish ankle boot of *c.* 1935 with exaggerated platform to showcase the constricted foot and increase the wearer's height.

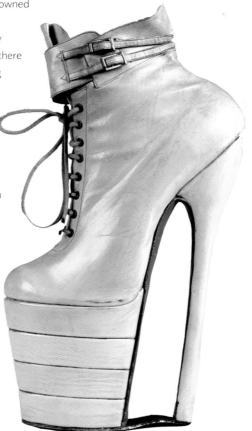

A. F. Vandevorst (Fall/Winter 2009)

The concealed platform is a popular 2000s innovation, providing a visual and physical counterbalance to the extreme heel.

below:

Galliano *c.* **2000s**

A playful postmodernist design that combines a Belle Epoque front-laced upper with a high, needle heel and exposed platform.

fishy about it all? You're right. The shoe is not for sale, never mind wearing." Like the "Gina Wheel-Heel" stiletto of the 1950s—an unwieldy shoe with a tapered heel ending in a wheel, supposedly to prevent damage done to floors with metal heel tips—the "El Padrino" seems to have been a publicity stunt.

Platforms were also popular in the 1990s; the first out of the blocks in this decade were Vivienne Westwood who launched her "Elevated Court Shoe" in the Portrait Collection (Fall/Winter 1990), and John Fluevog who designed the iconic "Munster Shoe" worn by singer Lady Miss Kier on the cover of Deee-Lite's debut album *World Clique* (1990). Madonna also wore the Louis-heeled Munster in her film *Truth or Dare* (1991). Westwood's collections had become increasingly historical throughout the 1980s, beginning with her Pirate Collection in 1980, and her interest in shoes reflected her belief that clothes should embody the "idea of the heroic." Women did not have to be put on a pedestal by men—they could do it themselves when wearing her shoes.

Westwood provided a contrast to the dominance of minimalism encapsulated in the march of Prada, an Italian label that had caught the zeitgeist with its discreet black clothes, shoes, and neoprene bags. Westwood's collection could not have been more different; the models appeared to have walked out of a Versailles boudoir painting by Watteau or Fragonard in black stretch-velvet garments, rich with elaborate gold-painted Rococo detailing and photographic prints such as Francois Boucher's *Daphnis and Chloe* (1743)—Westwood had spent a great deal of time studying the eighteenth-century paintings in the Wallace Collection in London. The shiny, black patent leather or brown suede "Elevated Court Shoe" had a concealed platform in which the upper extended in one piece to cover it, unlike the overt 1970s shape that made a feature of its height by dividing it visually into layers. When the concealed platform was viewed from the front, it looked like the prow of a ship and had a thick, slightly flared heel to balance the shape—no other extraneous decoration was needed on such an arresting silhouette. The collection also included a platform Oxford with brown leather wings extending from the back of the upper—the "Elevated Wing Shoe."

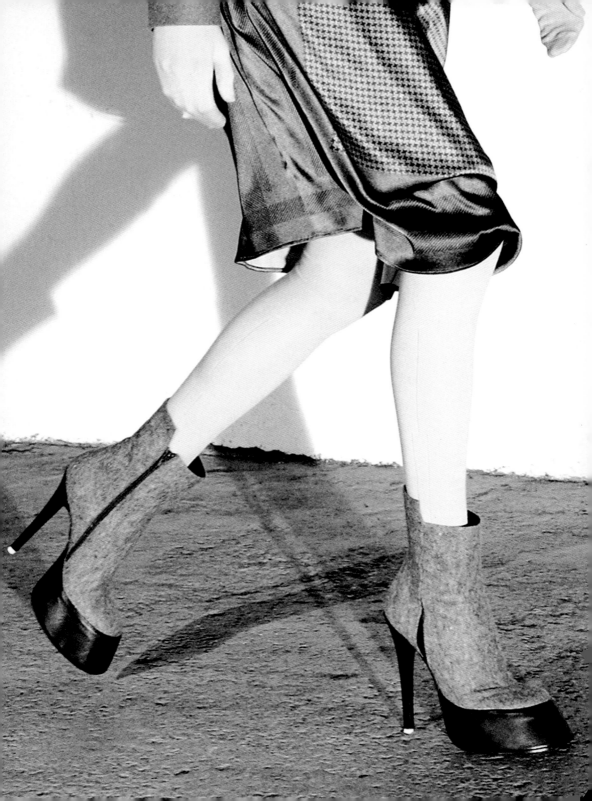

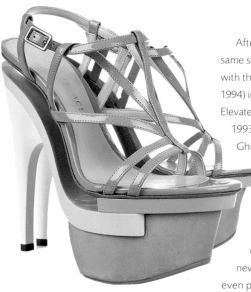

above:

Versace c. 2000s
A patent-leather platform whose
teetering heights are softened by
a color palette of the softest pastels.

After her Portrait collection, Westwood experimented with the
same shape; she made the concealed platform and heel even higher
with the "Super Elevated Fur Boot" (On Liberty Collection Fall/Winter
1994) in gray sheepskin; a teetering lime-green mock-croc "Super
Elevated Court Shoe" (appeared in Grand Hotel Spring/Summer
1993) and, most infamously, her mock-croc "Super Elevated
Ghillie" appeared on the feet of supermodel Naomi Campbell in
Anglomania (Fall/Winter 1993).

In 1991 the *New York Times* had heralded what
the reporter called "the reawakening of the platform,"
adding a few words of caution: "Platform sole shoes make
any woman feel taller and thinner. And they do look quite
wonderful with a long skinny skirt since they give a whole
new proportion to the silhouette. But this thick a shoe is tricky,
even potentially dangerous to wear. One stub of the toe and you
might be replacing the shoe with a plaster cast." Campbell would
have done well to watch out, for when sashaying down the catwalk
in Westwood's blue ankle-strap platforms (see page 63) she missed
her footing and did a spectacular tumble to the delight of the
photographers (and the fashion elite).

In 1992, Karl Lagerfeld at Chanel was also showing platforms,
though more modest than Westwood and Fluevog's. They were
cork-soled black suede platform sandals with a two-inch sole and a
four-and-a-half-inch heel with an ankle-strap that closed with Velcro.
Lagerfeld's take on the platform harked back to the 1940s originals
and prompted another analysis in the *New York Times* by journalist
William Grimes, who was clearly enamored of the trend: "The shoe
is paradoxical. It overturns the meaning of the sandal, a creature
of sunlight and fresh air, but here enlisted into sinister nighttime
service. The sole is bulky but lightweight, a natural untreated

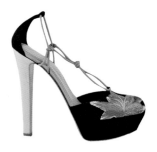

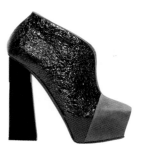

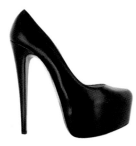

material put to the uses of artifice. With its elegant ankle harness, the Chanel sandal presents the foot as a beautiful slave."

In the Vive la Cocotte Collection (Fall/Winter 1995) Westwood swapped the thick, flared heel that accompanied her platforms with a spindle stiletto in metal with a disk at the bottom to aid balance. The combination of a stiletto rather than stack heel with a concealed platform was a revolutionary, if precarious one, and anticipated innovations in shoe design by well over a decade.

In 2009, the Yves Saint Laurent "Tribute" platform sandal started the reign of the power platform, a shoe with a vertiginous heel that needed a slab of platform underneath the sole to add balance and make the shoe physically wearable. In contrast to the chunky heel that marked out the 1970s and early 1990s platform, the power platform had an extremely high, fine heel that lent itself to a certain elegance; Victoria Beckham wore a pair of customized Christian Louboutin Daffodils dyed to match her outfit with a six-and-a-half-inch heel and two-and-a-half-inch concealed platform to the wedding of Prince William and Kate Middleton at Westminster Abbey in 2011. Nicholas Kirkwood, a shoe designer who designed many of the most deluxe and experimental power platforms reasoned in 2011, "A ten centimeter heel—I mean, it just looks a bit mumsy and low, doesn't it?" In an article in the same year entitled "The Rise of the Power Platform," journalist Jess Cartner-Morley wrote, "There is certainly nothing mumsy about the power platform. The traditional stiletto shape is a subtle form of power dressing; the new platform, by contrast, makes no bones about its ability to crush rivals underfoot. It is the 4 x 4 of the shoe world." Interestingly, this time around, men have refused to participate in the revival of the platform, unlike in the heady days of 1970s glam. It has become too overwhelmingly female.

Cutaway platform
Sergio Rossi cut away the sides of his platform shoe of Spring/Summer 2012.

Glam platform (Fall/Winter 2011)
1970s glam rock inspired this glittering shoe-boot by Aperlai.

Iconic platform
Christian Louboutin's "Daffodils" were famously worn by Victoria Beckham to the UK Royal Wedding in 2011.

Techno platform
A Pierre Hardy suede shoe breaks up its construction into distinct parts.

Power platform (Lorenzi, 2011)
A black suede platform pump with red-patent leather floral embellishment.

Art platform
Nicholas Kirkwood's homage to New York graffiti artist Keith Haring was designed in 2011.

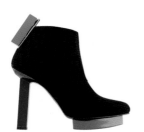

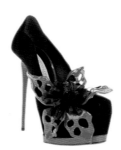

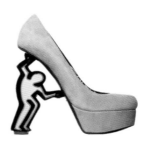

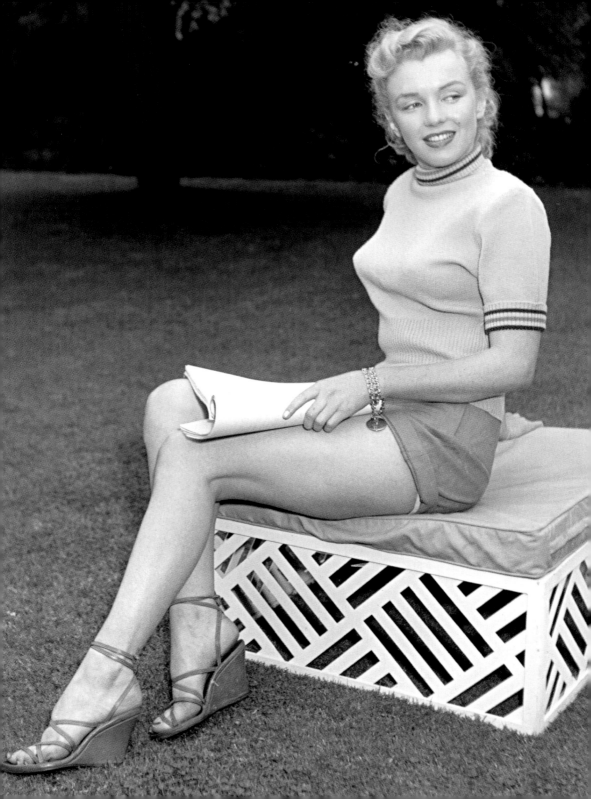

WEDGE

"Platform soles make short girls taller,
wedge heels make tall girls look short."
Life magazine, 1938

The first wedge shoe was the chopine, a shoe with a thick cork or wooden sole worn in Europe from the fourteenth to the seventeenth century and itself descended from traditional Turkish bathing clogs, called *nahn*. The height of the chopine's cork sole grew until it began to provoke comment; one pilgrim who journeyed through Venice wrote of women who "walk on great soles covered with cloth, three of my fists high, which cause them to walk with such difficulty that one pities them."

The tallest chopine were worn by courtesans in the public squares of Venice, a rich and cosmopolitan city where fashion was a prime indicator of wealth and rank. The chopine became a form of advertising for the sex trade—it made the working girls literally stand out from the crowd; lower chopine also known as *pianelle* were the footwear of respectable women who enjoyed being further away from the foul-smelling streets of the city. Wealthy women also liked that the extra material needed to cover their shoes accentuated their elaborate dresses and thus their social status.

The modern wedge was invented by Italian footwear designer Salvatore Ferragamo during the 1940s. The primary role of shoes in this era was to provide function and durability in wartime—the practical tweed suit conceived by British designers Hardy Amies and Digby Morton who worked for the government's Utility Scheme was the sartorial equivalent. The Ferragamo wedge evolved as a direct result of the Italo-Ethiopian War, when Mussolini's Italian forces invaded Ethiopia in 1935. Economic sanctions were imposed on Italy by the League of Nations, leading to the steel used in shoe arches being in short supply. Ferragamo was known for inserting steel plates into the arches of all of his shoes to give added support to the foot— he was a passionate believer in the notion that shoes should work

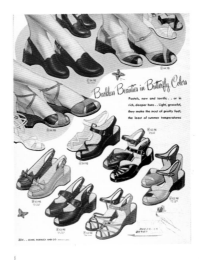

above:

Mainstream fashion
By the early 1950s, the practical wedge sandal was an accepted staple in women's wardrobes.

left:

The Hollywood wedge
Marilyn Monroe wears ankle-strap wedges for a photo session in Beverly Hills (1950).

ergonomically as well as look fashionably stylish. He said, "Women must be persuaded that luxury shoes need not be painful to walk in; they must be convinced that it is possible to wear the most refined and exotic footwear because we know how to design a supportive shoe modeled to the shape of the foot. Elegance and comfort are not incompatible, and whoever maintains the contrary simply doesn't know what he is talking about."

The wedge was a perfect example of this philosophy, born out of the absence of good-quality steel. In his Florentine workshop in 1936, Ferragamo came up with a simple solution—he filled in the space between the platform sole and the heel. To make the volume of the wedge light enough to be worn, Ferragamo fashioned it from layers of Sardinian cork, explaining that, "The comfort was in the cork. Rubber would have given a jerky, springy step; cork makes the feet feel as if they are riding on a cushion." The cork had to be carefully worked to achieve the right result; a specialist craftsman spent at least two days rubbing it down and then pressing it so that it remained stable. The wedge shoe was revolutionary in that it gave height but the wearer retained their balance, and Ferragamo filed for the patent in 1937, but as he ruefully recognized, "By that time every shoemaker in the world was making wedges and to have sustained my claims I would have been forced to sue everyone."

Ferragamo created many innovative wedges; in 1938 he combined the *babouche*—a Turkish design with a distinctive turned-up toe—with the backless mule, and attached a gold, kidskin-covered wedge after a drawing by Oliver Messel for a production of *The Thief of Baghdad*; a 1942 oval-toed design in patchwork suede with a four-tiered cork wedge covered in strips of turquoise blue, terracotta, mustard yellow, and deep purple suede; and the "Invisible Shoe" of 1947, a design that featured a slimline F-shaped, wooden wedge heel—originally designed by American Seymour Troy in 1939—and part ankle strap. The wearer's feet were held in by transparent nylon thread—hence the name—that gave a see-through effect to the shoe, inspired by the fishing line Ferragamo had seen being used by fisherman on the River Arno.

Wedges were manufactured by many companies in the late 1930s and 1940s in Europe and the United States, and ranged from

right:

Dolce and Gabbana (2011)
This ankle-strap wedge takes inspiration from the proportions of the 1970s version of the shoe.

below:

Lacroix (Spring/Summer 2007)
An ostentatious black-lacquered wooden wedge with a black-leather ankle strap and tassel decoration.

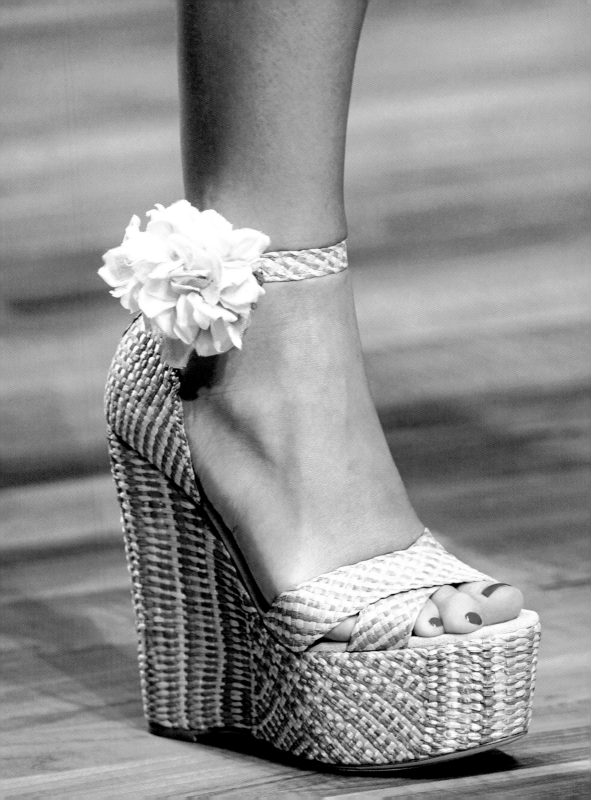

low wooden soles to high cork with the sides used as a surface that could be embellished in a myriad of ways. At the end of the war there was a widespread backlash against the wedge because of its association with the post-war years. American *Vogue* Editor Diana Vreeland hated both wedges and platforms, remembering: "Everyone was in wooden shoes, clack, clack, clack. You could tell the time of the day by the sound of the wooden soles on the pavement. If there was a great storm of them, it meant that it was lunch hour and people were leaving their offices for restaurants. Then there would be another great clatter when they returned."

The wedge rose again through the work of shoemaker Terry de Havilland in the 1970s, who magically reinterpreted the shape on the back of a wholesale revival of nostalgic shoes that had been instigated by Barbara Hulanicki at Biba. In 1969, he created the iconic "Leyla," a three-tiered wedge sandal in patchwork snakeskin, after finding one of his father's original designs dating from the 1940s in the attic, followed by the metallic snakeskin "Margaux" in 1975. De Havilland, born Terry Higgins in 1938, had inherited his family company, Waverley Shoes of London, and opened his shop, Cobblers to the World, on King's Road in London in 1972. Here he sold five-inch wedges to customers such as Britt Ekland, Bianca Jagger, and Angie Bowie. Beth Levine designed a printed leather boot with a crepe wedge heel in 1971, and towering three-buckled wedges were worn by aficionados of Northern Soul. In America the "Kork-Ease" cork wedge was a national phenomenon. By 1976, punk replaced glamor with grit, the stiletto heel was revived, and de Havilland resorted to catering to the subcultural market under the brand name Kamikaze Shoes.

In the 1990s, the wedge returned in a hybrid form with the ubiquitous Buffalo trainer, a towering wedge that made a mockery of sports shoes by being positively hazardous to walk in. The trainer was popularized by pop group The Spice Girls in 1996. Their call for "Girl Power" and the wearing of the "Buffalo Tower 1310-3" with its six-inch wedge gave the wedge an appeal that managed to imbue such an exaggerated shape with a brash sexiness, especially when worn with a neon-hued stretch mini. When Buffalo opened

below:

Prada "Rocket"

Prada launched a wedge in Spring/Summer 2012 with echoes of *Flash Gordon* sci-fi styling.

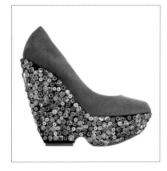
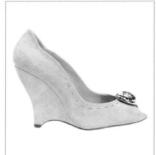
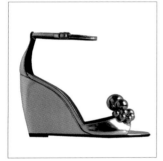
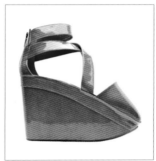

a store in London's Neal Street, it became a mecca for wannabe Baby Spices—even after the pop star had famously fallen off her pair in 1997 and broken her ankle.

Miu Miu, set up by Italian fashion designer Miuccia Prada in 1992 as an eclectic sister label to Prada, launched wedge shoes that strayed perilously close to the look of de Havilland's, irritating him enough to relaunch the originals. The "Leyla" and the "Margaux" were spotted on the feet of modern style icons such as Kate Moss and Sienna Miller, and the wedge was discovered by a new generation. The fashion for wedges reached its height in the 2000s; Patrick Cox designed a whimsical gold-leather strappy wedge in 2005 with miniature chandeliers dangling from the back; the Zabot label launched a hybrid shiny fuchsia-pink patent clog/wedge in 2008; Finsk, a label set up by Finnish-born Julia Lundsten, launched back-zipped wedge ankle boots in black pony hair and monochromatic suede in Fall/Winter 2009. Wedges have been attached to every shoe in the lexicon of footwear from Jil Sander's black-leather wedge ankle boots through Carven's wedge loafers, to Acne's wedge brogues.

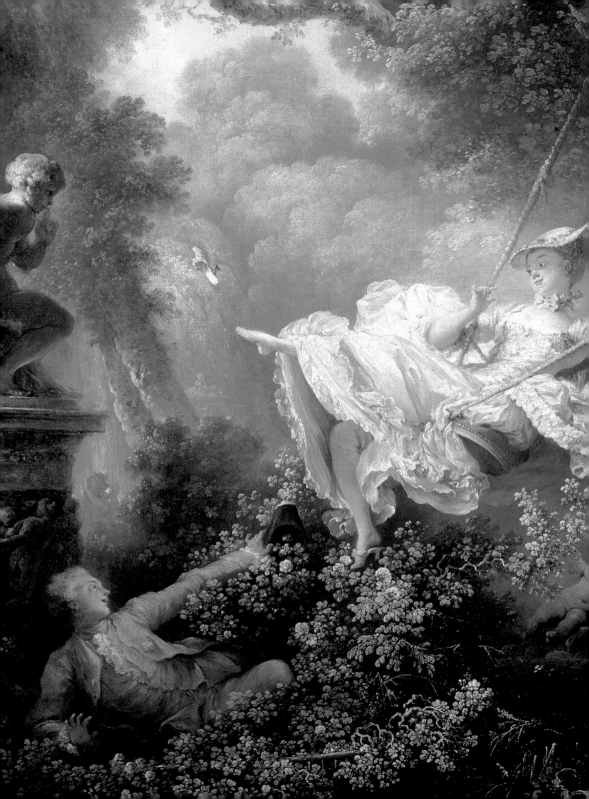

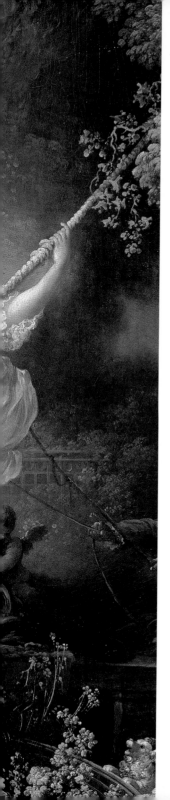

16–18th CENTURY

A certain flamboyancy began to enter into shoes during this period—high heels evolved, at first as a practical way of keeping a man's feet in the stirrups when riding, but later as a mark of social status that literally raised the wearer above the lowly masses. Footwear also becomes much more heavily gendered as women's shoes became increasingly delicate, fashioned from luxurious materials with curved Louis heels.

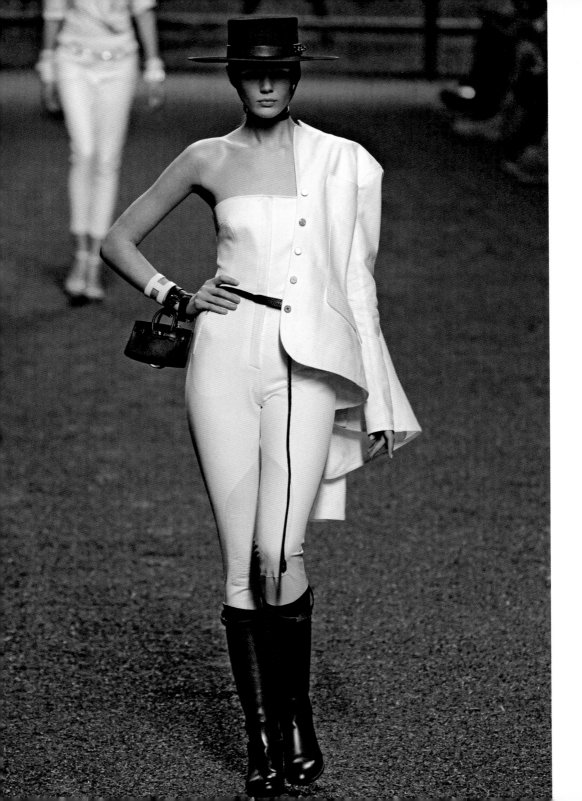

RIDING BOOT

"The tall, brown riding boots with a marvelous sooty glow, as if, though new, they had been worn a hundred years."
John Galsworthy, 1932

The riding boot is a heeled boot that fits and grips in the stirrup, is long enough to prevent the saddle from nipping the leg of the rider, and strong enough to protect the foot while on the ground. Tall riding boots were traditionally made of soft leather so the horses' flanks could be controlled by light pressure from the rider. As all gentlemen rode before the invention of the railway and motorized transport, they wore riding boots, and the boots became a mark of prestige, many highly decorated and richly wrought. Riding boots were at their most flamboyant in the sixteenth century; scalloped trims abounded as did intricately patterned uppers, together with turnover tops trimmed with lace. Today, a vestige of all this ornamentation can be seen in the combination of slick, black-leather riding boot with a contrasting brown leather top.

Many men's riding boots were given names that referenced military activity such as the "Napoleon," recognized by its high-cut front. After the French Revolution, men's riding boots became more serious, worn for function rather than fashion and made from waxed leather with a more rigid construction. For women, riding was a very different proposition, for equestrian equality is a twentieth-century achievement, much like women's right to vote. In many early societies such as Native American and Central Asian, women rode in the same way as men, astride their mounts—in the thirteenth century, writer Chaucer described the lusty spur-wearing Wife of Bath in *The Canterbury Tales* as riding in the same way as her male counterparts. As heavy decorative skirts entered fashion, women began riding behind men on a pillion or cushion that was set behind the saddle.

There was another issue at work here too—chastity became highly valued during the era of feudal rule, when women, especially

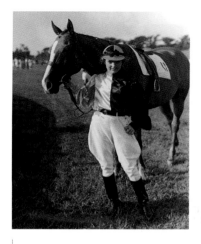

above:
Jackie, oh!
Fashion icon Jackie Kennedy, all cool patrician chic in riding boots at the East Hampton Horse Show.

left:
Sports deluxe
Luxury leather accessories are a Hermès specialty. These riding boots date from Spring/Summer 2011.

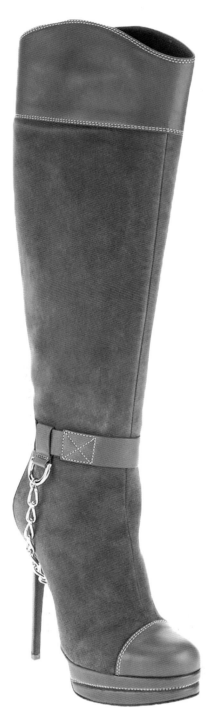

royal brides, were not allowed to own property. When Princess Anne of Bohemia journeyed across Europe in 1382 to meet her betrothed, King Richard II, she went side-saddle, sitting on a chairlike contraption with a front pommel to grip onto and a rudimentary footrest. Women were no longer allowed to control a horse (nor their own destinies) and were led by a male rider from the front. By the seventeenth century, the custom had become entrenched and no woman considered a lady rode astride; it was believed to be the height of wantonness. By the seventeenth century, a pommel was introduced to the front of the side saddle around which the rider could hitch one knee for stability and assert a degree of control, and a leather-covered stirrup was made available for one foot—women were thus strapped to one side of the horse. It seems unbelievable today that in such a precarious position many were able to ride to hounds and even take jumps, but accidents did happen—lucky male riders could be thrown away from their mounts and survive, but when a horse toppled with a woman in side-saddle, she could be easily crushed underneath.

Understandably, women's riding boots were slow to develop, since women were not necessarily "riding" in the accepted sense. In the eighteenth and early nineteenth centuries, women wore the same heel-less leather slippers they normally wore by day to present a pretty picture when on horseback. By 1848, *Godey's Lady's Book* wrote, "Dark boots should be worn for riding. Ladies who ride much will find the advantage of having a neat kid or Morocco boot" but there is scant evidence to suggest this was a fashion that had caught on. It took a group of pioneering women to create change, female travelers who were dubbed the "Long Riders" and included Isabella Bird, who was taught how to ride like a man by Mexican *vaqueros*, and Ethel Tweedie who rode astride like the local women when visiting Iceland, explaining, "Necessity gives courage in emergencies, so I determined to throw aside conventionality, and do in 'Iceland as the Icelanders do.' The amusement of our party when I overtook them, and boldly trotted past, was intense; but I felt so comfortable in my altered seat that their derisive and chaffing remarks failed to disturb me. Riding man-fashion is less tiring than on a side saddle, and I soon found it far more agreeable, especially when traversing rough ground. My success soon inspired Miss T. to summon up courage and follow my lead. Society is a hard task-master, yet for comfort and safety, I say ride like a man."

By the early twentieth century, riding was enjoying a rush of popularity among women, and the side saddle appeared both old-fashioned and patriarchal, particularly among suffragette-minded women who wanted no curtailment of their physical activities. In 1910, one such rider, the evocatively named Two Gun Nan Aspinwall rode astride from San Francisco to New York in a specially adapted split skirt, and in 1912, Alberta Clare rode across America in the same manner while calling on women to fight for the vote. Suffragette Inez Milholland rode astride her white steed, Gray Dawn, at the head of a huge parade of women in New York and Washington dressed in an outfit inspired by Joan of Arc in 1912 and 1913, charging on any men who opposed them as they made their way to Capitol Hill. In 1920, women's suffrage was granted in an amendment to the United States Constitution, and suffragettes rode into the polling stations on a side saddle and then after voting galloped out astride their horses.

Riding boots became practical and functional for both men and women—riding was now about sport not status. Boots with gaiters, puttees, or leggings began to be worn, including the ankle-laced flexible field boot, the cuffed hunt boot, and, later, short jodhpur boots with elastic sides. Today the tall riding boot is ever popular whenever it crosses over into fashion and its stack heel and sleek silhouette regularly appear in the winter. Designers love the boot's heritage appeal and it is frequently teamed with tweed and Fairisle knits to conjure a classic bucolic fantasy.

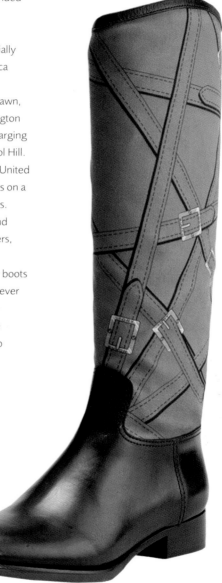

left:
Gianmarco Lorenzo (2011)
Lorenzo plays with the vocabulary of the traditional riding boot, adding a stiletto heel and toe cap.

right:
Boot straps
Tory Burch inserts a witty print into the leg of the riding boot to contrast with the practical toe and heel.

JACKBOOT

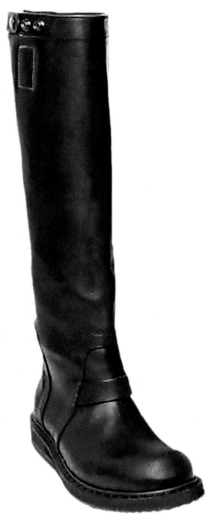

Today the jackboot is regarded as the footwear of totalitarian regimes, yet its origins are as a soldier's riding, rather than marching, boot. The name is derived from the French *jaque*, or chain mail, as the original tall, winged cavalry boot was jacked or reinforced by chain mail sewn into the lining of the leather, hence its general reputation for toughness. The cavalry jackboot was specifically designed for soldiers on horseback: the boot extended in length along the knee to protect it from injury during battles; widened out at the top for ease of access; had a high heel to fit in the stirrups; and a flat leather band around the ankle to which a spur was attached.

> "I think I've always had drive, and a kind of inner aggression that you have to have."
> Rick Owens

The jackboot was worn by cavalry units all over Europe from the seventeenth through the nineteenth century until it proved too cumbersome for soldiers on dismount. It remained as a form of ceremonial dress, most notably when worn by members of the Queen's Household Cavalry in London and produced by Schneider Boots of Mayfair. By the end of the nineteenth century, the term "jackboot" broadened to cover boots that came to mid-calf and were pulled on by means of straps inside the boot, having no zipper or laces.

During the First World War, the word jackboot began to refer to the combat footwear or *marschstiefel* (marching boots) worn by German storm troopers in the First World War, the SS during the Second World War, and the Russian army during the Cold War. Thus began the jackboot's associations with oppressive political and military ideology that remain to this day. The German version varied in length from mid-calf to knee, had hobnails in the soles, and iron horseshoe shapes embedded in the heels for extra longevity when marching long distances—this hardware also made a distinctive sound that came to symbolize oppression, especially when the heels were clicked together. Nazi troopers during the Third Reich were issued Model 1939 marching boots in brown leather that required the application of bootblack to acquire their shiny black finish.

After the Second World War, the jackboot became somewhat of a taboo; it went underground, appearing in sado-masochistic imagery, and overground by the end of the 1960s in movies such as Visconti's *The Damned* (1969), *The Night Porter* (1974), and *Salon Kitty* (1976). The jackboot has also made appearances on the 2000s catwalk alongside black leather trench coats, peaked caps, and boots such as Louis Vuitton's Spring/Summer 2011 collection. Raf Simons has been flirting with such elements since his Fall/Winter 2007 collection and for his Spring/Summer 2011 Anthem Collection, Rick Owens presented tall black-leather "High Jack" jackboots with stitch-panel detailing and three single snaps to alter the fit of the boot. Like their Third Reich predecessors, the Owens jackboots had the same vulcanized rubber sole and internal canvas pulls.

left:
The "High Jack" (2011)
Rick Owens' Anthem Collection launched this jackboot with stitch detailing and snaps to alter the fit.

below:
Anthem Collection
Owens is one of the few designers to rebrand the disturbing jackboot for a modern audience.

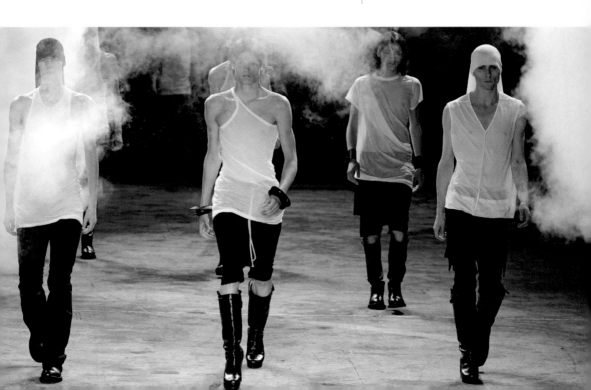

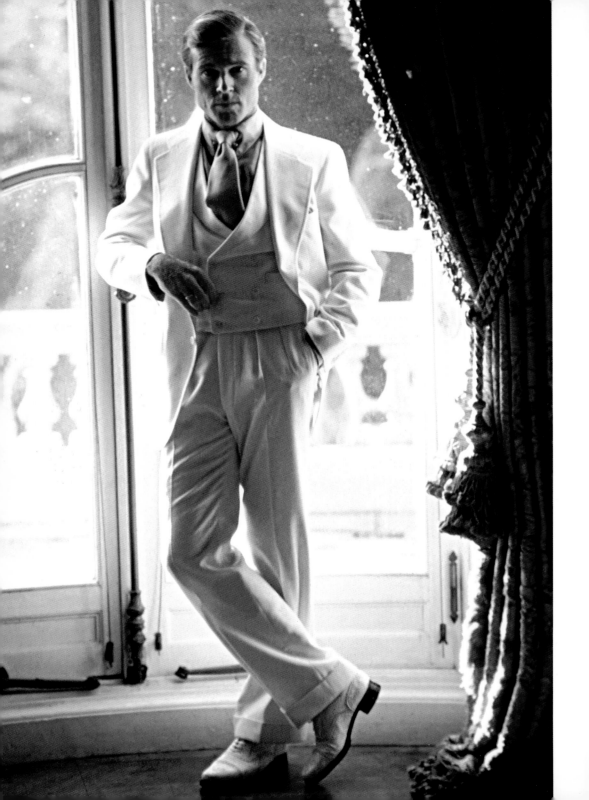

BROGUE

"It's time for sneakerheads
to graduate."

Matthew Chevallard, Del Toro president, 2011

Deriving from the Norse word *brók* or "leg covering," the brogue
is a low-heeled shoe or boot easily identifiable by the decorative
lacelike punched perforations (a.k.a. broguing), pinking, and
gimped edges on its leather upper. The seventeenth-century brogue
was originally an untanned perforated leather shoe designed for
walking the peat bogs of Scotland and Ireland, since the tiny holes
allowed the water to drain out. In 1779, writer Samuel Johnson while
traveling on the Isle of Skye off the coast of Scotland wrote of seeing
"brogues, a kind of artless shoe, stitched with thongs so loosely that,
though they defend the foot from stones, they do not exclude water.
Brogues were formerly made of raw hides, with their hair inwards,
and such are perhaps still used in rude and remote parts, but they are
said not to last above two days. Where life is somewhat improved
they are made of leather, tanned with oak-bark."

By the eighteenth century, this rudimentary footwear had evolved
into a heavier shoe of tanned leather with thick hobnailed soles. In
the nineteenth century, the shoe upper became double-layered and
the perforations were applied to the first layer only, thus allowing water
to drain from the shoe without compromising its water resistance. As
a result of its bucolic origins, the brogue has always been regarded
as footwear for the hunting, shooting, and fishing enthusiast. In the
2000s, however, it became a female fashion, an elegant heritage
alternative to the girlish ballet flat (see page 98), and versions have
been created by many of the leading shoe manufacturers and fashion
houses including Miu Miu, Tory Burch, Gucci, and Marc Jacobs who
inserted panels of gold glitter into an anthracite leather pair in 2011.

The foundation of the classic twentieth-century brogue is the
closed, laced Oxford (see page 90) or walking shoe, which is then
decorated in various ways. The toe cap is a focal point: it can be the

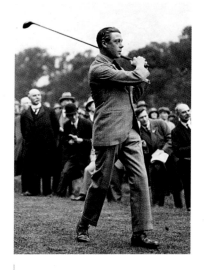

above:

By royal appointment
Edward, Prince of Wales, was a
fashion innovator in the 1930s and
wore brogues to play golf.

left:

Retro brogue
Robert Redford in *The Great Gatsby*
cuts a fine figure in suit, waistcoat,
and classic men's brogues (1974).

traditional full, semi, or quarter; or it can have a W-shaped wingtip or a longwing that extends through the whole length of the shoe. The formal Scottish dress brogue or "ghillie" is named for the assistant to the hunt or fishing expedition on the landed gentry's private estate, and is essentially a brogue with no tongue for fast drying, and with wrap-around laces that pass through leather loops sewn through the shoe's quarters, rather than eyelets on the vamp.

The brogue gained a little fashion fillip in the 1920s when the strict rules of etiquette determining gentlemen's clothes began to break down partly because of the sartorial experimentation of the Duke of Windsor. The brogue, once the preserve of gamekeepers and ghillies, was now being worn on the golf course by royalty. Brown shoes began to stroll nonchalantly into the city as an alternative to formal black, and in 1937, the British company John Lobb created the cap-toed semi- or half-brogue. This new shoe had the brogue's classic perforations and serrated edges on the toe-cap, creating a hybrid of Oxford and brogue that could be worn informally in town. The processing of leather had also improved and brown could assume the antiqued patina of a heritage pair of brogues even if brand new. Broguing detail also entered into women's footwear design, taking the form of perforated panel along the sides and across the toe of the shoe. A heel was added, and reached a height of popularity in the 1970s as a fashionable but sensible alternative to the platform.

Trickers, one of the old-school stalwarts based in Mayfair, London, that also includes John Lobb (established in 1885) and Edward Green (1890) are seen by many as the purveyors of the best brogues. In the United States, brogue brand names include Johnston & Murphy (1850) and Florsheim (1892), whose brogues are fashioned from shell cordovan hide— leather that is taken from the hind-quarters of a horse and is known for its strength and durability. More recently, Trickers have been working with Junya Watanabe of

below:

The "Creeper Brogue"

For Spring/Summer 2010 Prada launched a hybrid of brogue upper and brothel creeper, a curious mix of two classic men's shoes.

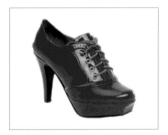
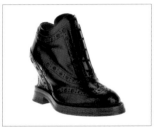
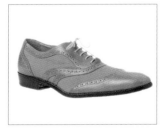
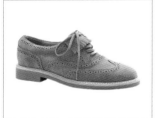

clockwise from top left:

High-heeled brogue

In the 2000s, the brogue has developed into high-heeled forms.

Brogue ankle boot

Acne stretched the traditional brogue detailing over an ankle boot.

Color-blocked brogue

F-Troupe made a focal point of the primary-colored sole.

Streamlined brogue

Vivienne Westwood extended the toe to give a streamlined silhouette.

avant-garde label Comme des Garçons to produce a range of modern brogues, as have Florsheim with menswear designer Duckie Brown, introducing unusual colors such as aqua blue and pale, flesh pink and longwing perforations. The lace-up closures have a five-eyelet vamp, piped trim to the cuff, perforated detailing to the sides, and a stacked and stained wood-effect low block heel, the whole constructed from calf leather with a leather sole.

In 2009, British company Grenson collaborated with Olivia Morris to create a range of Goodyear welted brogues for women including the "Eliza," a semi-brogue with toe-cap perforations with a slimmer silhouette to fit the proportions of the female foot. F-Troupe's brogues designed by Mick Hoyle are a contemporary take on this traditional shoe with their jewel-tone colors, and like many twenty-first century brogue designs, the emphasis is on immediate comfort rather than the owner having to go through the traditional "breaking-in" process—fitting for a generation that has grown up with trainers. Manufacturers such as Church's and Ludwych & Lodger have taken a lead from trainer design by using light, micro soles to transform the brogue into a summer rather than a fall or winter shoe. Bayode Oduwole of Soho-based tailor Pokit describes the brogue as "the stuff of myth and legend. It's folkish and glamorous, but also the footwear of choice for gangsters, spivs, dandies, and gentlemen of leisure. It has a romantic Gatsby image."

SLAP SOLE

Slap soles are a fashion that began in the 1630s and continued until the end of the seventeenth century. The shoe is derived from the practice of gentlemen wearing high-heeled riding boots that were eminently practical when on horseback because they kept the feet securely in the stirrups, but presented a problem when dismounting, since high heels had the tendency of sinking into the soft ground. The practice came into being of slipping shoes into flat-soled mules, and these rudimentary overshoes developed into a shoe in their own right—the slap sole.

> "I hope that the woman who wore these shoes would have felt elevated by them..."
> Bata Shoe Museum podcast, on the slap soles pictured below

This peculiar shoe had a high heel attached to a long, slender hinged sole that extended back from the ball of the foot to the heel itself. The sole was left free at the heel so that when walking, it slapped on the ground in the same manner as a flip-flop. The distinctive sound made by the slap sole shoe led to its name, and it became audible proof that the wearer was at the height of fashion. When women adopted the shoe for fashionable indoor daywear so the original function of keeping heels from the mud was redundant, the sound was even more necessary, since the shoe was invisible under long skirts. Eventually the sole and heel were attached securely and the shoe and mule hybrid assumed an unusual architectural shape that was fashioned from silk and embellished with beading and embroidery.

One would have thought that such a bizarre shoe silhouette would have been lost in the mists of time, but in 1938, Italian footwear designer Salvatore Ferragamo made a modern version with a wooden flat-through sole that linked the

below:

Original slap sole
A seventeenth-century hinged slap sole, a bizarre architectural shape derived from the overshoe.

wooden heel to a cork platform sole. This experimental slingback shoe had black velvet uppers edged with the same silver leather that covered the heel and a platform with alternating layers of silver and gold leather. This shape became associated with "arty" shoes and when platforms were at their highest it appeared again as a decorative device, first in the 1970s by manufacturers such as Romea of Italy and more recently in 2007 when Marc Jacobs showed his first "cut-out" wedge. This new version of the slap sole had a huge platform and heel attached by a sole that left a space or window between the join. Other labels followed, including Jil Sander and Donna Karan in 2007, and in 2011 the shape went mainstream for the very first time in its history, with some of the most extreme examples being designed by Giuseppe Zanotti.

Wedges were the height of fashion and the cut-out version was a way of making them look unusual while allowing more height as the cut-out shapes made them lighter. The cut-out was applied to shoes, ankle boots, flip-flops, and even trainers, and shapes ranged from the usual curved, cornered triangle to more prosaic shapes like stars and flowers. Instead of the uppers being the only canvas for a designer's imagination, the whole functional surface of the shoe became sculptural, spawning some of the most fascinating forms.

The rise, fall, and subsequent rise of the slap sole shows that anything is possible in contemporary shoe design. The most exciting footwear creators realize that looking backward can provoke a step forward in innovation. Joanne Stoker is a case in point; her "Bamboo" shoe of 2011 is a contemporary take on an antique shoe. As she puts it: "Never forget the timeless artifacts of the past but always look to the future when creating something new."

above:
The "Bamboo"
Joanne Stoker launched a new version of the slap sole in her Empire States collection (Fall/Winter 2011).

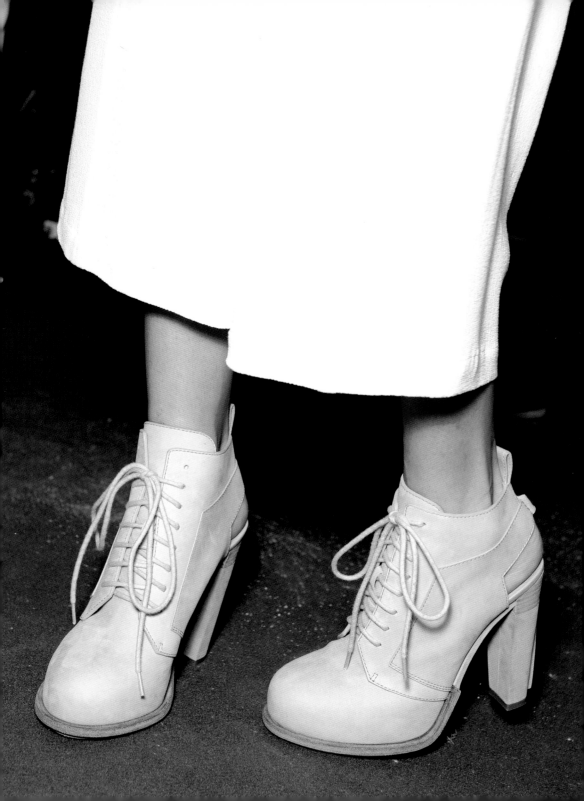

OXFORD

"I was now in possession of a shoe that for the past 100 years has been the second smartest in any man's wardrobe, trumped only by the Oxford."

Paul MacInnes on his brogues, the *Guardian*, June 9, 2008

The Oxford is a classic shoe that laces up the front through three or four pairs of eyelets with a tongue to protect the foot from the pressure of the fastenings. It has curved side seams and a low, stacked heel making it an ideal and practical walking shoe. A key feature of the Oxford is its method of closed lacing whereby the shoelaces are looped through eyelet tabs that are stitched underneath the vamp.

Until the beginning of the seventeenth century, the majority of shoes were fastened with straps or buckles, but in 1640 a brand new style of tailored shoe or half-boot with a lace-up front, square toe, and high heel emerged and was adopted by the students of Oxford University as a comfortable alternative to the heavy jackboot. It had a high tongue to protect the wearer from the splashes of mud that came from the unlined roads. The style spread rapidly and the shoe buckle industry based in Birmingham, with an estimated 20,000 workers, was devastated despite pleas to the King to prohibit lace-up shoes. President Thomas Jefferson was one of the first Americans to wear the Oxford despite accusations of foppishness, and by the end of the nineteenth century, the shoe had taken over from the boot as the footwear of choice in the city. It was a sober, businesslike style suited to the new middle-class industrialist who wanted, above all, to steer clear of any notions of vulgarity in his appearance. Vanity was disgraceful to a man who spent his time earning money to support a respectable household—sartorial frivolity was the arena of the female, who took the decorative role in the relationship.

The handmade Oxford shoe was the height of masculine taste by 1910, and successful manufacturers included Loake of Kettering, Northamptonshire, a business that was set up by brothers Thomas, John, and William Loake in 1880, and Church's of Northampton,

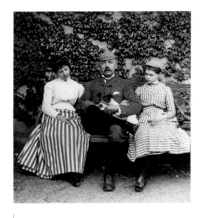

above:

The city shoe

By the end of the nineteenth century, the Oxford had become the favored shoe of the urban man.

left:

Runway Oxford (Spring/Summer 2011)

An avant-garde slingback Oxford with exaggerated lacing and extreme heel by Alexander Wang.

both of which are still in operation today. Loake and Church's gained recognition in the nineteenth century for their use of Goodyear welted construction, an intricate method that consisted of stitching the sole and the upper of the shoe onto a welt or strip of hand-cut leather before affixing it to the bottom of the shoe. Unlike the traditional method, where the sole and upper were directly stitched together, it meant that the sole could be easily detached if a repair was needed.

This method was also used by Italian house Berluti, based in Paris, who gained fame for their exquisite handmade men's shoes including the streamlined toe-capped classic Oxford. The upper was made from a single piece of leather with three eyelets and no visible stitching, and was worn by the Duke of Windsor in the 1920s. The trend-setting Duke was also the first to sport brown suede or

"Always wear expensive shoes. People notice."

Brian Koslow, Entrepreneur

"reverse-calf" Oxfords, causing a sensation by wearing them with a dark blue suit. When one gentleman expressed surprise at this fashion faux pas, one of the Duke's friends countered, "It would be wrong if it were a mistake. But he knows better, so it's all right." By the 1950s, the Oxford was a classic and the first shoe in which little boys were shod—in 1955, the Fortune shoe company that specialized in boys' footwear advertised the Oxford as "ideal for school and church wear" and informed potential consumers that they were "built to meet the strict standards of your Scouts organization." As men's magazine *GQ* put it in 2011, "These are shoes for chaps who like things the way they've always been, and when something's this good, why change it?"

By the early twentieth century, a revolutionary change occurred in women's shoes. Liberated from the shackles of home and hearth and no longer content solely with matters wholly domestic, women began to be a more tangible presence on the city streets and needed a comfortable

below:

Color pop

Jil Sander adds visual interest to her minimalist leather Oxford with a neon-yellow sole.

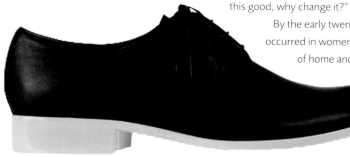

yet elegant walking shoe. The Oxford was the perfect shoe for excursions to the new department stores of the Champs-Elysées in Paris or to browse the windows of Macys, New York, or even to enjoy a theater's matinee performance.

By the 1920s, the Oxford was the most popular form of street shoe for women. The raised hemlines of women's fashion put the focus on the feet and the heel began to rise throughout the decade until a low-cut Oxford with high Cuban heels became a requirement for both day and evening. A few of the traditionally masculine references remained on the shoe such as the enclosed laces and toecaps but others were added, such as wingtips, named from their resemblance to the wings of a bird, and brogueing. Saddle Oxfords had a saddle-shaped section sewn onto the upper quarter of the vamp in a contrasting color to the rest of the shoe. Between 1925 and 1927, cut-outs appeared on the Oxford next to the eyelets and the toes of the shoe were elongated; this new version was renamed the semi-Oxford.

In the 1930s, the toe of the women's Oxford reverted to a rounder shape to fit the feminine curves that had reentered fashion and gained a sporty vibe—one star who favored this shoe was Katherine Hepburn, renowned in Hollywood for her athletic prowess. A journalist described the actress in 1940 "tipping back her chair to tie the lace of her Oxford shoe. These walking shoes studded with spikes, emphasizing her practical preferences in clothes, were worn with gabardine slacks in a greeny-fawn tone, a browny-fawn gabardine sporting coat, and a perfectly tailored white silk blouse."

In the 2000s, the sensible Oxford shoe attracted the attention of many designers who enjoyed subverting its dormant form. Alexander Wang created a directional stack-heeled cutaway version in textured eggshell leather in 2011 (see page 90), and in the same year Rag & Bone launched a minimalist pair in bright red suede on the back of the color-blocking fashion story that had dominated the runways. The 2000s recession stimulated an interest in practical shoes that denote a clear head for business, hence the revival of interest in such work-friendly footwear.

above:

Elegant lines
Vivienne Westwood's Oxford of 2012 has an elongated toe that echoes the shapes of the 1920s.

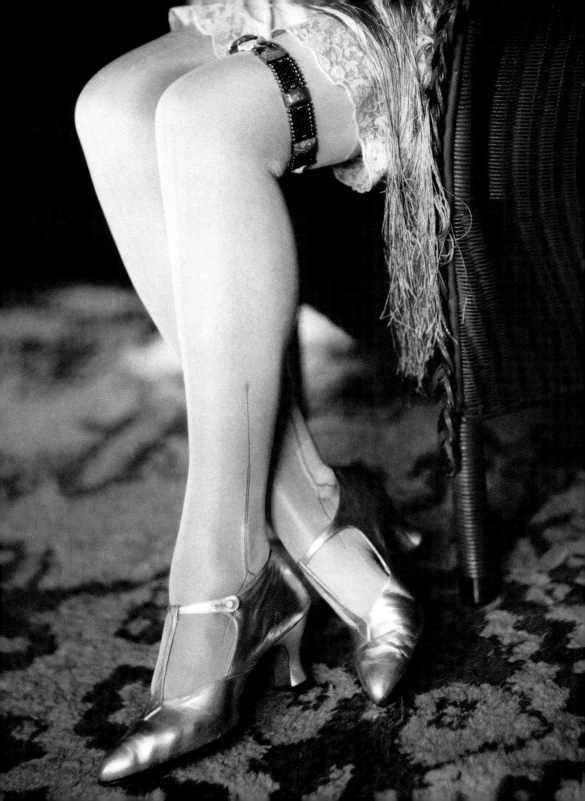

LOUIS HEEL

"My shoes are special shoes for
discerning feet."

Manolo Blahnik

The Louis heel is one of the earliest heel shapes, originally invented
by Nicholas Lestage in 1660. Heels were popularized by the rather
short French King Louis XIV (the Sun King), who at five feet three
inches wanted to increase his height and stature at the court
of Versailles. The height of the heel was significant because it
displayed social status by literally raising the aristocracy above the
masses and, by inhibiting movement, showed the wearer lived a
life of leisure. At the French court of the Sun King, attire played an
important role in displaying the absolute divine right and power of
the monarchy; it separated the rich from the poor. This passion for
courtly extravagance continued into the reign of Louis XV, who wore
the Louis heel. The Louis heel was fashioned of wood and had a
concave curve and an outward flare at the base of the heel that made
it graceful to look at and relatively sturdy to walk in. This early high
heel was one of the first to have a heel higher than the toe rather than
being an elevated platform like the patten or chopine (see page 63).
Throughout the eighteenth century, women's shoes had Louis heels
of varying thicknesses and heights, up to four inches high.

    Louis' favorite mistress Madame de Pompadour popularized a
higher, finer version of the Louis heel dubbed the Pompadour, and
it was worn with gowns that had tightly fitted bodices stiffened with
stays and skirts that were extended laterally to each side by paniers
or hoops. Rich materials were the norm, embossed, brocaded, and
shot through with gold thread, and the King's favorite had tiny shoes
with the elegantly waisted Pompadour heel offset with huge brocade
bows or jeweled buckles on the front of the vamp.

    A change in shoe shape was affected by the French Revolution
and, as Marie Antoinette went to the guillotine defiantly wearing a
pair of heels, they became associated with an aristocratic decadence

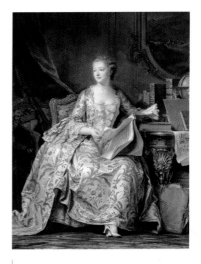

above:

The seductive shoe
Madame de Pompadour introduced
a higher, slimmer version of the Louis
heel in the eighteenth century.

left:

Vintage Louis heel
In the 1920s, the Louis heel was the
evening shoe of choice, worn by
fashionable and daring flappers.

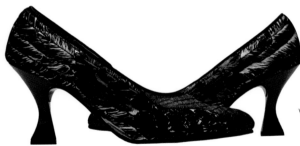

"Crow" Louis heel

The inspiration behind this embroidered Louis heel by Caroline Groves is Ted Hughes' poem "King of Carrion."

that was inappropriate in a modern Republican era. Thus flat slippers persisted in women's fashion throughout the first half of the nineteenth century. In 1854, Jean-Louis François Pinet patented the Pinet heel, a refined, lighter version of the Louis heel and attached it to open-worked leather and hand-painted silk boots covered with intricate gold embroidery. They were worn by a rich clientele of Parisian women who frequented the workshop of Charles Frederick Worth, couturier to the Empress Eugenie of France. Customers also included a new version of the Versailles courtesan—the *grandes horizontales* of the Belle Époque, a decadent time (1890–1900) before the carnage of the First World War. They were the established "queens of the erotic" and included La Belle Otero, Lianne de Pougy, and Emilienne d'Alençon who amassed huge fortunes, a just reward for their talents in the bedroom. The Pinet and Louis heel conveyed all the seductive connotations of the eighteenth century, conjuring up the erotic delights supplied by a pampered flirt in a Versailles boudoir.

When the Louis heel was combined with an oversized buckle on the front, the shoe had an even stronger eighteenth-century resonance, especially when Pietro Yanturny used eighteenth-century Valenciennes lace, gold threadwork, and diamond buckles on exquisite handmade Louis-heeled shoes for his prestigious customers, who included divorcée and millionairess Rita de Acosta Lydig. Her shoes were kept on wooden shoe trees sourced by Yanturny from the wood of antique violins and were kept in a custom-made Russian leather trunk lined with cream velvet. The Louis, then, was a sexy heel shape, especially since it was also the heel of choice of can-can dancers at the Moulin Rouge in 1889.

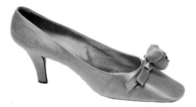

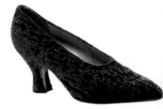

The Louis heel was at the height of its popularity in the 1900s when the dainty feminine foot was still prized, for it had the added effect of optically shortening the foot when viewed from the front. In the mid-1920s, as the Cuban heel began to take over by day, the Louis took to the night as the shape used for evening shoes, becoming higher and more tapered until supplanted by the platform and wedge. Its next incarnation was in the hands of footwear designer Roger Vivier in the 1950s, who understood the heel's seductive and luxurious origins. His low-rise Louis, a hybrid of the stiletto and the Louis heel, was affixed to the most coquettish of beaded shoes in the 1950s, when designing for couturier Christian Dior. In 1962, Vivier attached a low Louis heel to evening mules with vamps of jewel-encrusted velvet, causing the magazine *L'Aurore* to write: "Vivier's evening shoes are the work of a goldsmith, not a shoemaker. They can only be made for empresses and movie stars."

The Louis heel has never regained its early-twentieth-century popularity, save a brief renaissance in the late 1980s through the work of Christian Lacroix, Manolo Blahnik, Emma Hope, René Caovilla of Venice, and American footwear designer Stuart Weitzman, who created retrospective styles including a Louis-heeled, Edwardian-style ankle boot. Canadian John Fluevog designed avant-garde splayed versions of the heel, known as the "Guignol," in the early 1990s, and Christian Louboutin has used the heel throughout his career and, like Vivier before him, understands its coquettish connotations.

The beauty of the Louis lies in its supreme ergonomics—the heel is placed directly under the natural heel of the foot, which gives a balance and even distribution of weight that keeps the back and legs aligned. After a decade of unwieldy heels, the Louis could be poised for a comeback.

below from left to right:

Vivier for Dior (1957)
A luxurious Louis-heeled shoe in pink and black brocade silk.

Vivier for Dior (1957)
A shoe that displays its eighteenth-century origins, fashioned from mustard satin silk.

Yves Saint Laurent (1992)
An exaggerated Louis in embossed Bordeaux-colored velvet silk.

Christian Dior (1965)
A white satin-silk Louis with mesh, sequin, and bead embellishment.

Christian Dior (1964)
A black-and-beige crêpe de Chine silk pump with bead and sequin detail.

Rossimoda (1996)
Rococo-inspired pink satin-silk with glass beads, sequins, and embroidery.

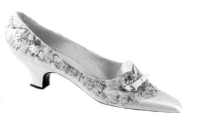
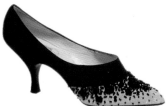
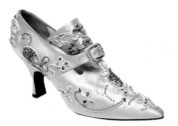

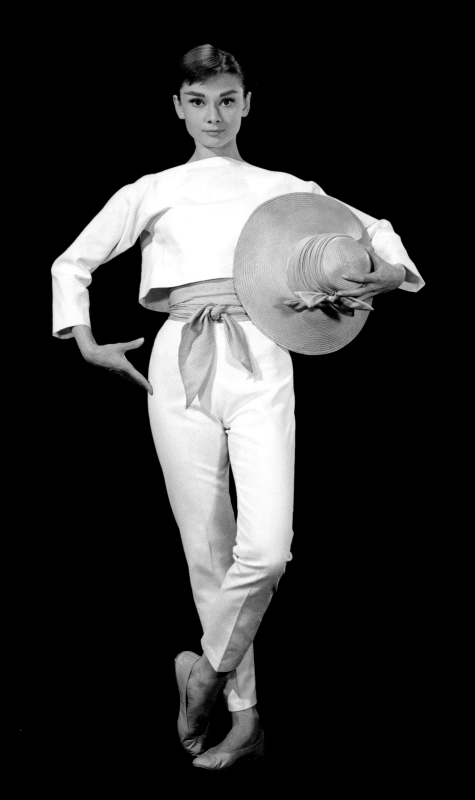

BALLET FLAT

"Maybe [ballet flats] are getting last year's flip-flop customer."

Richard Olicker, Nine West Group

The ballet flat is a hard-soled shoe derived from the slippers worn for classical ballet. Ballerinas need a shoe with the finest of soles in order to be able to feel the floor and arch the foot. Unlike most other forms of footwear, there is no difference between the left and right shoe—they are designed to mold to the contours of the individual's feet.

In early ballet, female dancers were hampered by heavy headdresses and buckled shoes, unlike men who were free to leap around in tights, but by the eighteenth century, women began to achieve principal roles and thus their footwear had to change. By the nineteenth century when the Byronic artists and poets of the Romantic movement demanded the ethereal from their female muses, ballets began to depict a myriad of water nymphs, fairies, and swan maidens—supernatural women who were clearly not bound to the earth. Thus the fashion for dancing *en pointe* began, an advanced form of ballet where the dancers literally moved on the tips of their toes; Marie Taglioni is said to have been the first ballerina to dance a full-length ballet—*La Sylphide*—entirely *en pointe* in 1832, wearing satin ballet slippers with leather soles darned on the sides rather than the tips to provide support.

As dancers tried to give the illusion of defying gravity, the more specialized pointe shoe emerged to help support their movements, and its flesh-pink coloring helped to create the illusion of the body's stunning uninterrupted lines. The shoe was constructed of layers of burlap and canvas stiffened with glue then covered in a layer of satin. The bottom of the slipper consisted of a stiff spine of three soles or shanks of leather and cardboard sandwiched together with glue and nails. The sole was designed to be shorter and narrower than the sole of the foot, ending under the metatarsophalangeal articulations

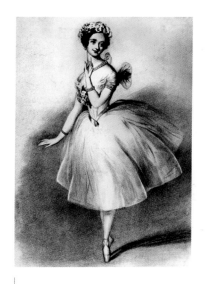

above:
Ballerina Marie Taglioni (1832)
The first to dance a ballet entirely *en pointe* wearing ballet slippers darned on the sides to provide support.

left:
Audrey Hepburn (1957)
She famously argued with *Funny Face* (1957) director Stanley Donen that flats would make her feet look too big on screen.

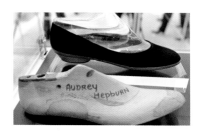

Ferragamo and Hepburn

Salvatore Ferragamo had wooden lasts for every celebrity customer. Here Audrey's model is displayed with her ballet flat.

and thus freeing up part of the arch. The pointe shoe had a wooden block at the end with lambswool padding that allowed the dancer a heightened lightness by enabling her to pirouette and arabesque on the very points of her toes.

The most renowned purveyor of ballet shoes was Salvatore Capezio, a native of Italy who had immigrated to America in the 1880s. He became a cobbler and opened a shop on New York's Broadway and 39th Street. Situated directly opposite was the Metropolitan Opera House and he found himself repairing a range of theatrical shoes including ballet pointes. Believing he could improve on their construction, Capezio started making his own, which were so beautifully engineered that they were snapped up by prima ballerina Anna Pavlova in 1910, who ended up buying pairs for every member of her company.

Freed of London Ltd was founded in 1929 and went on to become the biggest distributor of pointe shoes in the world, making up to 1,000 pairs per day for demanding ballerinas, who are known to wear out more than five pairs per week. Another prominent name, Jacob Bloch, began hand-crafting ballet shoes in 1932, and the renowned Repetto company launched in 1947. Madame Rosa Repetto, at the behest of her son, dancer and choreographer Roland Petit, sought to design a more comfortable pair of ballet shoes. She came up with a new method of construction, the innovative "stitch and return" technique, whereby the shoes were made by stitching under the sole that was then turned inside out. This resulted in an almost invisible join between the sole and the upper and a much higher degree of ease—said to feel almost like wearing no shoes at all. Rudolph Nureyev wore Repettos throughout his career—apart from one of his worn-out pairs by Gamba that sold at Christie's in 1996 for $18,619 USD.

Perhaps the irony of the ballet slipper is what lies beneath—years of pain and calloused feet. Yet once the foot is in its natural position, the shoe becomes eminently practical. American designer Claire McCardell was one of the first to realize the ballet slipper had fashionable appeal when she chose to use Capezio flats in her 1941 collection, and asked the manufacturer to add a hard sole. When Lord & Taylor department store began showing shoes for daywear built on models designed for dance shoes, the ballet slipper became the ballet flat, making the transition from dance to fashionable footwear.

The ballet slipper made its first appearance as a counter-cultural shoe of teenage rebellion in the 1950s when worn by beatniks. Young people turned on by the existentialism of philosopher Jean-Paul Sartre and writer Jack Kerouac's beatnik prose sought a new form of sartorial expression that symbolized the lack of understanding they found in the adult world, a feeling vehemently expressed in Allen Ginsberg's seminal 1955 poem *Howl*. The pristine grooming and bandbox neatness of 1950s fashion was avoided in favor of a casual, relaxed Bohemian style; most notably they were the first teenagers to wear jeans. The ballet shoe was the footwear of choice for the Boho beatnik woman and found cultural expression in one star, Brigitte Bardot, whom proto-feminist writer Simone de Beauvoir called "the finest example of liberated woman in post-war France." Bardot studied dance and had learned of Repetto's reputation; on gaining the role of the free-spirited Juliet in Roger Vadim's directorial debut, *And God Created Women* (1956) she asked the company to design her a specially adapted ballet shoe with a durable sole that could be worn outside as everyday wear. The resulting red leather "Cinderella" ballet flat was worn both on and off screen by Bardot to accessorize Capri pants and a striped Breton top that seemed to sum up the sun-drenched shores of Saint-Tropez. Repetto was no longer a niche dancewear brand and was to go on to become a mainstream fashion look for thousands of young women. The ballet flat retained a few references to the original ballet shoe, such as the ribbon binding around the low top of the slipper and the gathering at the front part of the vamp. The string tie used by ballerinas to adjust the shoe to fit the foot was converted into a functionless decorative bow and remains a focal point of the flat today.

The ballets flat's celebrity endorsement continued when Hollywood icon Audrey Hepburn played a beatnik turned top model in *Funny Face* (1957). Hepburn was unsure about her screen wardrobe, complaining to the director Stanley Donen before a key scene that flats combined with white socks would draw attention to her large feet. He was insistent, explaining that the socks would allow the camera to focus on the movements of her feet in a pivotal song-and-dance sequence set in a Left Bank jazz club. She capitulated and after the film was released sent an apologetic note: "You were right about the socks. Love Audrey." Audrey's flat shoes off screen were by Capezio and Salvatore Ferragamo, whose label fit her from

below:
Sex kitten in flats
Brigitte Bardot wore "Cendrillon" flats with durable soles by Repetto both on and off screen.

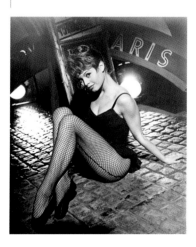

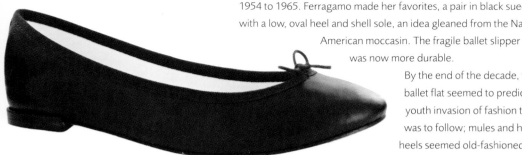

1954 to 1965. Ferragamo made her favorites, a pair in black suede with a low, oval heel and shell sole, an idea gleaned from the Native American moccasin. The fragile ballet slipper was now more durable.

By the end of the decade, the ballet flat seemed to predict the youth invasion of fashion that was to follow; mules and high heels seemed old-fashioned, vulgar, and overblown compared to this youthful shoe. Ironically though, the 1960s spelled the death of the ballet flat; its feminine softness was unsuited to the pop art-inspired fashion and the slick chic of mod street style. Other styles of flat shoe took over—more tailored styles such as the Pilgrim Pump (see page 238) and, for teenagers, the Mary Jane (see page 132), a style with the requisite youthful connotations to fit with the graphic designs of Mary Quant, John Bates, and André Courrèges.

The ballet flat was resurrected by the late 1980s, helped by Diana, Princess of Wales being frequently photographed wearing them. Footwear designer Franco Fieramosca, who launched his own line in 1991, made her influence clear when he said "A ballet slipper in pale pink suede looks refined and ladylike. When I designed my ballerinas, I was inspired by the image of Lady Diana getting into a jet. She was wearing tight gabardine pants and a blazer, and you might have thought that masculine shoes would be appropriate for those clothes, but her ballerinas looked phenomenal!" The delicate lines of Diana's ballerina flats by French Sole, her favored label, were a counterpoint to the minimalist lines of much 1990s fashion, and also suited the dressed-down, grunge-inspired look that could be seen both in the grunge rock style from Seattle and the unkempt vibe of Kate Moss in her advertising for CK1.

above:

Classic ballet flat

Repetto has been manufacturing ballet flats since 1947. Today they have become a shoe classic.

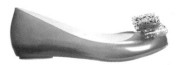

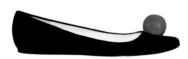

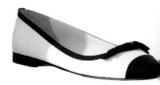

French Sole is a global label that started in 1989 as a concept mail-order company founded by the designer Jane Winkworth to sell only ballet-style footwear. After the patronage of Princess Diana, the label was successful enough to expand into its first store in Fulham, London, in 1991. Style is the operative word for this company, which produces ballet flats in over 500 different combinations of colors, textures, and styles. They retain the look of the original ballet slipper but with more functional hard-wearing soles and uppers that range from the bestselling leopard-printed pony skin to woven bronze leather—uppers that mold to the contours of the owner's feet in the same way the slipper does to the prima ballerina, and their "Low-cut" and "Henrietta" styles are worn by Kate Moss, Madonna, and Sienna Miller. In the 2000s, the ballet flat has become a city classic with most labels launching their own versions including Lanvin, Tory Burch, Miu Miu, Chloe, J. Crew, Marc Jacobs, and Pretty Ballerinas. In 1999, Repetto was bought by Jean-Marc Gaucher, former head of Reebok, France, who reinvigorated the original dancewear label with a series of designer collaborations for the catwalk including Karl Lagerfeld, Kenzo, and Comme des Garçons.

In 2009, original ballet slippers rather than ballet flats emerged into fashion consciousness when spied on the feet of singer Amy Winehouse. Hers were by Gandolfi, a dancewear business with a shop on London's Marylebone Road, a label that had been in existence since the early years of the twentieth century manufacturing handmade ballet shoes. Winehouse's ballet slippers were uncanny, their baby pink innocence and image of grace completely at odds with the singer's self-destruction. By the 2010s, the ballet flat was a shoe that stood out amid a sea of towering heels, a classic example of footwear that has withstood the test of time, managing to move from the stage to the street.

below from left to right:

Nude flat
Vivienne Westwood gives the flat a luxe edge with its subtle nude tone and embellished detail.

Black suede flat
Witty ballet flat by Larin with bright-red pom-pom to the front.

Monochrome flat
A smart city flat by Chanel in contrasting black-and-white leather.

Stacked flat
Acne rejects the traditional light feel by adding a rubber platform and heel.

Tutti frutti flat
Charlotte Olympia gives a fresh feel to the flat with fruit detailing.

Color-blocked flat
A stunning ballet flat by Pierre Hardy in bright-blue and jade-green suede.

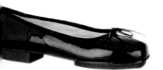
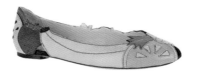
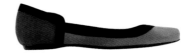

SPATS

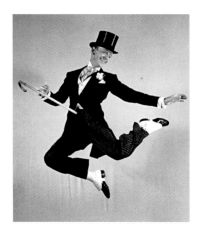

Spats, a.k.a. gaiters, are derived from the "spatterdash," a protective foot and ankle cover first worn in the eighteenth century by soldiers and farmers to protect their boots and legs from the mud. The spatterdash was constructed of a stiff fabric buttoned up the side with a buckled or elasticized band under the shoe. By the nineteenth century the most functional became known as gaiters; the most decorative became spats, and the spiffy, monochromatic effect of white spats on black shoes has made this footgear a feature of many marching bands and military dress uniforms.

> "You shave with your spats on?"
> "I sleep with my spats on."
> Officer Mulligan to Spats Columbo in *Some Like it Hot*, 1959

above:

Formal spats

Fred Astaire is "Puttin' on the Ritz," clad in top hat, tails, and spats for the movie *Blue Skies* (1946).

In the early nineteenth century, the widespread use of gaiters by men led to the introduction of the gaiter boot that mimicked their effect. The side-laced gaiter boot had a cloth and leather upper and was so popular, a distinction had to be made between the boot and its origin, the protective overshoe that was briefly renamed the over-gaiter. Women began to wear gaiters by the 1830s, and the cloth of the boot could be designed to match the color of their dresses. However, as front-laced and button boots became fashionable, the gaiter boot declined in popularity.

Gaiters or spats became popular again in the early twentieth century after a series of Factory Acts gave responsibility to employers for protecting their workforce, making them one of the earliest forms of footwear used for the purpose of health and safety. Gaiters buttoning up to the knee were also worn by female bicyclists because they were a cheaper alternative to the specialized and expensive front-laced cycling boot with grooves in the sole to keep feet from slipping from the pedal. Gaiters covered the lower leg rather shockingly exposed by cycling bloomers, and when covering the gap between bloomer and boot were called leggings.

As the more decorative spats fell out of fashion, they gained a new image as an eccentric form of footwear worn by men trying to appear classier and more sophisticated than they actually were. The minstrel show is a case in point—a nineteenth-century form of entertainment where Caucasian men in "blackface" ridiculed what was believed by Caucasians to be African-American culture. The gross stereotype was of an African-American man in loud clothes, including a swallowtail coat, top hat, cane, and spats. His inappropriate dress was used to suggest an inability to function as a free man; in *Some Like It Hot* (1959) directed by Billy Wilder, one of the Most Wanted Chicago gangsters wearing spats has the moniker "Spats Columbo" and appears throughout the film as a man trying to rise above his bloodthirsty occupation through high-class sartorial references.

Today spats have become the fail-safe option for stylists wishing to give an impression of gentlemanly "elegance" to a fashion shoot or pop video, most notably sported by Michael Jackson in the promo for "Smooth Criminal," an ironic twist of fate in that the star's popularity reframed spats as an urban fashion trend, rather than a formal one that was fit only for retro-themed weddings. An attempt has been made to bring them back into fashion in women's footwear as an alternative to the legwarmer, and zebra- and leopard-print spats can be purchased from The Spats Factory based in Vicenza, Italy.

below left:
Stiletto spats
In the 1950s John Kirby designed a pair of female spats in leopardskin with a quilted lining for warmth.

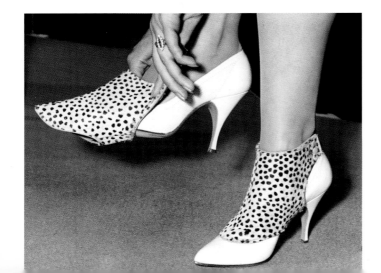

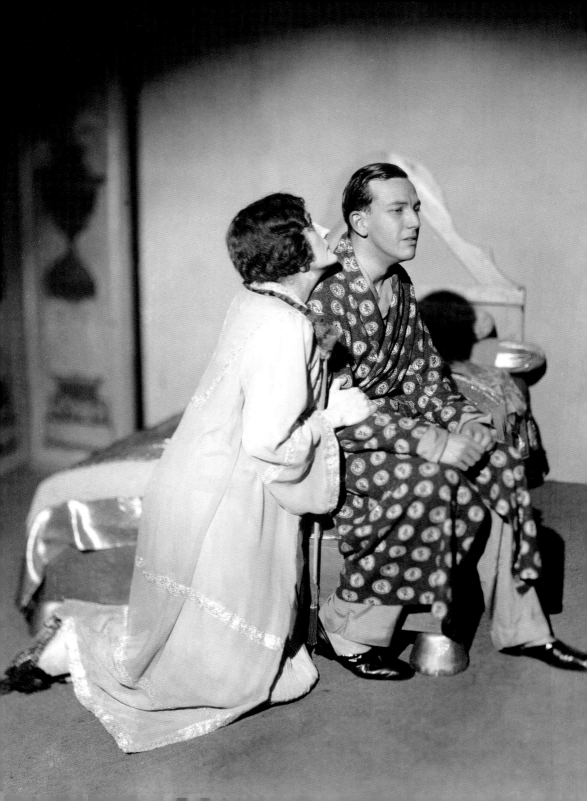

SLIPPER

"Don't you stay at home of evenings? Don't you love a cushioned
seat in a corner, by the fireside, with your slippers on your feet?"

Oliver Wendell Holmes

The term "slipper" was originally applied to any shoe that slipped
on. At the beginning of the twentieth century, the term was
exclusively applied to an indoor informal slip-on shoe with no
fastening or closure. Today we associate the slipper with informal
evenings at home when we change into our comfy clothes,
but the genesis of the slipper is a fascinating one, tied to
radical cultural changes in notions of femininity in the mid-
nineteenth century.

In their early form, slippers were among the most decorative of
footwear types, particularly the boudoir slippers of the eighteenth
century, fashioned of silk and lavishly embroidered with metallic
thread. The boudoir was a domestic space that, by the eighteenth
century, had evolved into a highly decorative sitting room where
a woman of fashion entertained female friends, potential beaux,
and business associates. An aesthetic of informality dominated the
design of the boudoir: white paint and gilding, lots of mirrors, and
Rococo curves—Madame de Pompadour's room in Versailles was
described as "crammed to bursting point with pictures, bibelots,
furniture, embroidery, cosmetics, all buried in flowers and smelling
like a hothouse." The favorite mistress to Louis IV would "sit in a
cloud of fragrant lace" according to historian Gertrude Arentz and
display an enchanting little foot in a dainty slipper scattered with
precious gemstones. The slipper was thus the most feminine of shoes
designed to show off tiny, delicate feet—a cult taken to its most
extreme with the Chinese Lotus foot (see page 63).

From the 1790s through the 1810s, brightly hued leather and silk
slippers with stripes or repeating patterns were popular, the more
expensive embroidered with silver threadwork interspersed with
sequins, or ruched, fringed, and crowned with rosettes. The tiny and

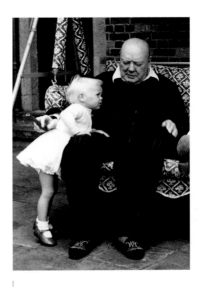

above:

Masculine attire

Sir Winston Churchill relaxes in a pair
of gentlemanly monogrammed Albert
slippers in 1951.

left:

Casual chic

Noël Coward, in a scene from *Vortex*
at the Everyman Theatre in the 1920s,
wears a pair of smart leather slippers.

exquisitely slippered foot was a sign that its delicate female owner labored little and did not venture much outside, so it was an obvious symbol of wealth and social status that invaded popular culture. Little girls lapped up tales of Cinderella who went to the ball in the most brittle of footwear, a glass slipper—the epitome of fragile femininity and a shoe so small only the woman destined to marry a prince possessed the miniscule foot to fit it.

Such notions continued into the nineteenth century; man the provider and the working-class woman in the laundry or mill wore boots; the genteel woman was clad in impractical, lightweight, low-cut, leather-soled slippers made out of silk taffeta, wool serge, or soft leather, and if venturing outdoors wore what was dubbed a slipper-sandal with ribbons tied around the ankle to hold it in place.

Dress slippers were imported into the United States from French companies, including the exporters Vault-Este and Thierry and Sons, and the fad for French footwear was such that firms based in the United States referred to a Gallic connection. In the 1858 *Boot and Shoe Manufacturer's Assistant and Guide*, author W. H. Richardson wrote: "Most of the so-called French manufacture is the product of American artizans. This 'amiable deception' is practiced in order to gratify the whims of those who lack confidence in the skill and taste of American manufacturers." To achieve the appearance of tiny feet, women squeezed them into the smallest slipper possible, and the pain they had to endure further limited them outside the confines of the home. *Godey's Lady's Book* described how a wealthy woman on a typical evening out in 1850 was forced to wear a gown, "as uncomfortable as stiff laces and tight corsages can make it and steam over the soup, or faint in the odour of roasts, with [her] hair in Jenny Lind bandeaux, and [her] feet in excruciating French slippers."

The slipper-sandal fell slowly out of favor from the 1850s on as a move toward social change began to be apparent, with the first mobilization for women's rights in the United States, the formation of the Rational Dress Movement in

below:
Pom-pom slippers
Topshop's "Vava" bottle-green velvet slippers with low stack heel and pompom have a subtly pointed toe.

the United Kingdom that called for less physically restricting fashion, and women's increasing participation in sport. As women sought power, their shoes became more practical, the thin-soled slipper-sandal was swept aside, and thicker-soled boots were worn by day with practical, sturdy heels. The slipper was worn in the home but it was still not the informal house shoe of today; slippers were there to enhance the feet, as women's publication *Mme. Demorest's What to Wear* attested in 1883: "The chaussure is another item of house dress, which should never be neglected, for it is certain never to escape observation. A shrewd writer says, 'Many a man's heart has been kept from wandering by the bow on his wife's slipper.' Daintily dressed feet are always admired, so we would advise all young wives, and older ones too, for the matter of that, to look well to the ways of their feet and dress them in pretty hose and neat slippers."

By the late nineteenth century, the slipper was back in its rightful place, in an informal domestic setting, although it took a little longer to catch on as a concept in the United States. Shoe expert Nancy E. Rexford believes this was due to the fluid class structure in the United States, which made clothing a much more important indicator of status than in the hierarchical class structure of the UK—there, the concept of class had been rigidly determined for centuries and all instinctively knew their place. If, heaven forbid, a housemaid dressed like a duchess, she would become the object of ridicule for getting "above herself." Thus Rexford says in the United States, "when society rewarded women who managed to dress like ladies, and being ladylike meant cultivating an aura of physical delicacy and restricting oneself to indoor pursuits, then thin indoor footwear was bound to be widely worn while heavy shoes would be shunned even when it made sense to wear them."

By the early twentieth century, slippers were back in the boudoir, the most exquisite pairs handcrafted by Michonet, the master embroiderer at the House of Worth in Paris. Michonet was renowned for ribbon embroidery, a three-dimensional style that used a combination of ribbon and silk floss with traditional embroidery stitches to give a sumptuous, padded effect. His color combinations were luxurious and designed to be highly sensual, such as pink, cream, and red with insets of black jet beading, and were beloved by the scandalous *grandes-horizantales* such as La Belle Otero famed for her erotic dancing at Maxims de Paris and the divine Liane de

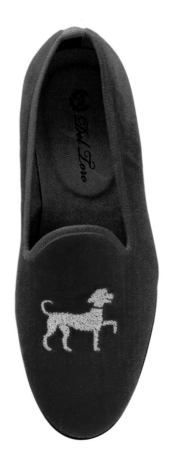

above:
Street slipper (2005)
The Albert slipper was reworked and rebranded after the Del Toro company was set up by Matthew Chevellard.

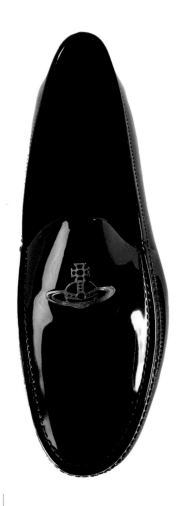

above:

Slick slippers

Vivienne Westwood turns her gaze on the slipper and gives it a super-shiny black patent surface.

Pougy. Many middle-class women sewed their own boudoir slippers following patterns in popular women's magazines catering to the domestic market, and one popular practice was to embroider the soft uppers at home and then take them to the local cobbler to have thin leather soles attached. A successful manufacturer of boudoir slippers in the early twentieth century was the American company Daniel Green. Green was originally a traveling shoe salesman for the Wallace Elliott Company in New York; on visiting a mill, Green saw workers wearing flat slippers made from pieces of discarded felt to shield their feet from the cold of the factory floor. He persuaded the mill owner to manufacture the slippers to sell to the shoe trade with himself as sole agent and, in 1885, when appealing colors, white felt soles, and heels were added for the boudoir, he sold 75,000 pairs. 100 million pairs of shoes later, the company is still in operation.

Men's slippers had also become fashionable thanks to Prince Albert, Queen Victoria's husband, who popularized the Albert, a tab-fronted black velvet slipper with a quilted lining and leather sole that he wore while relaxing at the palace. By the Edwardian era, a gentleman would arrive home and change from his formal work clothes into a relaxed smoking jacket, black tie, and trousers, signifying his entry into the domestic space, and his feet would be slipped into a pair of comfortable monogrammed Alberts. In 1908, the *Washington Post* published an article entitled "The Joy of Slippers" by one Mr. Millington who extolled their virtues: "Smoking jackets and slippers are synonymous with comfort but if I could have only one of these I should take slippers." He went on to say, "I have known my feet so long now that we have come to be as you might say friends, or at least I have a friendly feeling for them. I know that they seem grateful to me when I take off my shoes and release them from their day's imprisonment; and then my feet and I sit back in my particular chair and smoke a stogie and read the evening paper." This at-home combination of smoking jacket and slippers with the substitution of a cravat for black tie persisted into the 1930s and 1940s as worn in Hollywood by Noël Coward, Fred Astaire, and Cary Grant. Many companies produced male slippers for indoor use such as L. B. Evans established in 1804, and Trickers Ltd set up in 1829 in Northampton. The company is known today for its handmade leather shoes for men as worn by Prince Charles and his sons William and Harry, as well as its handmade leather-lined velvet Albert slippers.

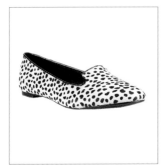

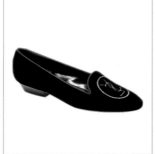

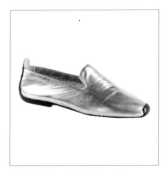

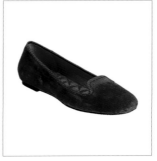

In 2005 the Albert slipper was reworked and rebranded after the Del Toro company was set up by Matthew Chevellard. While a student, he had wanted to sport a spiffy pair of black velvet Albert slippers embroidered with his high-school crest to his graduation, but was put off by the stratospherically high price. After having sourced his own, Chevellard sensed a gap in the American market and set up Del Toro, whose headquarters are in Miami with the slippers manufactured in Madrid. Del Toro have been instrumental in turning the slipper into a street shoe by making the vamp higher, replacing the quilted interior with sturdier leather, replacing stuffy monograms with embroidered skulls and crossbones, and introducing a range of neon colors. Global success was assured when they were spotted on the feet of rapper Kanye West in 2011.

Women's slippers take many forms today including the clog, moccasin, and Ugg, which like the boudoir slipper and mule, have moved from the home to the street with similar problems of wearability because of their inherent unsuitability in extreme conditions. The hard-soled slipper-sock is a recent development, often worn with the Snuggie, a blanket that is also a wearable garment.

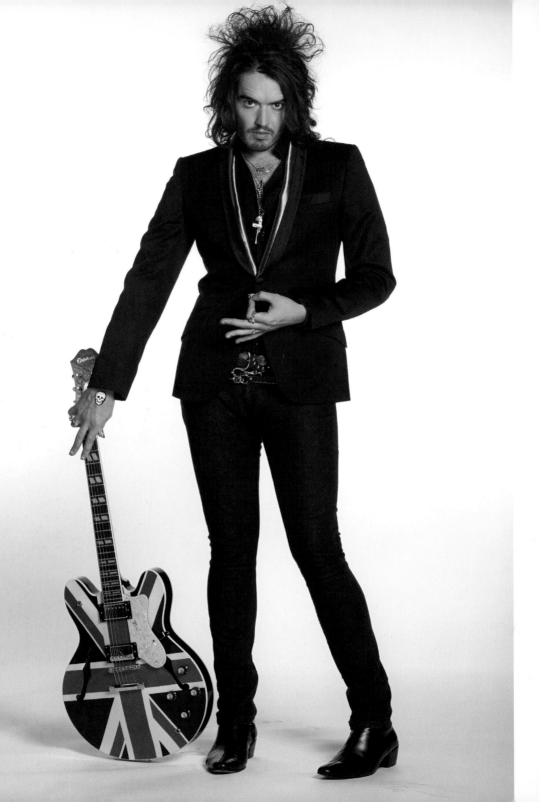

CUBAN HEEL

"People say I'm wearing heels because I'm short.
I wear heels because the women like 'em."

Prince

In 1977, a white-suited John Travolta strutted his stuff in a pair
of Cuban-heeled boots in the disco-fueled movie *Saturday Night
Fever*. A star and a footwear fad were born and the late 1970s were
dominated by men in high heels. Travolta's swaggering machismo
reflected the Cuban heel's origin as a style worn by the gauchos
of South America. When riding a horse, the Cuban heel kept the
gaucho's foot securely in the stirrups, its angled shape preventing
it from sliding forward, particularly when roping steers. Today the
relationship between men and the Cuban heel is more complex;
for some they are rock-star sexy, for others an obvious device for
disguising restricted height.

The Cuban heel is a chunky one: broad, of moderate height,
and wider at the top than the bottom. It is characterized by a slightly
tapered back and straight front and is used in both shoes and boots
such as the 1960s Chelsea or Beatle boot, which incorporated a
Cuban heel offsetting its slim, ankle-high top. The distinctive heel
gave added height, but more importantly, it provided a flashpoint for
1960s pop styling.

The Cuban heel was attached to women's footwear a little
later than men's—around 1905—and stood out as a streamlined
heel amid a sea of Louis heels. The Louis mirrored the Edwardian
silhouette—all hourglass curves—but by the 1920s, the Cuban heel
suited the masculine shape that had entered fashion as shown in the
work of Parisian couturier Coco Chanel. Its clear lines were suitably
androgynous and modernist and, when affixed to evening shoes, it
could be dazzlingly decorated with scatterings of rhinestones, mock
tortoiseshell, or decorative enamel. New energetic dance crazes
such as the Charleston and Black Bottom required shoes that fixed
more securely to the feet, so the sensible width of the Cuban heel

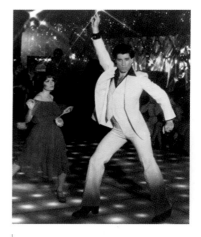

above:
Disco strut
John Travolta as Tony Manero in
Saturday Night Fever (1977) helped
foster the macho image of the
Cuban heel.

left:
Russell Brand
Hedi Slimane's skinny silhouette,
developed at Dior Homme, was the
perfect foil for the contemporary
Cuban-heeled boot.

was perfect; by day they were added to smart Oxford walking shoes, adding a hint of style to a formerly masculine shoe.

In the 2000s, the Cuban-heeled boot came back into fashion when men's trousers became skinnier in cut, inspired by the silhouette developed by Hedi Slimane during his stint at Dior Homme. Heeled boots lengthened and streamlined this elegantly attenuated look, giving it an extra-sexy swagger, and were designed by—among others—Patrick Cox, whose Cuban-heeled boots were worn by actor Russell Brand and singer Lenny Kravitz. Cox believes that "Rock stars love Cuban heels because a lot of them tend to be diminutive. And I've never met a man who doesn't mind having an extra inch or two anywhere on his body."

Other designers who incorporate Cuban heels into their collections include Vicky Haddon for Hudson; Jeffrey West, whose inspirations include Beau Brummell and the actors Richard Harris and Oliver Reed, and whose flamboyant boots incorporate hand-burnished uppers and Goodyear welted soles; and Australian manufacturer R. M. Williams, established in 1931 and renowned for their oil-infused cowhide or suede Cuban-heeled boots, as worn by Russell Crowe, Bill Clinton, and Ricky Martin. The most flamboyant pair were created by Gareth Pugh in 2011—high-shine black patent leather with a three-inch heel and a bright gold zipper.

right:
Rock-star style
Rolling Stones guitarist Brian Jones reclines on a bed wearing rebellious Cuban-heeled boots in London, 1964.

below left:
Elegant attenuation
Jeffrey West's mock snakeskin boots have a high Cuban heel and back zip.

below right:
Cow-print Cubans
R. M. Williams' signature Cuban-heeled boots, here in a striking black-and-white cow-print fur.

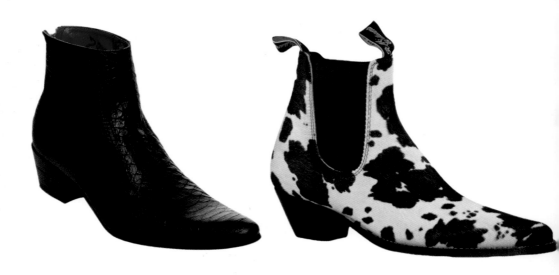

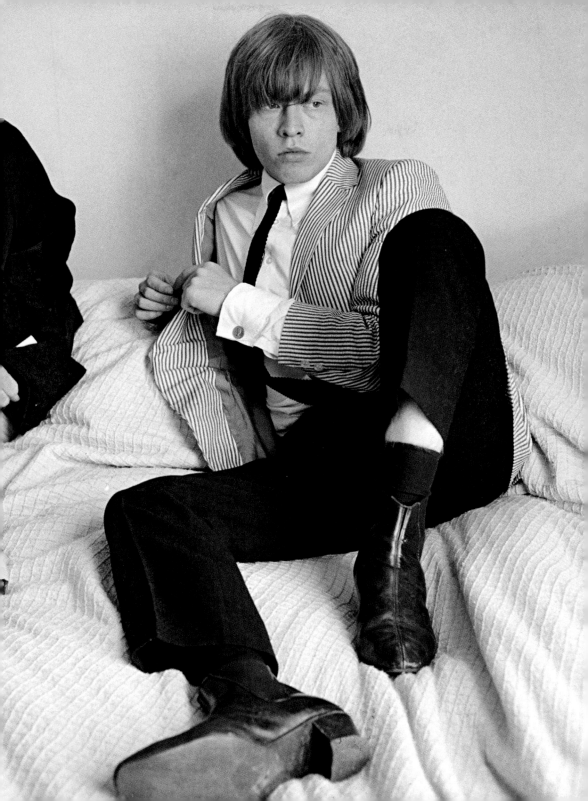

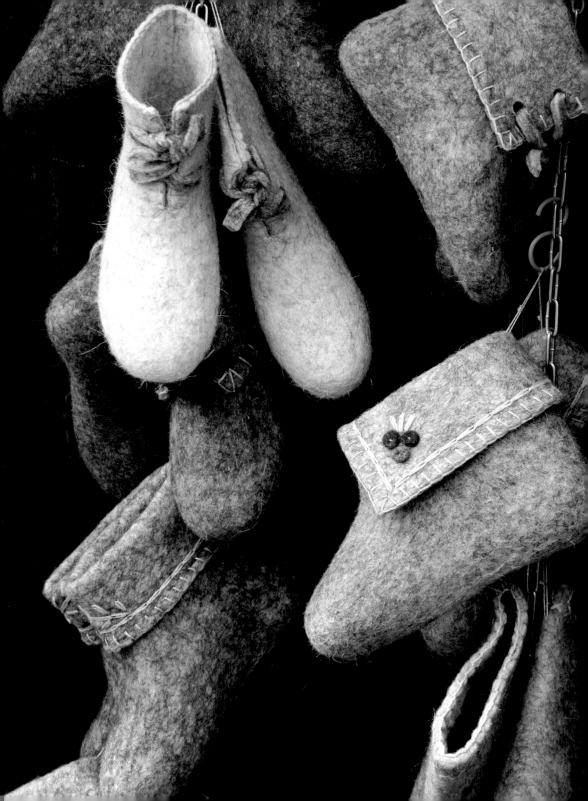

VALENKI

"I painted gray felt boots with orange and red gouache, which turned into a terrible scandal."
Vyacheslav Zaitsev, designer and artist

The valenki is a flat, knee-high, and wide-topped flat boot developed over 300 years ago to cope with walking on the dry snow of the harsh Siberian winter. The name is derived from the Russian *valenok*, meaning "made by felting," an ancient technique of transforming wool into a thick cloth by dipping it into boiling water, causing the fibers to shrink and bond together. Valenki are handmade from a large piece of felted lambswool that is pummeled into a boot shape before being dried in an oven—the resulting free-standing rigid sock has no differentiation between left and right. Valenki are designed to be worn without socks both indoors and outdoors as the felt molds to the shape of the owner's feet, making them among the most comfortable and insulating of footwear. As the boots lack waterproofing in wet weather, they are traditionally covered with galoshes. Russian valenki are either black, gray, or white; in Norway and Sweden, brightly colored versions called *lobben* have protective leather soles and are heavily embroidered on the uppers with folk motifs.

In the nineteenth century, the production of valenki began to be industrialized; as numbers increased they became cheaper and thus more readily available. When rubber soles were added in the early twentieth century, valenki were made standard winter issue for the Russian army. Today it is estimated that 4.5 million pairs are produced every year in Russia.

Valenki are regarded as therapeutic because the texture of the felt is said to stimulate circulation in the feet, and the restorative properties of a pair of valenki were legendary; Peter the Great's hangover cure was reputedly a bowl of steaming cabbage soup and a stroll around the palace in his favorite pair. The boot has fortune-telling properties too—on Christmas Eve it is traditional to go outside

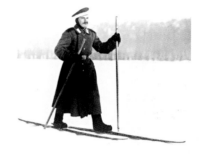

above:
Snow boot
The traditional Russian valenki was originally created for ease of walking in the snow of harsh Siberian winters.

left:
Warm and snug
Valenki are constructed out of thick felted wool and take the form of a sock.

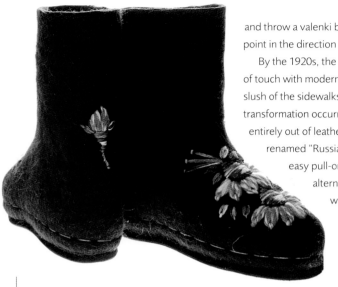

and throw a valenki boot into the air. Wherever it lands, it will point in the direction of a single girl's prospective husband.

By the 1920s, the rustic qualities of the valenki seemed out of touch with modern city life. They were also unsuited to the slush of the sidewalks, and fell from favor. However, a fashion transformation occurred when felt valenki were constructed entirely out of leather, given a low stack or Louis heel, and renamed "Russian boots." The open-topped shape and easy pull-on/pull-off style made the boot a modern alternative to the old-fashioned button boot and were first worn in 1916 by Denise Poiret, style icon and wife of the designer Paul Poiret. Paul Poiret had designed the boot to accompany his flamboyant ethnic-inspired designs and they were handmade by the French *bottier* Favreau in white, red, and tan leather with a low stacked heel and square toe. Hems were still too low for this style to be practical though, and it wasn't until the early 1920s that they began to catch on.

above:

Next generation

Olga Chernikova has updated the traditional valenki for young modern Russians, as with this blue hand-felted version.

In 1922, the *Boot and Shoe Recorder* referenced the trend in an article, recognizing that the Russian boot could spell the end of the unsightly galoshes that were being worn by young flappers. The magazine reported that, "The Russian boot stands for utility, not for beauty. It can hardly be said to be a fitting and beautiful part of the costume of the modern American girl, whose skirts are short and whose feet in Russian boots are far from being petite. No merchant expects the Russian boot to become a landslide proposition, but if the Russian boot could be made the complement of the winter season and could be worn instead of flapping galoshes, there might be something in the Russian boot as an item of utility." Little did the journalist know that flapping galoshes were the least of their worries—the Russian boot was to become infamous when used by the heavily painted female companions of Chicago's notorious gangsters to smuggle illegal liquor into clubs—the origin of the term "bootlegging."

The wide-topped Russian boot fell out of favor as the hems of daywear dresses became almost ankle-length and fashions generally more traditionally feminine and figure-hugging in the 1930s—there was literally no room between hem, knee, and ankle for this bulky shape. Its origins from behind the Iron Curtain were also politically inappropriate at the height of the Cold War in the 1950s, when Joseph McCarthy's hounding of anyone with Communist sympathies obsessed America. Russian boots with their taint of "red" were denounced, but perhaps more prosaically, the wide-topped shape completely worked against the fitted, tailored looks that were being created in the workshops of Parisian couture.

The Russian boot reemerged briefly at the end of the 1960s when footwear manufacturers were casting around for ethnic styles to rebrand as "hippie deluxe," but it was to really find its feet as a mainstream fashion for both men and women in the 1980s on the back of the New Romantic movement. The followers of this early 1980s style tribe were post-modernist plunderers of fashion, raiding history's image bank for theatrical garments that could be used to create looks of eccentric individuality. Quaffing cocktails in an underground bar alongside singer Boy George in a nun's habit or club promoter Steve Strange in an Elizabethan ruff were budding Cossacks, their feet shod in black leather Russian boots with low stacked heels. As the look went mainstream, many footwear manufacturers and store brands such as Dolcis, Sacha, Lilley & Skinner, and Ravel produced their own versions of this simple shape that were worn by fashionistas over black leggings or under the shortest of dirndl skirts.

The original valenki, unlike its derivation the Russian boot, was pretty much unknown outside of Russia until the Australian Ugg (see page 128), a similar-shaped sheepskin boot emerged on the global marketplace with unprecedented success. The popularity of the Ugg led to a new generation of Russians embracing their home-grown boot, and contemporary designers include Olga Chernikova, who showed her first handmade collection at Russian Fashion Week in 2007. She said: "At first, a lot of people think that they're something for the village or the collective farm. But why shouldn't we remember that we're Russians? The Scottish have their kilts, and we have our valenki."

below:

New Ugg

Zdar have created the "Nico" as a luxurious Russian alternative to the ever-popular Australian Ugg boot.

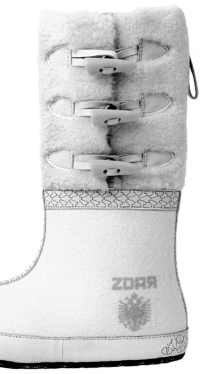

GALOSH

A galosh is a covering worn over indoor shoes to protect them from severe weather conditions. The word "galosh" derives from the Latin *gallica solea*, or Gallic shoe, and originally referred to a wooden sole or sandal fastened to the foot with straps. By the end of the eighteenth century, the name described an overshoe of waterproofed or japanned leather. Japanning was a method by which the leather was covered in layers of varnish and oil, resulting in a glossy finish that withstood the damp. In the early nineteenth century, the first rubber galoshes were imported into Europe and America from Brazil, created by pouring layers of latex over clay

> "Whenever it's wet underfoot I must put on my galoshes."
>
> Mrs. Conroy in "The Dead," from *Dubliners*, James Joyce, 1914

"feet" that were then smoked and cured over a fire of palm nuts. After curing for several days, the clay was simply removed with water, leaving a pair of rubber forms that could be worn to protect the feet. This rather rudimentary process had its drawbacks; the rubber was still in an unstable form and could become sticky in summer and brittle and liable to cracking during cold snaps. Despite this, the imported galoshes were incredibly successful—500,000 pairs a year were being sold by 1842.

In 1839, Charles Goodyear managed to stabilize the properties of Brazilian rubber by heating it in combination with sulfur—a process called vulcanization. The improved temperature-resistant rubber galoshes were launched in 1844 and were a hit in the male market, becoming a key part of a gentleman's working wardrobe. For a woman, it was a very different state of affairs; if she was in any way refined, she wore leather slippers that offered no protection outdoors or front-laced or button boots for improved protection while

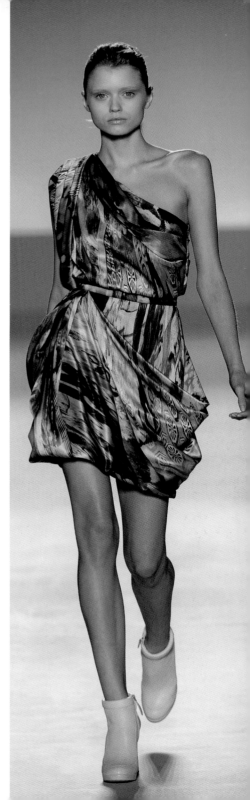

walking. The large dimensions of the galosh were an affront to dainty feet and indicated a social mobility that was frowned upon by the middle-class woman who was so conscious of her social status that she was not prepared to enter town without a male chaperone to escort her. Servants were there to run errands, and if one had servants, one had money. It would take the new woman of the 1920s to wear the galosh—the flapper, a woman who presented a more sportif silhouette that implied a youthful, outdoorsy modernity.

The flapper was a headstrong woman whose lone appearance on the city streets mimicked the actions of the prostitute. A visible woman in a short skirt, cloche hat, and painted face had an outlaw status when moved away from the traditional sphere of the domestic and her role as wife and mother. A woman in galoshes was a woman who was prepared to go outdoors whatever the weather and was also making a practical choice in an era when boots were deemed old-fashioned. Flappers added an extra rebellious touch too by refusing to fasten the buckles of the rubber galosh so that they flapped around their calves and ankles—some say this informal look gave birth to the term "flapper" itself.

left:
Anglomania
Vivienne Westwood experiments with rubber footwear as in the Melissa boot (2010) that mimics the galosh.

right:
New boots
Fashion designer Matthew Williamson gives the humble rubber boot an edgy catwalk chic in 2011.

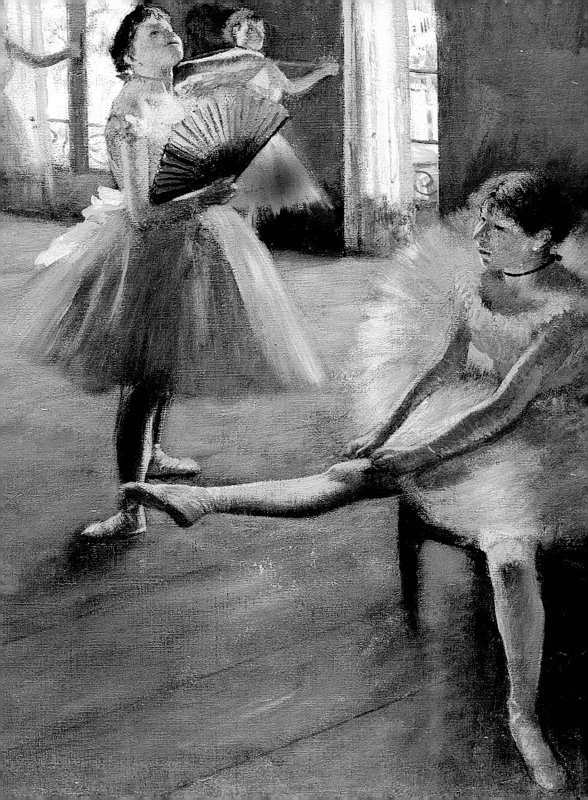

19th CENTURY

The cult of celebrity affects the popularity of shoes and boots, as in the innovation of the Wellington, named after the Iron Duke because of his prowess on the battlefield. It was in the nineteenth century that the shoe's seductive properties become more obviously appreciated with the development of the first fetish shoe or "staggerer." Many key men's styles evolved during this period including the Oxford day shoe, and an array of practical boots including the Chelsea boot and button boot.

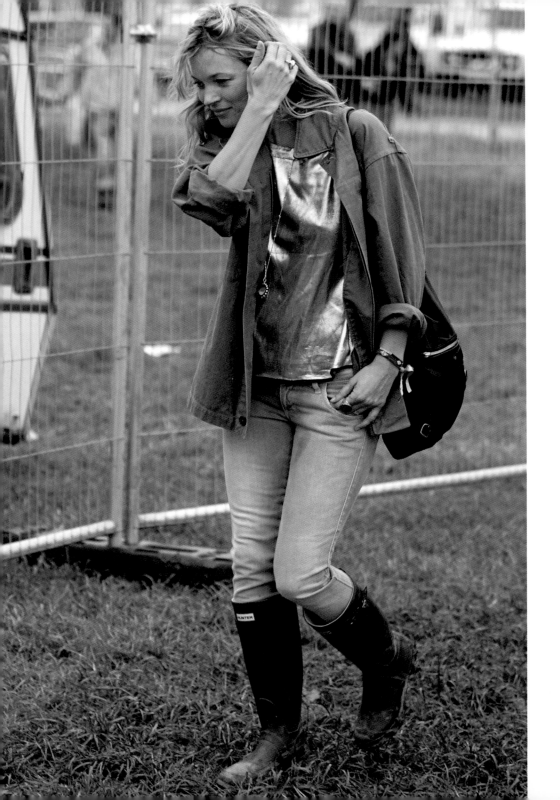

WELLINGTON

"We're obsessed with the way Kate [Moss] looks—Wellington boots with shorts? Who else could get away with that?"

Rachel Zoe, fashion stylist

The Wellington—a.k.a. gumboot—is a pull-on boot designed by Arthur Wellesley, the first Duke of Wellington (1769–1852) to sharpen up the appearance of his troops on the battleground when facing up to Napoleon. At the time of the Wellington's development the Hessian boot held sway, named after the German state of Hesse and worn by Beau Brummell among others in the 1790s. The Hessian boot's curved top and decorative tassel were deliberately showy, drawing attention to a finely modeled masculine leg when worn with tight breeches. George Cruikshank wrote in 1851 of seeing "the dandies of that day take out a comb, and comb out the tassels of their fire-bucket-looking boots as often as they got into disorder."

Wellington as a dedicated follower of fashion wanted to wear trousers, a new birfircated garment that had entered the lexicon of nineteenth-century menswear. The curved top of the Hessian boot and its heavy, decorative braided trim and tassel caused unsightly lumps and bumps in the line of the new trouser silhouette, so Wellington put his style sensibilities to work. He wanted a boot that would stand up to the rigors of battle but look good and feel comfortable when off the battlefield too. The Iron Duke, a.k.a. the Beau on account of his slick good looks and fashion sense, commissioned shoemaker Hoby of St James Street, London to create a soft calfskin, trim-free, close-fitting version of the standard Hessian boot. His streamlined version was a great success, one of the first celebrity-influenced fashions as men strove to copy the footwear of this military hero. The boot had a surge in popularity after the Iron Duke's military success in both the Peninsular War and the Battle of Waterloo in 1815, and when dubbed the "Wellington boot" it became the most popular boot of the 1840s, eventually being superseded for daywear by the ankle boot (see page 202) in the 1860s.

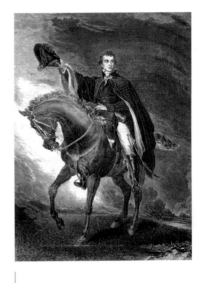

above:
Boot innovator
The Duke of Wellington pictured on his charger and wearing the original Wellington boot (c.1825).

left:
Festival fashion
Kate Moss attends the Glastonbury Festival in England in 2008 and makes the Hunter wellie the height of chic.

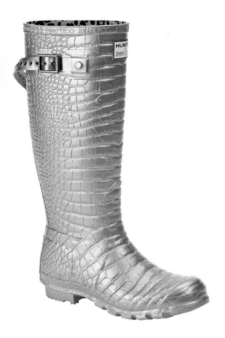

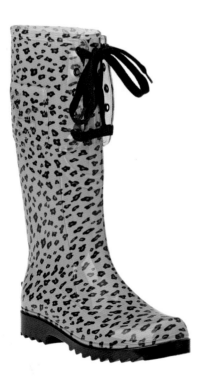

In 1852, entrepreneur Hiram Hutchinson bought the patent for the production of the boot in natural rubber from Charles Goodyear using his vulcanization process, and rubber Wellingtons were sold through the French Aigle company. Other manufacturers began experimenting with rubber versions of the boot, such as Henry Lee Norris who traveled from the United States to Edinburgh, Scotland, in 1856, where he set up the North British Rubber Company to manufacture boots and shoes.

By the early twentieth century, the rubber boot was catching on; European farmers had grown to love this footwear innovation because it kept their feet dry in muddy fields and it began to replace the traditional clog; similarly it gained a reputation during the First World War because it protected soldiers from trench foot in the flooded trenches. The North British Rubber Company manufactured well over a million pairs for the British Army during 1914–18 and Wellingtons were issued again during the flood conditions in Holland during the Second World War. The unavailability of boots and shoes as a result of rationing during the 1940s meant such a durable boot was widely worn and it became standard wet-weather gear for men, women, and children by the 1950s with a wider fit and more rounded toe. In 1958, the North British Rubber Company introduced the most iconic of Wellingtons aside from the Iron Duke's originals, which evolved into fashion brands by the 2000s—the "Green Hunter" and "Royal Hunter" boots.

In the 1960s, Wellington boots were made from PVC (polyvinyl chloride) with a super-shiny surface that fitted the space-age fashions of the decade, and fashion designer Mary Quant designed matching combinations of raincoat, rain hat, and Wellingtons. Quant launched a range of footwear in 1967 with the brand name Quant Afoot, including a chisel-toed ankle boot in injection-molded crystal-clear PVC with a colored jersey lining that showed through. Her signature daisy motif was molded into the heel so that traces would be left behind on the pavement after splashing through a puddle or tramping through snow—a motif that held much poignancy for the designer, for as a teenager she had fallen for an older man and wished his girlfriend dead. To Quant's absolute horror, the girlfriend died of appendicitis: her name was Daisy. Italian fashion label Fiorucci also produced brightly colored Wellington boots during this era and a bright-red PVC pair with a shiny black kitten heel in the early 1980s.

Hunters became a must-have fashion item in the 2000s; in 2005 Kate Moss was spotted at Glastonbury Festival in a black pair and in the same year Angelina Jolie wore red Hunters in the film *Mr. & Mrs. Smith*—Hunters gained such fashion cachet they collaborated with lifestyle shoe brands such as Jimmy Choo. Fashion houses jumped on the Wellington bandwagon—it was clearly a cheap and cheerful canvas on which to easily print distinctive logos such as the Burberry checked print, the Pucci psychedelic swirl, and the Missoni zigzag, and then charge premium prices. The myriad of designer versions made it clear that the humble wellie had moved from country pursuits to festival wear, and it was only one small step into mass-market fashion. Wellies are now so completely removed from their utilitarian origins that they have even been spotted being worn in clubs in the south of France at the height of summer. In 2011, journalist Bryony Gordon wrote: "Wellington boots are currently the ultimate symbol of city stupidity. Everywhere you go in London, women are clomping along the streets in a dizzying array of red wellies, patterned wellies, wellies with high heels. If you are especially stupid, you can even spend £275 on a crocodile-print pair by Jimmy Choo—the modern equivalent of a dunce's cap. It started with the snow, of course, despite the fact that a pair of six-inch stripper platforms provides more grip than most of the pink floral wellies the high street has to offer. The snow melted long ago, but the march of the Wellington-boot army continues."

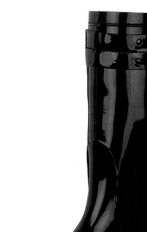

clockwise from top left:

Designer collaboration
A silver crocodile-embossed wellie—a Jimmy Choo–Hunter design.

Brazilian brand
Havaianas, a flip-flop brand, have moved into the lucrative wellie market.

True Brit
This glossy black "Plaque" wellington is by Burberry, the classic British label.

Rubber glamour
Chloe's diffusion line See launched a lace-up, leopard-print festival boot.

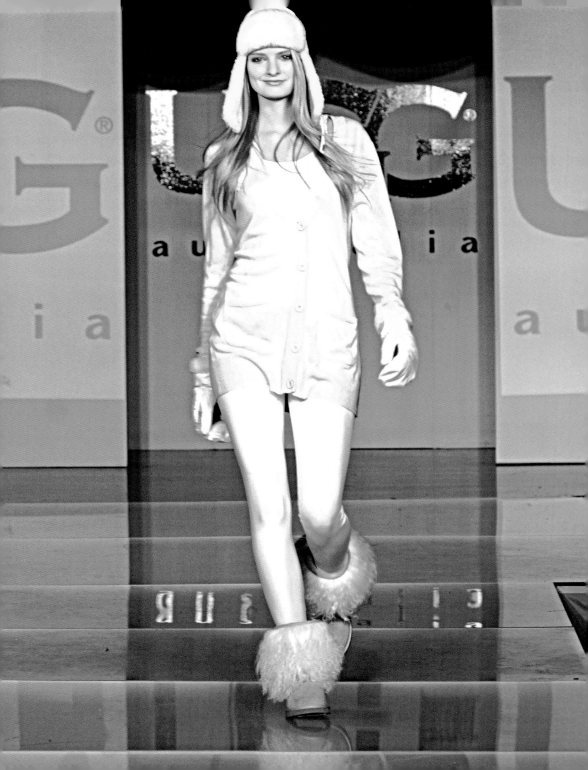

UGG

"There is nothing acceptable about the Ugg: It is girlishly fluffy... and it is such a tediously obvious means of making one's legs look thinner."

Hadley Freeman, the *Guardian*, November 12, 2007

Although the Ugg boot seems a contemporary entry on the footwear scene, it is over 200 years old, with its genesis as a generic sheepskin boot or "footie" worn by farmers and drovers in Australia and New Zealand. The Ugg is twin-faced in that it is constructed of one piece of sheepskin with the inside made from the fleece side of the skin and the outside of the boot from the tanned leather side. Once the sheepskin is cut, it is sewn together in the shape of the boot and soles are glued inside. A heel counter made of leather is attached to the outside of the boot to give support to the heel, and the bottom of the boot is attached to a molded rubber outer sole.

There is a debate over the derivation of the name—whether it is short for "ugly" or because the sheepskin-lined boot comfortably "hugs" the foot as a more fitted version of the valenki (see page 116). Blue Mountains Ugg was the first known company to commercially produce Uggs in the early 1930s, but the boot was yet to gain any fashion cachet and was usually worn at home as a domestic slipper.

The boot began to gain popularity in 1973 when Australian Shane Stedman created a version that he sold to surfers. Its easy pull-on style, the fact that it could be worn without socks, and the way the fleece absorbed the moisture from damp feet made it the perfect boot to keep feet warm between sessions. Stedman explained: "The sea is bloody cold in the Aussie winter, which is June time. I used to wear football jerseys to keep warm. Trouble was, they nearly drowned you. You couldn't wear wetsuits back then because they were big, thick, rubber things for professionals only. Your feet used to freeze, so I thought boots for surfers was a brilliant idea. People in the outback have been wrapping their feet in sheepskin for years."

Stedman's first boots were so rudimentary they still had flesh and sinews attached to the sheepskin and had the reputation for being

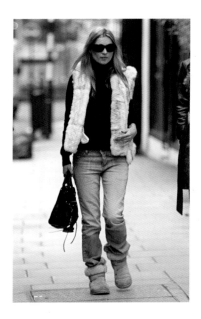

above:

Street chic
Kate Moss appears in Uggs on the streets of London in 2003 and helps start a footwear revolution.

left:

Winter warmer
A model takes to the runway for Ugg Australia's Fall/Winter 2010 collection at the Palais Royale, Toronto.

rather malodorous. By attaching rubber soles and using improved sheepskin, the boots became a success, not least because they gained a rebellious reputation when worn with ripped jeans, which saw them banned from Sydney's cinemas and nightspots. The sheepskin boot began to be associated with the slouchy downtime of a sexy sport, and girls wore their boyfriends' Uggs as a mark of being one half of a cool couple.

In 1978, enterprising surfer Brian Smith began importing and selling a similar sheepskin boot to Californian surf shops from San Diego to Santa Cruz under the label Uggs Australia—they were a niche success, which was duly noted by the Deckers Outdoor Corporation. Deckers had a seasonal shoe, the "Teva" sandal, and wanted a winter boot to complement it and keep their sales force employed all year round, so in 1995 they bought Uggs Australia for $15 million USD—they had also quietly acquired Stedman's concept in 1983 for $10,000 USD plus three pairs a year for life. It was around this time that Uggs began to gain a more mainstream status as a result of one female star—actress Pamela Anderson, who had discovered the boots while working in Australia and used them to keep her feet warm during breaks in shooting the popular TV series *Baywatch*. The paparazzi photographed her out and about in a cut-off mini and Uggs and her stratospheric popularity meant the boot gained an aspirational celebrity status among young women who loved her mix of California beach babe and glamor model. When It-girl Paris Hilton began wearing them with tucked in sweatpants and a pair of oversized shades, Uggs became the uniform of most young actresses (and their wannabes) off stage. In 2000, talk-show host Oprah Winfrey raved about the boot on her show—that at the time had a daily audience of 7,000,000—and its success was sealed.

The Ugg is perhaps the most faked boot in footwear history with, it is estimated, over 4,000 international Web sites selling counterfeited pairs as well as legitimate labels that sell a similar Australian boot including Aussie Dogs, Emu, Koolaburra, Bearpaw, UGG, and Warmbat—there have been several attempts over the years to overturn Ugg Australia's rights to the trademark, since the boot is seen as part of Australia's cultural heritage.

The Ugg's strangely oversized proportions, particularly the overly rounded stitched toe, are considered ugly by many—this plus their tendency to

below:

Studded suede

Jimmy Choo toughened the Ugg with the striking studded black suede "Mandah."

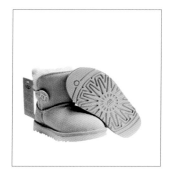

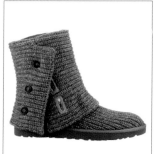

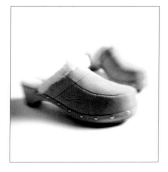

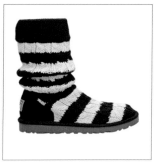

clockwise from top left:

Uggs in miniature
Ugg expand their market share by manufacturing baby Uggs.

Knitwear
The side-buttoned "Cardy" boot is the winter version of the Ugg.

Striped Ugg
An Ugg that provokes a double-take—is it a shoe or a striped sock?

Ugg clogs
An Ugg combining the comfort of sheepskin slippers with the durability of the clog.

become what has been dubbed "street crippled" has led to much media debate. Podiatrists point to the lack of arch support that leads to the sides of the boots being trodden on instead of the sole, causing the so-called "Ugg shuffle" where the wearer is barely able to lift her feet from the floor. The boot also takes in vast amounts of moisture in wet weather and retains water stains on its sheepskin uppers—but this does not seem to have detracted from its success. The boot's all-round comfort may well be its downfall though; it has become such a popular alternative to the formerly ubiquitous trainer that it is now associated with the "pajama run," a name bestowed on the practice of slovenly women dropping their children off at school gates in pajama bottoms and cheap, high-street copies of Uggs. The huge number of synthetic copies have also made what was considered the height of casual luxe incredibly downgraded so the Ugg Australia label is rebranding. In 2011, an attempt was made to get the boot's luxury status back by collaborating with high-end lifestyle brand Jimmy Choo. The Ugg began a metamorphosis from completely flat to high with heels or with platform wedges added, the only recognizable component being the original sheepskin lining.

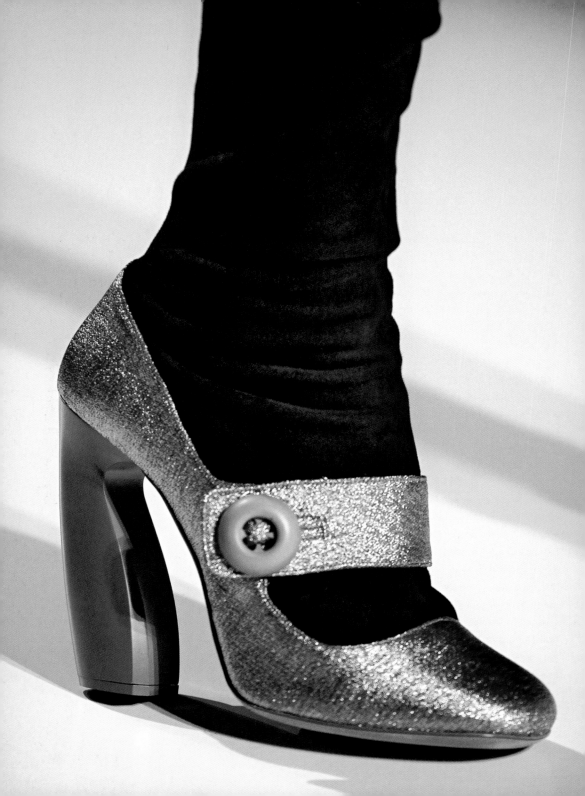

MARY JANE

"Manolo Blahnik Mary Janes! I thought these were an urban shoe myth!"

Carrie Bradshaw in "A Vogue Idea," *Sex and the City*, 2002

The Mary Jane is a broad, closed-toe shoe with a flat, single-buttoned strap that fastens across the instep, and a low heel. The ubiquitous broad toe and one-bar strap date back to Tudor England—King Henry VIII can be seen wearing flat satin strap shoes with a "latyn," or metal buckle, in his official portraits.

By the nineteenth century, the practicality of this shoe made it the perfect choice for the growing feet of children, because the flat sole and secure strap helped toddlers to take their first tentative steps away from adult arms. The compelling resonance of this important rite of passage imbued the unisex shoe with its powerful associations of childhood, a bond forged even further when two popular childhood characters were pictured wearing the style: Lewis Carroll's "Alice" of *Alice in Wonderland* in the iconic illustrations by Sir John Tenniel of 1865 and Christopher Robin as illustrated by E. H. Shepherd in A. A. Milne's *Winnie the Pooh* (1926).

The shoe derived its distinctive moniker in the United States. In 1902, the Buster Brown cartoon strip made its first appearance in the *New York Herald* newspaper drawn by writer and artist Richard Felton Outcault. It featured a boy, Buster, with an unquenchable thirst for mischief, his sister Mary Jane, and his talking bulldog Tige. On publication, the cartoon was so popular that Outcault decided to cash in on his creations by searching around for marketing possibilities. In 1904, he met George Warren Brown, founder of the Brown Shoe Company, at the St. Louis World's Fair and negotiated the licenses to use Buster Brown as a children's shoe brand—an early example of cartoon merchandizing that predated Walt Disney. Brown bombarded the United States with a publicity blitz of little people wearing replicas of Buster's Little Lord Fauntleroy-inspired outfits, who toured the country visiting department and shoe stores. He

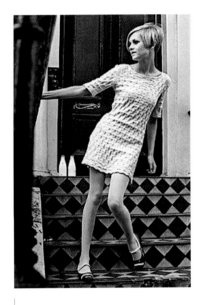

above:

Twiggy in Mary Janes

The pre-adolescent "little girl" look of the 1960s had Mary Janes as the perfect foil.

left:

Prada Fall/Winter 2011

Trompe l'œil suede boots give the appearance of wearing pink-metallic brocade Mary Janes.

soon established a shoe empire that today has an annual turnover of more than $40 billion USD. The Mary Jane shoe was one of the most successful of the company's styles—a hard-wearing, well-fitting, leather example of the traditional single-strap shoe launched in 1909. The feminization of the style led to the shoe gradually transforming into an item of female dress rather than male, and its doll-like appeal was assured on celluloid when the style was worn by the world's most popular child star, Shirley Temple.

In the same decade, Mary Janes were adopted by flappers, whose fashionable masculine style emanated from the French fashion houses of Coco Chanel, Elsa Schiaparelli, and Madeleine Vionnet. The streamlined schoolgirl silhouette with flattened breasts and short skirts deliberately rejected any hint of the pre-war Edwardian Gibson Girl, and the Mary Jane was the perfect form for the modern foot. Throughout the decade though, the style of Mary Janes subtly shifted, so that by the early 1930s, the shoes had higher, tapered heels, and the plain leather and cloth uppers of yesteryear had been supplanted by colored satin, ornate brocade, and Art Deco silks.

During the 1940s, the schoolgirl style was clearly inappropriate for wartime women in times of trial. By the early 1950s, the stiletto had taken over as a more powerfully sexy form of footwear, and the Mary Jane had retired to its former role as a child's shoe—considered the first step in the progression to womanhood in shoe fashion. Author Charlotte Nekola described this trajectory in *Dream House* (1993), her memoir of a girlhood spent in the 1950s: "Mary Janes to flats to pumps with a small tasteful heel, and finally to the realm of pure sex and authority, 'spike heels.'"

Mary Janes reappeared in the early 1960s as a perfect foil to the newfound youthful fashion that surfaced in London with designers such as Mary Quant, and were made high fashion when showcased on the slender feet of supermodels such as Twiggy. André Courrèges, Yves Saint Laurent, and Christian Dior all featured patent leather bar shoes in their runway collections of this era, too, with the trademark low heel but a slightly more tapered toe. It took the earth mothers of the hippie counterculture, the radical feminists, and the aggressive punks of the 1970s to reject the inherent meanings of such a childish shoe.

It was not until the 1990s that the shoe reappeared in women's fashion again—this time in one of its most

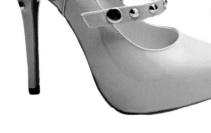

below:

Tough love

Louboutin's "Mad Mary Jane" has a pink leather upper and is toughened up with biker studs.

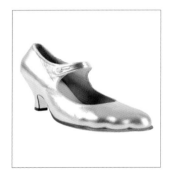

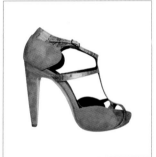

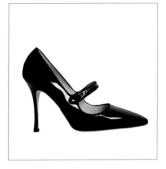

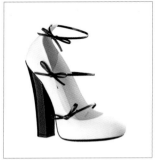

clockwise from top left:

Surrealist Mary Jane
Vivienne Westwood's molded-toe
buttoned Mary Jane in silver leather.
Watersnakeskin and suede
Pierre Hardy's turquoise suede Mary
Jane with watersnakeskin strap detail
for Spring/Summer 2012.
Be-ribboned Mary Jane
Louis Vuitton substitutes sturdy straps
with delicate bows for Fall/Winter 2011.
Modern classic Mary Jane
Manolo Blahnik's signature Mary Jane
with stiletto and winklepicker toe.

memorable forms. Singer Courtney Love subverted the "little girl"
look in a grunge style. Wearing a baby-doll dress with a pink ribbon
sash, with a knitted toy hanging from her waist and Mary Janes on
her feet, Love appeared on stage with "witch" and "slut" scrawled
on her forearms and a red lipstick-smeared mouth. The little girl had
grown up and clearly had a voice entirely of her own.

Since then, Mary Janes have appeared in many guises, from
the runway shows of Anna Sui through Manolo Blahnik, Narcisco
Rodriguez, Marc Jacobs, and shoe designer Tokio Kumagai for
Commes des Garçons. Heels can now be flat, wedge, or platform as
long as the round toe and bar strap are in evidence. Mary Janes have
also found their place in the enduring subculture of Goth, where the
innocent look of the shoe is overturned by the addition of decorative
details such as painted skull and crossbones or orange flames. More
recently, the Mary Jane has been adopted by a visually arresting style
tribe in Japan, dubbed Goth Lolita. Goth Lolitas take on the persona
of a porcelain Victorian doll in knee-length frilled gowns, knee socks,
and high platform Mary Janes. The Mary Jane has evolved from its
cartoon origins, and its universal popularity shows no sign of fading.

STACKED HEEL

Stacked heels are simple in construction, made of sections of leather that have been literally stacked on top of one another. Each layer of leather is commonly called a lift. They are used for very practical footwear such as the Oxford (see page 90) because they are usually low and follow the heel shape at the back with a straight edge at the front. Stacked heels were common from the 1820s in both shoes and boots and were usually just under an inch high; when the fashion for flat slippers took over, the stacked heel disappeared in women's footwear until the 1860s, when it became a permanent fixture of walking shoes.

right:

Postmodernist stacking

Yves Saint Laurent adds a stacked rubber platform and heel to his 1992 sandal that artfully exposes its construction.

below:

Stacked high (Spring/Summer 2011)

Pierre Hardy negated the functionality of the stacked heel with this sky-high pair in blue-and-white suede.

> "I walked around that way, wherever I could without falling over."
>
> Bobby Darin on his shoes with 3-inch lifts and $2^1/_2$-inch heels

The stacked heel was the focus of shoe fashion in the 1970s with its combination of height and chunkiness. In 1972, men's magazine *Penthouse* was effusive in its praise for the heel and in an article entitled "Heel Thyself" wrote, "today's stacked shoes don't let anyone go short," and went on, "the most popular look in higher heels is the stacked heel. In natural leather, often unstained to give a 'raw' look, the heel ranges in height up to as much as three inches."

This raw look was perfectly encapsulated in the Frye "Campus" boot in banana- or light-tan-colored leather with a Wellington vamp, leather sole, and two-to-three-inch stacked heel. Still in production today, the "Campus 14L" conjures images of the end of the hippie era when American students protested on campus to the tunes of Jimi Hendrix or Janis Joplin. The first rugged Frye boot was made in 1863 by English bootmaker John A. Frye and was worn by soldiers during the American Civil War and pioneering homesteaders heading West in the late nineteenth century. Like Levis, the heritage of the Frye boot

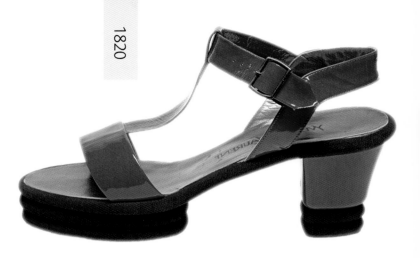

chimed with the "authenticity" required by the fashionable in the recession-hit years of the 1970s, and the hard-wearing "Campus," a reissue of the 1860s original was worn alongside the clog, moccasin, and espadrille.

The extreme height of the stacked heel could be easily balanced with a platform that made the shoes surprisingly comfortable and relatively easy to walk in, and they became a feature of the towering styles associated with glam rock. The stacked heel gave wobble-proof support and the layered lifts were made a feature with alternating colors, as worn by singer Elton John in 1973. Faux-wood stacked heels made from plastic were a lighter and cheaper alternative to leather, and many had flared bases that gave even more support to the feet and ankles. In the early 2000s, Stella McCartney and Miuccia Prada revived the 1970s stacked heel as a fresh alternative to the stiletto with no elevating platform under the front of the foot.

In male footwear, the stacked heel still appears on many classic boots including the biker and engineer, yet stacked heels or shoe lifts have another function—to elevate the height of diminutive men and, as such, they have a history in Hollywood. Pasquale di Fabrizio, also known as the "Shoemaker to the Stars," made stacked heels for Frank Sinatra, Michael Douglas, Sylvester Stallone, and Michael Jackson, among others, working out of a store on Fairfax Avenue in Los Angeles. More recently, TV mogul Simon Cowell has been ribbed over his thick stacked heels and Nicolas Sarkozy has added inches to his shoes while his four-inches-taller wife Carla Bruni-Sarkozy wears flats.

below:

Jackson stacks

Michael Jackson and the Jackson Five appearing on the Sonny and Cher television show in the mid-1970s.

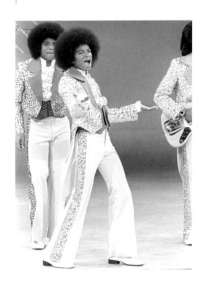

TENNIS SHOE

A tennis shoe—the forerunner of the sneaker—is a type of athletic shoe with a canvas upper and rubber sole, and was the first type of sports shoe to be worn at the Paris Olympics of 1924. The original tennis shoe, called "plimsoll" in the UK, was manufactured by the Liverpool Rubber Company (acquired by Dunlop in 1925) in the 1830s and was marketed as a sand shoe. The expansion of the UK railways in the early nineteenth century had made a vacation by the sea possible for thousands of working-class families, and products began to be targeted at this new audience. The leather boots habitually worn by day were unsuited to the beach, so inexpensive

> "Shoes are the first adult machines we are given to master."
>
> Nicholson Baker

light canvas-topped shoes with leather or jute soles were worn. As the original form of the sand shoe tended to wear out pretty quickly, the Liverpool Rubber Company combined a cotton canvas upper with a rubber sole, and a thin rubber band was wrapped around the whole shoe as reinforcement for the join between the canvas and rubber sole.

In the UK, the shoe was given the nickname "plimsoll" in the 1870s because the rubber band resembled the Plimsoll Line invented by Samuel Plimsoll as a safety measure for merchant ships. In 1876, the Board of Trade recorded the loss of well over 800 ships at sea within sight of the British coastline despite good weather conditions—they were dangerously overloaded and the slightest swell caused them to capsize. The Plimsoll Line was painted on a ship's hull to show how much weight a ship could carry before it became unstable—thus, in footwear terms, if the water got above the line on the plimsoll shoe, the wearer's foot got soaked.

As women began to participate more actively in sports such as tennis in the early

below:

Mixed messages

Stone's canvas trainers play with the notion of a "sports" shoe by adding a tapered stiletto heel.

below right:

"Amber Flash"

Classic Dunlop tennis shoe based on the "Green Flash" launched in 1929 and endorsed by tennis star Fred Perry.

twentieth century, the tennis shoe was widely worn on court and patterns were added to the rubber sole to add grip, helpful when they were worn on a yacht, so the shoes became known as "deck shoes." Tennis shoes also became a compulsory part of the physical education uniform in schools. The shape of the shoe also reflected the increased physicality of women's bodies. The shoes underwent a series of changes: a rubber strip was added to give more life to the toe, since the big toe could easily rub through the canvas; molded studs were added for hockey, eventually developing into a separate category of hockey boot; and in 1912, the US company Spalding made a high-top sneaker with a gum rubber suction sole, and an upper of black kangaroo leather—the forerunner of today's basketball shoes.

In the United States, the tennis shoe dates back to 1893 when it was first mentioned in *The Household Magazine*. The name "sneaker" was coined by Henry Nelson McKinney, who worked for the advertising agency N. W. Ayer & Son, because the rubber sole made them perfect for "sneaking" around. Keds were the first to market their tennis shoes as sneakers in 1916 and gave the term common usage.

The tennis shoe has remained a footwear classic with no innovation necessary—that's left to the trainer—apart from in Spring/Summer 2006 when the chain Topshop introduced a hybrid—a stiletto tennis shoe—a sports shoe that couldn't be more unsporting, for it had the most physically restricting of metal stiletto heels.

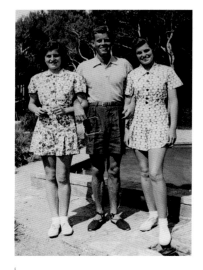

above:

Sports casual

The Kennedy sisters pose poolside with their brother John in American tennis shoes and sun dresses.

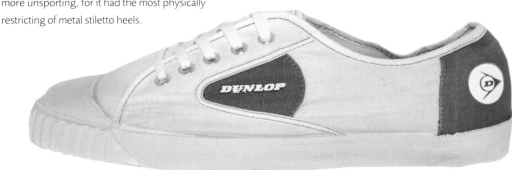

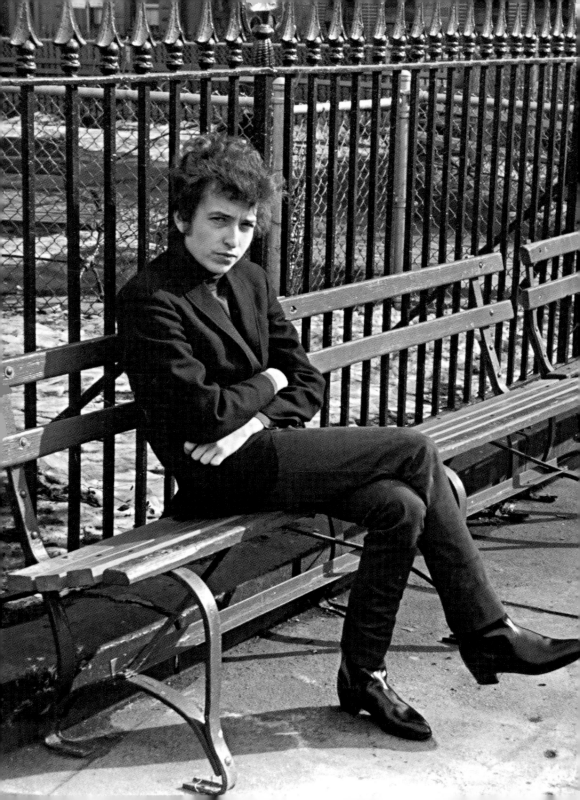

CHELSEA BOOT

"They're an endlessly adaptable design, usefully located on the border between smart and casual."

Alexis Petridis, the *Guardian*, August 8, 2009

The Chelsea boot is a fitted ankle boot with elastic inserts up the sides invented in 1837 by bootmaker to Queen Victoria, J. Sparkes-Hall of Regent Street, London. The boot was eminently functional, since the elastic vulcanized rubber made for ease in pulling the boot on and off. It was originally worn by nineteenth-century women who found it a comfortable alternative to the button boot (see page 145), and Sparkes-Hall described how the Queen was quite enamored of her pair, explaining how "she walks in them daily and thus gives the strongest proof of the value she attaches to the invention." Sparkes-Hall patented his boot in 1851, the year of the Great Exhibition at Crystal Palace, a showcase for the British Empire's advances in design and engineering. The pioneering Sparkes-Hall Patent Elastic Ankle Boots were advertised as requiring "neither lacing, buttoning, nor tying; they can be put on and off in a moment without trouble or loss of time" and did away with "the constant annoyance of laces breaking, buttons coming off, holes wearing out and many imperfections in the ordinary modes of fastening." The boots caught on for horse riding and became known as paddock or Jodhpur boots, after the colonial capital of Rajasthan, India, and were an everyday staple up to the First World War in 1914. A heavier version also evolved in Australia in the nineteenth century known as the "blunnie" or Blundstone boot.

It wasn't until the 1960s that the elastic-sided boot was adopted as a fashion. The King's Road was the epicenter of the swinging London scene, and Chelsea was the nickname applied to whatever was considered the height of cool; the boutique Chelsea Girl for instance opened in 1965. The elastic-sided boot was worn by the new street tribe—mods—and renamed the Chelsea boot. Mods appeared on the Soho scene in the late 1950s and were renowned for their

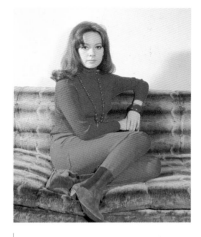

above:

The boot that swung

By the end of the 1960s, the Chelsea boot was a signifier of youthful cool for both men and women.

left:

Rock 'n' roll bohemian

The high-heeled Chelsea boot was worn by the coolest names in 1960s rock, most notably Bob Dylan (1965).

fastidious tailoring and fascination with English country dress. They subverted tailored suits, having them made in houndstooth check or mohair rather than the customary tweed and adopted the riding boot for a lifestyle that revolved around the hedonism of consumption and an ironic statement of the class divide.

Once the Beatles adopted the fashionable mod boot it hit the big time, and was renamed the Beatle boot, starting an association with rock 'n' roll that continues today. John Lennon had found the boots in Annello and Davide, a company founded in Covent Garden in 1922 that specialized in handmade shoes. A flamenco-inspired Cuban heel was attached to the Chelsea boot and the resulting masculine high heel—the first for decades—had fans literally lining up around the block to buy them from this small bespoke shoe shop. The boot was worn by such titans of rock music as the Rolling Stones, Bob Dylan, and, more recently, the Kings of Leon. George Lucas even dressed his Stormtroopers in them for the first three movies of the *Star Wars* franchise—they had to be spray-painted white to convey a suitably futuristic look. Aside from Anello and Davide, the company Frank Wright established in 1885 in Kettering, UK, were a major part of the Carnaby Street scene in the 1960s as manufacturers of the Chelsea boot, and still produce their "Adler" and "Yorke" models in the 2010s. Today the Chelsea boot has become a staple of the male wardrobe, and ironically, women rarely wear them except for horse riding.

right:
Power platform
The Akris Chelsea boot streamlines the traditional elastic sides and heel to give a futuristic feel (Fall/Winter 2011).

below left:
Star styled
Actress Chloë Sevigny designed the high-heeled "Nana" Chelsea boot in napa leather for Opening Ceremony.

below right:
Classic Chelsea
Hasbeen, a brand best known for clogs, show their prowess at recreating traditional footwear types.

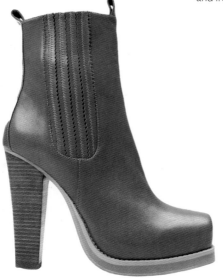

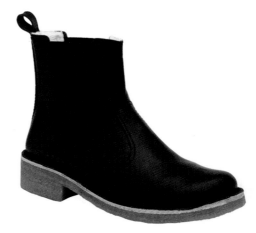

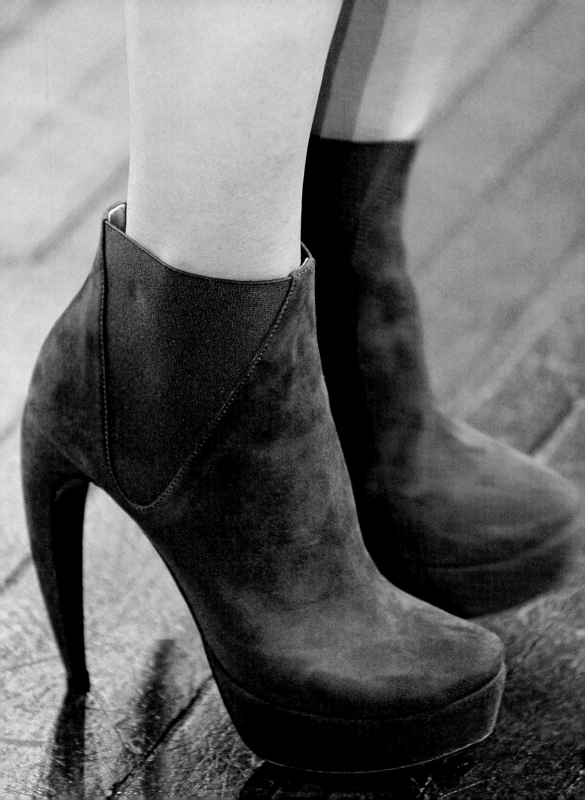

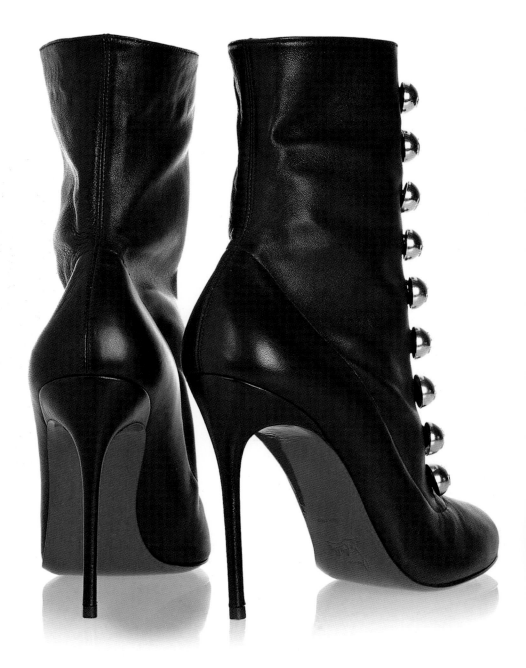

BUTTON BOOT

"The shiny red color of the soles has no function other than to identify to the public that they are mine."

Christian Louboutin

From the mid-nineteenth to the early twentieth century, boots or *bottines* were the accepted everyday footwear for all classes of men and women. Button boots were made of leather, or a lighter canvas in the summer, and had a row of buttons that fastened over a flap of leather at the front, and a low heel. The button closure gave the boot a tight fit that kept the foot warm and dry, plus it provided good ankle support. Women's button boots evolved into a corset for the foot and were at their most elaborate in the period 1870–1914, with up to twenty-five buttons on each boot.

A buttonhook—a steel prong of differing lengths with a hook on the end— was used to get them on, and buttonhooks became extremely decorative items during the Victorian era, the most expensive fashioned from precious metals and studded with gems. The prong was pushed through the boot's buttonhole and positioned around the shank of the button. One swift tug and flick of the wrist and the button was through the hole and tightly fastened—some hooks were a foot in length and used by women who were too tightly corseted or portly to bend over. Buttoning boots was a difficult task, compellingly described by writer Eileen Elias in 1910: "The buttonholes were so hard and slit-like that they hurt your fingers, and you didn't always have a buttonhook. Even if you had, it invariably hooked the wrong button into the hole. I would sit wrestling with my button boots and choking back tears. As often as not I would be forced to walk out into the road with the buttons half undone, and pretend not to notice the grins and glances."

The close fit of the boot looked extremely elegant, but once on, it had to stay on all day with no adjustment possible—painful if the foot was inclined to swell. At home, the head servant, housekeeper, or nanny kept a buttonhook about their person at all times attached to

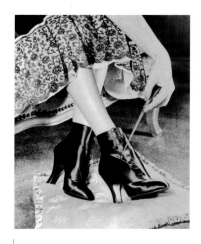

above:
Revival
The boot made a brief return in the 1950s with nostalgic New Look fashions. Julianelli's black satin pair came with a button hook.

left:
Fetish meets fashion
Louboutin recalls the great mistresses of the Belle Époque with this supremely sexy boot.

a chatelaine, a chain belt worn around the waist from which dangled all manner of household tools including keys, scissors, and a bottle of smelling salts.

By the turn of the century, as the boot gained more buttons it became more difficult to fasten, unless one had the tiniest and most dexterous of fingers, and it fell from male fashion. Fastenings of tiny buttons took over womens' clothes and footwear, necessitating a variety of buttonhooks. Writer Gwen Raverat, in her evocative biography of a late nineteenth-century childhood *Period Piece*, felt "there must have been something aristocratic about buttons for everything that could possibly button or unbutton was made to do so; buttons all down the front of one's nightgown, buttons on the sleeves, buttons on one's bodice and drawers, buttons everywhere. That anonymous genius who discovered that clothes could be slipped over one's head, had not yet been born; nor had his twin

"The core of my work is dedicated not to pleasing women but to pleasing men."

Christian Louboutin

brother who discovered elastic." Buttons, as Raverat realized, showed that one had time and money—money to pay for a servant to help in dressing and time to have all those buttons fastened up—time that the city's poor spent laboring in front-laced boots. Front-buttoned boots were clearly becoming gendered objects and Raverat relates how "I wish I had been allowed to have proper boys' boots with little brass hooks for laces; for I wanted them so passionately. I always had button boots, which I thought effeminate. There was a grand row once when Charles was made to wear a pair of my old button boots and we both thought it an insult to his sex."

As the button boot moved away from male footwear fashion, it began to gain the reputation as a sexy item of clothing, in part due to the popularity of the "Gibson Girl." Illustrator Charles Dana Gibson had invented this Edwardian character in 1890, and she became an incredibly popular representation of new American femininity, with her pin-tucked blouse, huge dressed hairstyle, bustled skirt, and button boots with scalloped edges.

By the 1920s the button boot began to be eclipsed by the rise of the city shoe and didn't appear again until the 1970s when they, together with front-laced nineteenth-century-style ankle boots, were dubbed "granny boots." The previously ornate loops were constructed out of elastic, and a low stack or Louis heel was attached. Today they have a retro appeal that remains popular at weddings, but their appeal is limited because it takes time to put them on—and that's incompatible with the fast pace of twenty-first century culture. There are exceptions; Christian Louboutin's "Ronfifi 100 Button Boots" play on their modern fetish appeal by mixing gold metal buttons and military references on a high, black leather boot with his signature red sole and four-inch stiletto heel, and button boots have also become the counter-cultural uniform of some street tribes including Goth and Steampunk.

Followers of Steampunk, an offshoot of the Cyberpunk genre, are fascinated with Victorian science fiction, in particular the work of Jules Verne and H. G. Wells and the writers' relationship with early technology, scientific exploration, and industrialization. Instead of imagining the future, Steampunk looks back to the Victorian to create "what-if" scenarios such as situating the computer or atomic bomb in Dickensian London. This futuristic retro-Victorianism has its natural home on the Internet and has had its effect in Japanese anime in movies such as *Howl's Moving Castle* (2004) and the elegant gothic-aristocrat offshoot of the Goth-Lolita movement. Aficionados follow no strict rules over their clothing choices, but certain Victorian garments are favored, including corsets and crinolines for women and frockcoats or military-inspired outfits for men, accessorized with fob watches, parasols, futuristic goggles, and robotic body parts. The button boot has the right nostalgic appeal, plus the original version is so far out of fashion that it appears suitably eccentric. Pleaser Shoe sells a side-buttoned retro-Victorian boot with an almond toe and low, Louis heel and UturnUtopia have bypassed the button fastening by adding an invisible zipper.

left:
Fitted foot
A red velvet side-buttoned boot with Louis heel that dates from the nineteenth century.

below:
Military discipline
Louboutin's "Ronfifi" mid-calf buttoned boot has a military appeal, with its navy flannel and gold buttons.

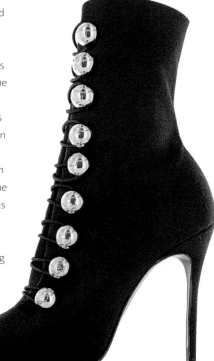

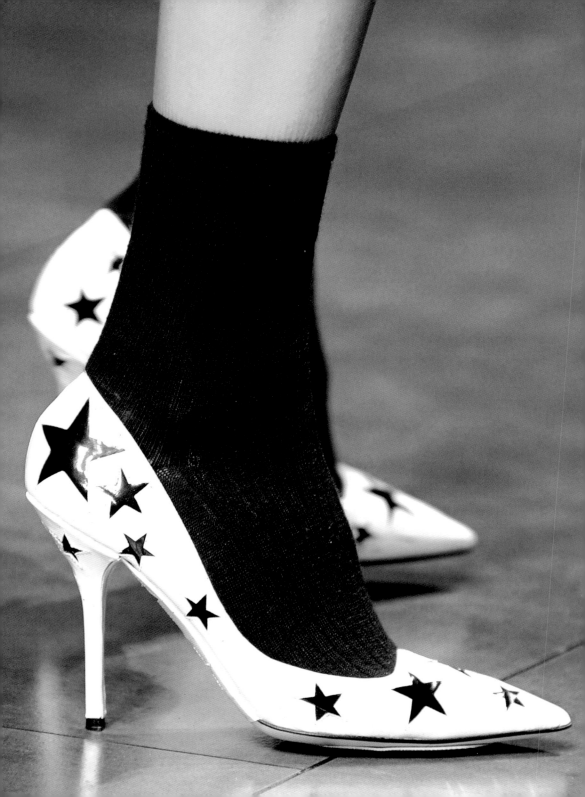

PUMP

"You put high heels on and you change."

Manolo Blahnik

The pump—or court shoe as it is known in Europe—is a practical, formal, smart shoe without fastenings and a low-cut front that can be slipped on and off with ease. Its name is derived from the French *pompe* or "pump," allegedly because the first French shoemakers made the leather buckets for Paris' fire departments. The plain shape means that the pump can take many kinds of decoration or heel, which is why the style has never gone out of fashion.

The rise of the pump in the 1860s mirrors the advances being made in the technology of shoemaking as it morphed from a small-scale localized industry of cobblers or the more expensive *bottiers* (shoemakers who collaborated with couturiers of Paris) to factory-based production. Pumps required careful construction to fit and to stay on the feet without the aid of buckles, straps, or ties, which made them expensive shoes. Well-heeled Victorian gentlemen wore shiny black-patent, low-heeled pumps for dancing, but they were not considered a day shoe like slipper-sandals or button boots. In the 1850s, an American machine for sewing leather came into use, and by the 1860s, the sewing of soles and welts was mechanized, putting the large-scale manufacture of shoes and pumps within grasp of a larger audience. Its heel increased in height, the instep was cut higher, and the upper was constructed from leather, canvas, or cloth.

The word "pump" began to be used when slippers with a welted sole and heel began to be worn regularly on the street, rather than confined to the boudoir. The name was generally used as a footwear term for women's shoes, rather than for men's dancing pumps around 1906. When in the hands of the *bottier*, the pump could become an expensive proposition with embroidered and beaded hand-dyed silk vamps, a Cromwellian buckle on the front, and a high carved heel. In the 1900s, Louis-heeled pumps were worn, the toe

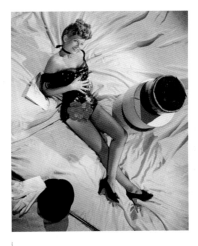

above:

Haute Hollywood

Rita Hayworth wearing pumps on the set of *Cover Girl* (1944). Throughout her career she was shod by David Evins.

left:

D&G (Fall/Winter 2011)

The proportions of a typical 1950s pump shape are exaggerated with a killer heel and winklepicker toe.

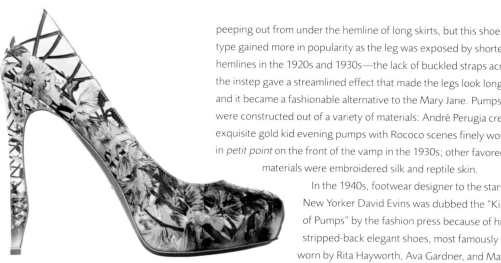

peeping out from under the hemline of long skirts, but this shoe type gained more in popularity as the leg was exposed by shorter hemlines in the 1920s and 1930s—the lack of buckled straps across the instep gave a streamlined effect that made the legs look longer, and it became a fashionable alternative to the Mary Jane. Pumps were constructed out of a variety of materials: André Perugia created exquisite gold kid evening pumps with Rococo scenes finely worked in *petit point* on the front of the vamp in the 1930s; other favored materials were embroidered silk and reptile skin.

In the 1940s, footwear designer to the stars, New Yorker David Evins was dubbed the "King of Pumps" by the fashion press because of his stripped-back elegant shoes, most famously worn by Rita Hayworth, Ava Gardner, and Marlene Dietrich. Evins began his career in footwear almost by accident when as a fashion illustrator for *Vogue* he altered the style of some shoes he was drawing to make them look more elegant. He was fired by the editor for turning out work that "reeked of artistic license," adding that if he liked shoe designing so much he should do it instead. After learning the trade with a number of manufacturers, Evins opened his own factory in New York in 1947, and by 1948, he had won the Coty Award for his "Shell" pump, a court shoe with a plunging vamp that was the first to show toe cleavage. In the early 1950s, Evins' goal was to make women's pumps lighter and more comfortable, which lead to the creation of the "6 ounce" pump, a deluxe handmade shoe that sold at three times the standard price of a quality shoe. The style was revisited by the designer in 1987 with the launch of the "Cashmere" pump, advertised as "A very special innovation in lightness, fit, and floating comfort." The shoe came in black patent or navy kid and had a one-and-a-half-inch "walking" heel—it was the perfect executive shoe. Nancy Reagan, wife of the

above:

Sky high

Nicholas Kirkwood creates a super-high concealed platform, floral-printed pump with a Vivier-inspired sculptural heel for Spring/Summer 2012.

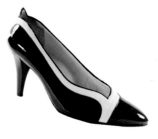

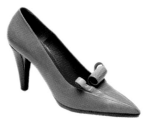

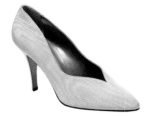

late American President Ronald Reagan, wore Evins' pumps to her husband's inauguration, and throughout her time as First Lady, she ordered six pairs of Evins pumps per year; two styles in three sizes to be worn in different climates and latitudes, depending on how her feet reacted to her environment: Size 6 were worn in cold places, 7 for Washington, and 8 for Air Force One.

The pump reigned in the 1950s as it took over from the platform and could be worn by day with a leather-covered wooden heel and in seductive black shantung silk with a stiletto heel for cocktail hour, together with a witty bibi hat. Roger Vivier's were the lowest cut and most extravagantly beaded, and his ubiquitous "Pilgrim Pump" (see page 238) was a 1960s phenomenon, as were Beth Levine's transparent vinyl pumps with rhinestone toes of 1966. The suede stiletto pump was popular in the 1970s, and in the 1980s, the kitten or red leather cone-heeled pump by Maud Frizon marched through many a boardroom at the height of power dressing. Today, Manolo Blahnik is famed for his pump design and Christian Louboutin's Very Prive pumps are notorious for their towering heels. The pump may seem an innocuous, understated design, but many of the world's most iconic shoes have been pumps, from Nancy Reagan's Evins inaugural pumps to Grace Kelly's pearl-covered wedding pumps for her marriage ceremony to Prince Rainier of Monaco. Gossip columnist Walter Winchell commented at the time that "David Evins is making Grace's wedding shoes. Low heels. So his Serene Highness won't look like a shrimp at the altar." Winchell was wrong however, as Grace's shoes were classic pumps with two-and-a-half-inch heels. In 1939, sixteen-year-old Judy Garland clicked her heels together in a pair of ruby pumps with a stack heel (even though they are referred to as slippers) for *The Wizard of Oz*—these most famous of shoes were designed by legendary Hollywood costumier Adrian and were sold at auction in 2000 for $666,000 USD.

from left to right:
YSL 1987
Graphic pump in blue patent kid and white lizard-pressed calf.
YSL 1988
Pointed-toe pump in gray kid with fuchsia and yellow furled kid detail.
YSL 1990
A V-neck, scallop-edged pump in yellow moiré grosgrain silk.
Larin 2011
Larin shoes come with trademark "click and twist" so the accessory can be changed.
Louboutin 2012
This nude lace pump is from the trademark Very Prive collection.
Hardy 2012
Pierre Hardy creates a streamlined pump in a color alchemy of cyan and petrol suede kid.

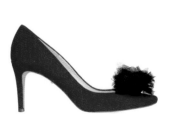
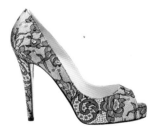
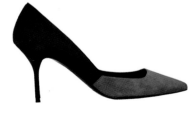

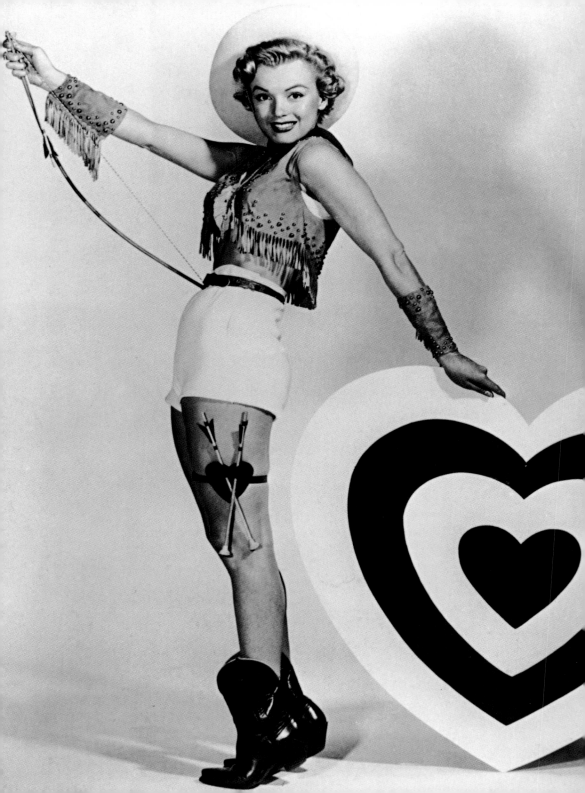

COWBOY BOOT

"You make noise when you walk, and it's a powerful, ominous sound. Nothing gets attention like a great pair of cowboy boots."

Jennifer June, author and cowboy boot expert

The skillful, rugged Texas cowboy riding the trails of the Rio Grande while driving his herd of Longhorn cattle is a character of incredible resonance in American culture. The prototype cowboy was the Mexican *vaquero*, a horseman revered for his prowess in cattle herding. Every year the *vaqueros* drove huge flocks of sheep from the sprawling *haciendas* of New Mexico over 1,000 miles to Chihuahua, a grueling journey that needed expert skills. By the eighteenth century, their skills were called upon in Texas to manage the state's vast herds of Longhorn cattle, skills that were passed on to both Native Americans and white settlers, the first cowboys.

At the end of the Civil War in 1865, as more and more cattle began to be exported out of the state, a boot was developed to cater to the needs of the cowboy: It had a slim toe to slip easily into the stirrup, a low undercut heel to keep it there, plus an arch with a steel shank to rest on the stirrup's bar. The heavy leather protected the cowboy's feet from rattlesnake bites, cacti spikes, chafing from the saddle, and the high sides prevented him from having his pants torn by the brush and mesquite thorns. Most importantly, the wide boot top and slick leather sole safely enabled the cowboy to pull his foot quickly out of the boot, or his boot out of the stirrup, if he was thrown from the horse.

In 1870, John Cubine of Coffeyville, Kansas, took the design a step further by combining the Wellington and military boot to create the high-topped unlined, waxed leather, Cuban-heeled Coffeyville with stitched-on pull straps. From the 1870s onward, the Coffeyville was copied and modified by many boot makers such as Charles Hyer of Hyer Brothers Boots of Kansas (1880). Innovations included the rounded scalloped top and a higher Cuban heel. Hyer introduced one of the early decorative details on the boot: the toe wrinkle, a line

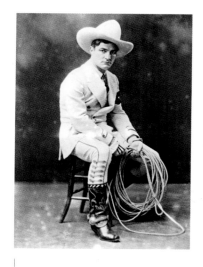

above:

Cowboy star

Tom Mix, the Hollywood cowboy (*c*.1920), heralded the era of the highly decorated cowboy boot.

left:

Valentine cowgirl

Marilyn Monroe sports cowboy boots as part of a cowgirl ensemble for an early publicity shot (1952).

right:

Uber American

For Spring/Summer 2011, Ashish paired cowboy hats and Western shirts with boots emblazoned with skeletons from the Mexican Day of the Dead.

below:

Cuban heeled

Delhi-born, London-based fashion designer Ashish launched a range of cowboy boots in 2011.

of stitching on the front of the boot that took the form of flowers or the fleur-de-lis, and it became the personalized signature of the bootmaker. The stitching also had a function: it stiffened the leather of the boot so that it stood straight, rather than becoming stretched over time.

The boot really took off in Hollywood as a form of fantasy footwear fabricated by movie studios that had only a little connection with its roots in the Wild West. The cowboy became one of the first popular radio and movie heroes: Bronco Billy, Tom Mix, and singing cowboys Roy Rogers and Gene Autry became household names, and highly decorative boots in a cornucopia of colored leather formed part of their masculine appeal. In the 1920s, cowboy boots were inlaid with geometric decorations, but by the 1940s, they had spiraled off into flights of fantasy including eagles, bucking broncos, butterflies, and even oil derricks.

In the 1950s, America's cowboy heritage found expression in the rodeo, where an exaggerated cowboy look was adopted by the participants to appeal to the crowds of adoring fans in the stands. Bronco riders wore flashy decorated boots that found their way into the burgeoning country-and-western music scene in Nashville, Tennessee, where they were worn by men and women alike. June Ivory, a rodeo celebrity, wore a pair in purple calfskin with the vamps and uppers covered with pink roses and zigzags inlaid with gold leaf.

Key manufacturers included Justin, a firm that started in 1875 as a small boot-repair operation at the end of the Chisholm Trail, where cowboys would drop one pair of boots off to be repaired and pick them up on the way back. Other boot-makers included Tony Lama, a cobbler who joined the US army to mend the boots of soldiers stationed at Fort Bliss, Texas. In 1911, Lama set up a business in El Paso making custom-made boots, which took off in the 1930s when Westernwear stores began to stock them in order to cater to tourists vacationing at dude ranches. Acme (1929) and the Nocona Boot Company (1925), along with Hyer (see page 153) make up what is known today as the Big Five, purveyors of the finest authentic cowboy boots. In the 1940s, the Lucchese Company of Texas created what many believe to be the pinnacle of cowboy-boot design, a series of forty-eight boots in homage to each American state with inlays of the state house, flower, flag, and bird.

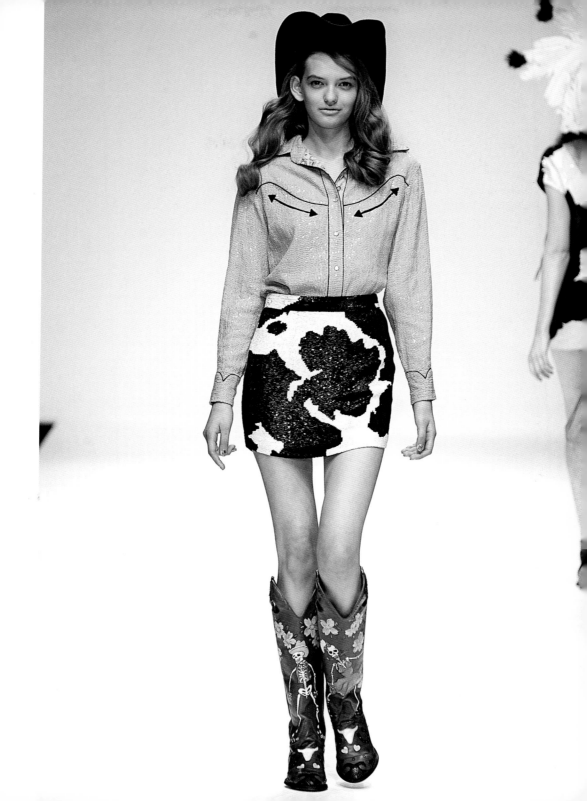

The cowboy boot was yet to hit mainstream fashion, remaining a truly American phenomenon throughout the post-war years and into the 1960s when the knee, kinky, and go-go boots held sway in women's fashion. By the late 1960s, the cowboy boot downsized, becoming more rugged and authentic, less decorated, and with a lower heel. It became a more serious heritage item, emblematic of the lost America that was celebrated in hippie counterculture and accordingly was worn by some of the main style leaders of old-time rock 'n' roll including Jimi Hendrix, Frank Zappa, and Janis Joplin.

Outside of Nashville and the rodeo, the cowboy boot remained a serious footwear proposition throughout the 1970s—the first cowboy boots on the runway were shown by Ralph Lauren in his 1970s Western collections. All changed in 1980 with the release

"The West would have been conquered earlier, if they had boots like these."

Cecil B. DeMille on Salvatore Ferragamo's 1920s cowboy boots

of *Urban Cowboy*, starring John Travolta and Debra Winger, both clad throughout the film in cowboy boots. The global success of the film popularized the cowboy boot and an estimated 17 million pairs were sold in the United States as a result. Sales gained another boost with *Top Gun* (1985), in which Tom Cruise strutted his stuff in a pair of vintage inlaid boots. Women wore low-cut, rhinestone-studded versions in white leather with miniskirts and push-down socks; boys with faded Levis and a bright white T-shirt—the decorative details even entered into shoes to create a hybrid cowboy-shoe with the same stitching and metal toecaps.

Sales dropped dramatically as the urban cowboy fad passed, until 1990 when Americans bought 12 million pairs as recession hit and a new authenticity entered fashion. Ralph Lauren continued to look to the Wild West for inspiration as an answer to the glamorous *Dynasty*-inspired style that had dominated the late 1980s. His patchwork blanket coats worn with blue jeans and cowboy boots were a refreshing alternative to power suits and high heels—they would always be redolent of an American heritage of rugged independence. Other designers followed suit including Michael Kors who launched the Sundance Chic Collection in

Fall/Winter 1999, but perhaps the most bizarre manifestation of the cowboy look was by Andrea Pfister, who created a surreal pineapple-print cowboy boot with a pineapple-shaped heel.

Heavy-metal stars including Guns N' Roses, Mötley Crüe, and Bon Jovi also popularized the boot in a more renegade statement, rather than fashion form, and the boot was in rebellious black leather with a pointed toe with a silver-metal tip. Cowboy boots went mainstream in a myriad of shapes, including low shoe-boots manufactured by Guess and Kenneth Cole; Laredo Boots launched over seventy styles of boots for women in a vivid color palette, including hot pink and red with black polka dots.

Today cowboy boots come in three basic categories: those handmade in custom shops such as Charlie Dunn's of Austin, Texas, that are fitted to the individual; authentic shapes made in large factories such as Tony Lama and Justin that have developed from their lowly nineteenth-century origins; and cowboy boots that change with the whims and vagaries of fashion by manufacturers such as Fly, La Redoute, and Schuh. Fashion designers who have dipped their toe in and out of Western style in the 2000s include Anna Sui in 2009, Givenchy, who recreated the classic tall cowboy boot in shimmering gold leather in 2011, and Robert Cavalli who regularly shows the style. Cowboy boots can be made from hard-wearing calfskin or deluxe exotic materials such as alligator, stingray, lizard, ostrich, and even water-buffalo skin, with elaborately decorated uppers favored by urban cowboys in oil-rich states like Texas. Rather ironically, they are very rarely, these days, worn by anybody who rides a horse.

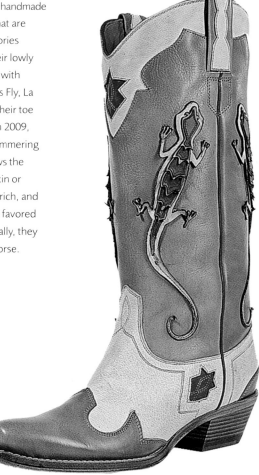

left:
Parisian cowgirl
A green and brown suede cowboy boot by Yves Saint Laurent with tassel detail.

right:
Urban cowboy
A high cowboy boot in cognac and cream leather by Ralph Lauren, embellished with a lizard detail.

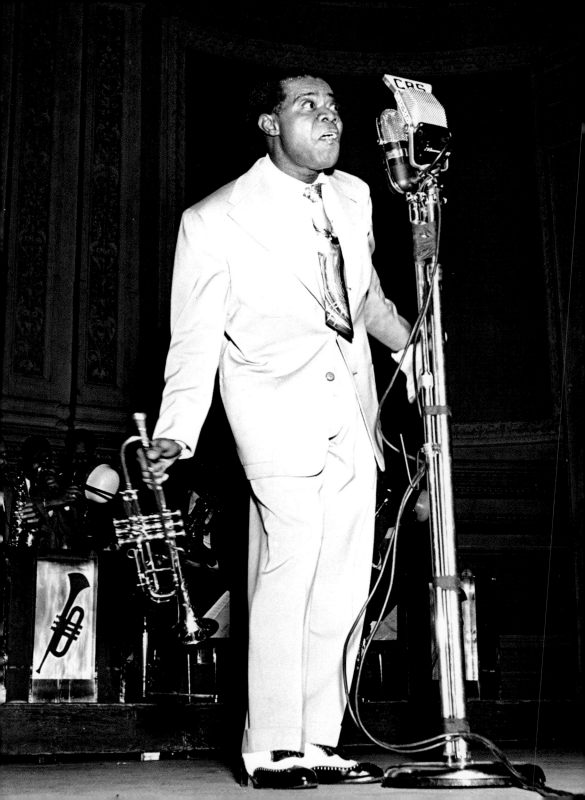

SPECTATOR

"Look at the outfit: Astaire is wearing a single-breasted suit with two-tone spectator shoes and a turtleneck. You wish you could look that stylish!"

G. Bruce Boyer in "Shall We Dress?" *Forbes*, May 3, 1999

A spectator is a unisex shoe associated with sport, since the name derives from a spectator standing on the sidelines at an event. The original two-tone form is said to have been invented in 1868 by John Lobb as a cricket shoe that combined a white accent with different-colored leathers or leather mixed with colored canvas or gabardine. Today the term "spectator shoe" refers to a two-tone Oxford shoe with black, brown, or tan leather at the toe-cap, back quarter, and instep, and white or tan suede or buckskin at the front and sides.

The spectator began its rise in popularity in the 1920s, when it was worn by that decade's arbiters of cool, African-American jazz musicians, disreputable night owls who played in backstreet nightclubs owned by Chicago mobsters and bootleggers. These men looked stylish and sharp: Earl Hines used his appearance as a form of showbiz advertising to get much-needed work as the Great Depression loomed; Jelly Roll Morton turned his clothes into an integral part of his act—one observer noted that he would come on stage and "take his overcoat off. It had a special lining that would catch everybody's eye. So he would turn it inside out and, instead of folding it, he would lay it lengthwise across the top of the upright piano. He would do this very slowly, very carefully, and very solemnly as if the coat was worth a fortune and had to be handled very tenderly." Spectator shoes were a spin on the Oxford day shoe and had the right brand of flashiness that these rakish performers wanted to project; the shoes were worn by many musicians including Count Basie, Duke Ellington, and Louis Armstrong.

Stacy Adams, a company founded in 1875, created some of the most flamboyant spectator styles in the 1930s, including the classic "Dayton Spectator" still available today using combinations of shiny red or black patent leather on a white leather upper. Cole Haan was

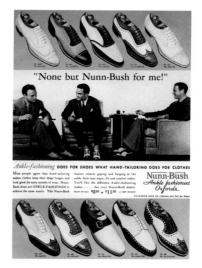

"None but Nunn-Bush for me!"

Ankle-fashioning DOES FOR SHOES WHAT HAND-TAILORING DOES FOR CLOTHES

above:

The 1940s spectator

Nunn-Bush has been manufacturing shoes since 1912 and is a popular purveyor of spectator shoes.

left:

Jazz spectator

Louis Armstrong sports the spectator shoe in 1940, a key style of footwear among dapper jazz musicians.

set up in Chicago in 1928 and, after having been bought by Nike in 1988, still manufactures shoes inspired by their original designs of the inter-war period.

Outside of the jazz community, black Americans employed in menial work as maids, factory workers, and laborers shook off their uniforms on the weekends and gained back control of their own bodies by dressing up in their finery and going to church before strolling down the city streets. The spectator shoe became an important sartorial symbol during both social interactions, a flamboyant form of footwear that caught the eye and made one stand out from the crowd. It has remained so ever since, rising to the fore during the disco era as well as the "ghetto-fabulous" look of R&B consecutively. Bernard Edwards and Nile Rodgers of the

> "I always wear flat shoes, because
> I can't walk in anything else."
>
> Sadie Frost

below:

Cuban heel spectator
Camper updated the traditional spectator by adding a Cuban heel and minimalist lacing.

disco band Chic remember wearing black tie to a Grace Jones gig at the infamous Studio 54 in 1977: "I had a Cerutti dinner jacket and Bernard had an Armani. We were killin'. I probably had a wing-collar shirt with a decorative front, but not lacy. Pleated, with studs. The whole bit. Spectator shoes. You know, two-tone! We wanted to look Chic. We wanted to smell Chic!" Today the shoe is still beloved by African-American superstars such as rapper Snoop Dogg, for whom they became a trademark.

In mainstream pop culture, the spectator gained ground in the 1930s as a casual sport shoe worn in the spring and summer; the broguing helped cool the foot in hot weather, and the leather inserts protected the white of the shoe from grass stains and scuffing. The Duke of Windsor popularized the look among bohemian young men, much to the consternation of the conservative British public, by wearing a spiked pair on a British golf course. The devil-may-care rakish image of the shoe was such that it led to a renaming in the UK—the co-respondent, after the adulterous partner in a divorce court. It took

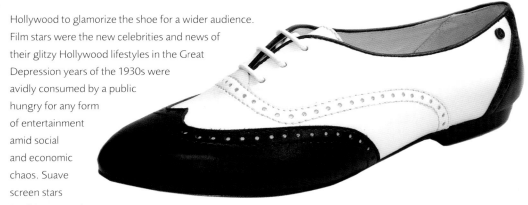

Hollywood to glamorize the shoe for a wider audience. Film stars were the new celebrities and news of their glitzy Hollywood lifestyles in the Great Depression years of the 1930s were avidly consumed by a public hungry for any form of entertainment amid social and economic chaos. Suave screen stars Fred Astaire and Jimmy Cagney whirled across the dance floor wearing spectators, their two-tone effect perfect for drawing focus to the feet in a black-and-white movie. In women's fashion, tailored pleated skirts demanded a smart day pump—the spectator had a smart, sassy, and sporty image that looked just right, and the most fashion-forward pairs were a mix of shiny black patent leather and brightly colored reptile skin. The shoe was adopted by Ivy League college students in the 1950s and gained a preppy image, then it disappeared from fashionable female footwear during the 1960s only to regain its hold in 1977 after the film *Annie Hall* was released. Actress Diane Keaton caused a style sensation in a look that took its inspiration from classic menswear and included spectator shoes. Manufacturers transformed them with heels and bold color combinations, and they reached the height of popularity in the 1980s in the form of the heeled spectator pump.

In 1971 Stacy Adams was bought out by the Weyco Group, a major manufacturer, purchaser, and marketer of mens' and boys' footwear who marketed the company as a purveyor of authentic retro styles from its back catalog to appeal to the vintage crowd, in particular lovers of swing. It was a success and an average of 200,000 pairs were sold every year—a substantial boost to the company's profits. Johnston & Murphy, founded by William A. Dudley in 1850 in Newark, New Jersey, picked up on the trend and their spectator shoe became available in white buckskin with tan or black trim. The company has also shrewdly reached back to the jazz roots of this shoe style by using musician Wynton Marsalis in its advertising.

above:
Bass "Joyce" spectator
A shoe in monochrome leather with a softly curved toe that gives a feminine feel to a formerly masculine shoe.

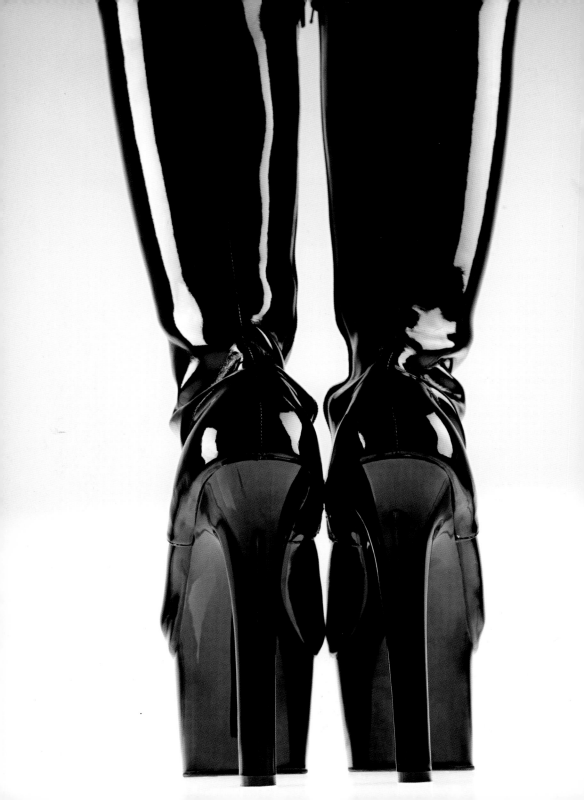

FETISH SHOE

"There is no more unfortunate creature under the sun than a fetishist who yearns for a woman's shoe and has to settle for the whole woman."
Karl Kraus

The origins of the fetish shoe are complex and many-layered. The impulse to treat a shoe as an object of the erotic stems from childhood, according to psychoanalyst Sigmund Freud, who described in 1927 how a fetish object was the result of a male child recognizing the absence of a penis in his mother during his early sexual development. Fearing the possibility of his own castration—if it has happened to his mother it could happen to him—he invents a surrogate, which becomes his fetish object without which any sexual pleasure is beset with anxiety.

In one of the earliest examples of shoe fetishism in literature, the writer Rétif de la Bretonne (1734–1806) writes of how the shoe becomes the substitute for the corporeal presence of his lover, Colette: "Dragged away from the stormiest, completely adoring passion for Colette, I imagined seeing and feeling her in body and spirit by caressing the shoes she had worn just a moment ago with my hands. I pressed my lips on one of the jewels while the other substituted as woman during a frenzied fit... this bizarre, mad pleasure seemed to—how should I say?—seemed to lead me straight to Colette herself." Colette's shoes inspire passion, they are fetishistic surrogates for her imagined body and de la Bretonne's choice of shoe is common for, as Freud explains, it is the object most usually glimpsed by a boy beneath his mother's skirts as he inquisitively peers up at her genitals. The shoe becomes a tantalizing talisman and its accidental exposure causes a man's heart to race—especially during historical periods when the revealing of a foot and leg beneath fashionably long skirts was a taboo.

What constitutes the most erotic foot and shoe has been debated for generations, but across history and culture, particular features recur. The foot should be dainty, perfectly formed, and, for many,

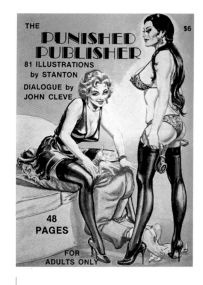

above:

Submission
Illustrator Eric Stanton worked for many underground fetish titles during the 1950s depicting the spikiest of heels.

left:

Complete control
The high heel of the fetish shoe is designed to exaggerate the female body while restricting its movement.

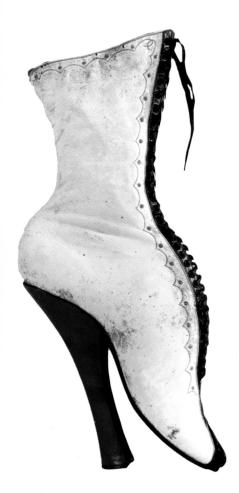

above:

Leg bound
A mid-nineteenth-century staggerer in white and red leather, one of the earliest fetish shoes, designed for posing rather than walking.

tightly shod. From the very outset fetish shoes were exaggerated versions of standard shoe shapes; heels are extremely high, lace-up boots have an inordinate number of eyelets, platforms are towering, colors bright, surfaces super-shiny, and buckles oversized. The first consciously designed fetish shoe entered the bedroom in the 1890s and "staggerers" or "boudoir shoes," as they were dubbed, were based on a romantic fantasy of a seventeenth-century Cromwell shoe. The ultra-high wooden heel meant that they could only be worn at home—they were impossible to walk in, hence the name. They were designed to tip the body forward into an exaggeratedly feminine shape and peep slyly from beneath the skirt, presenting the tiniest of feet.

In the 1930s, a more formally organized fetish movement began when magazines such as *London Life* and *Bizarre* were launched by photographer John Willie—magazines that acknowledged the power of the fetish shoe when worn by a whip-wielding femme fatale. The same trampling harridan can be seen in the work of Eric Stanton, an illustrator whose fetish shoe of choice was the extreme high-heeled mule. By the 1950s, the stiletto heel entered the lexicon of fetish footwear and according to one Paula Sanchez, who wrote for *Bizarre* magazine in that decade, one of the important features for enthusiasts was the way in which it changed the wearer's walk: "The slight jar produced by extra-high heels results in an eye-catching quivering wave in the plump, protruding breasts. There is an alternate side-to-side movement of the hips, a sway in the direction of whichever foot appears to be carrying the weight... this hula-like movement becomes automatic."

When the points of the fetish shoe's heels are at their smallest, the support for the heel is drastically reduced. The ankle then has to take compensatory action leading to a "lateral quiver" as David Kunzle puts it in *Fashion and Fetishism* (1982). Fetish shoes are designed to exaggerate the female form while restricting movement—the woman appears at her most sexually alluring while unable to leave—their very design limits the range of action in the foot and restricts the walk of the wearer, while at the same time pushing the body into a most appealing feminine shape with breasts thrust out and bottom behind for balance. The extreme height of the heels gives a psychological power, and a dominant phallic presence of sexual power is produced.

In the 1960s, fashion was prepared to flirt with this forbidden territory. Kinky clothes, knee-length boots, and leather catsuits crossed into the mainstream, with many garments created by specialist companies such as AtomAge run by clothing designer John Sutcliffe. By the 1970s, an exaggerated platform and ankle strap made the fetish shoe reach dizzying heights and by the end of the decade, Vivienne Westwood made direct reference to the sado-masochistic underground in her Bondage Collection of 1976. Inspired by Louise's, a Soho sex club frequented by exotic dancers, drag artists, and bondage enthusiasts, Westwood used straps, buckles, leather, and leopard skin to create shoes and boots that shocked Middle England, announcing that "sex is the thing that bugs English people more than anything else, so that's where to attack."

Shoe designer Christian Louboutin understood the power of the fetish shoe too; one of his earliest memories was being in Lunar Park, Paris, at the age of ten and seeing "a woman, quite shabby, all in black, big hair like Kim Novak. She was wearing a black *tailleur* and black stockings with a seam up the back. She had spiky heels—I could not believe it! I followed her, I was really following her shoes for half an hour. At one point a guy grabbed me by the shoulder, kicked my arse and said, 'You! Move!' I was following a prostitute." He successfully took the components of the prostitute's fetish shoe—the ultra-high heel and shiny black and red patent leather—and converted it into shoe couture, a pair of which was worn by Victoria Beckham at the wedding of Prince William and Kate Middleton in 2011. In 2007, Louboutin teamed up with film director David Lynch to create fetish shoes for a series of photographs exhibited at the Galerie du Passage in Paris with the title Fetish. With no pressures on practicality, Louboutin pushed his designs to the limit and included ten-inch heels and Siamese heels, where two shoes were fused at the heel.

below:
Behind the mask
The "Naked Lady" shoe of 1978, adapted by Rodolfo Azaro for the UK Crafts Council, depicts a narrative of sado-masochistic sexuality.

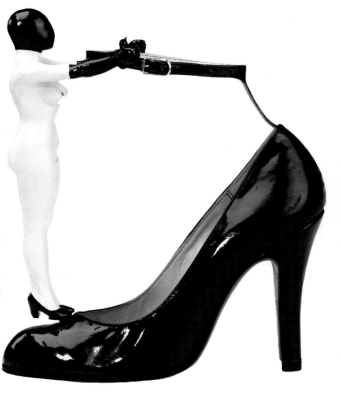

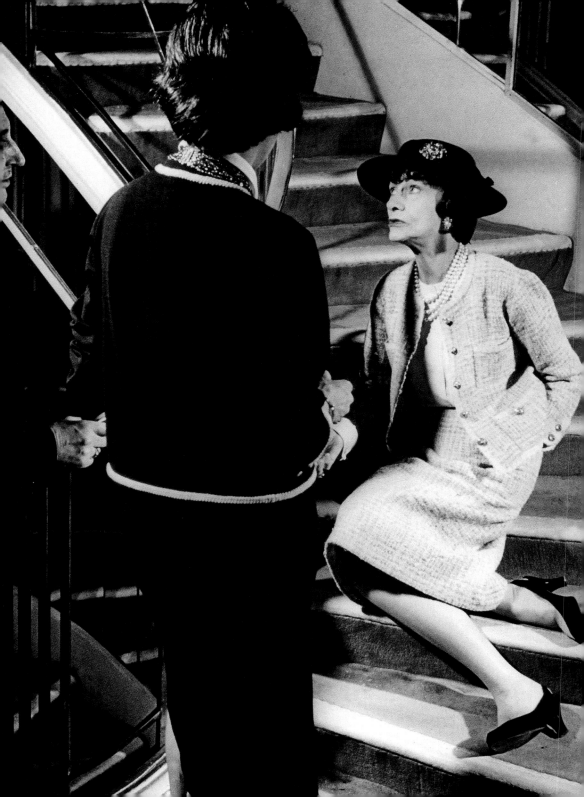

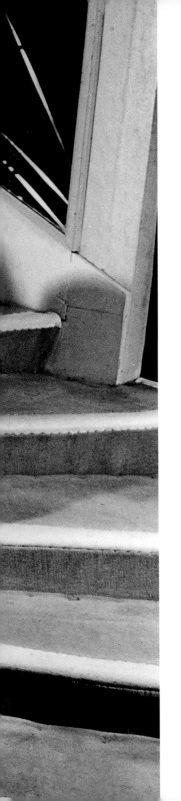

20th CENTURY

A rich cornucopia of shoe and boot styles evolved during this period and the shoe designer began to be known by name rather than regarded as a mere artisan cobbler pandering to the needs of his customers. Production was mechanized and streamlined, making cheap shoes available to the masses and speeding up changes in fashionable style. From 1910s tango shoes through 1930s platforms to 1980s cone heels, this was a period of magical innovation when shoes came into their own as a most innovative form of fashion.

SADDLE SHOE

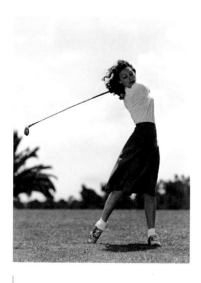

above:

Sports saddle

Actress Ava Gardner takes a graceful swing at the golf ball wearing sporty saddle shoes in 1942.

In the 1950s, an established form of footwear invented in 1906 by sporting goods company Spalding began to sweep teenage America: the saddle shoe, a sassy all-American shoe that was unisex, practical, and sporty. The saddle shoe was derived from the buck, a tennis shoe of the 1870s, fashioned from the suede buckskin of Brazilian or Chinese deer. The buck was all white whereas the saddle shoe had a low stacked heel, a front-laced fastening, and a saddle-shaped panel on the vamp that gave it its name.

The saddle shoe was originally considered a racket sports shoe —essentially the Edwardian equivalent of the trainer—and by the

> "Boys are looking stylish right now— especially when they are wearing a pair of my multicolored Saddled Oxfords."
>
> Rupert Sanderson, 2009

1920s, it was used for sports such as fencing, tennis, and golf. The saddle panel, today an entirely decorative feature, was placed at the part of the shoe that suffered the most stress during such physical activity to give extra strength and support as a reinforced instep that held the foot tightly against the shoe while running. The most popular color combination was white with a black saddle and white or coral crepe sole; when the saddle was colored, usually red, it was called a duotone saddle.

When the sporty saddle shoe began to be worn as a street shoe, it presented a problem because the rubber sole tended to attract dirt that was then carried into buildings, discoloring the floors. Spalding commissioned a manufacturer of brake linings to come up with a solution, which led to the development of the distinctive coral-colored sole.

In 1936 and 1937, *Life* magazine featured the shoes prominently when investigating college life and fashion, even showing a pair on its cover. So crucial to campus life were the shoes that after they were worn by cheerleaders, they were dubbed "rah rah" shoes and in the 1947 publication, *How To Look Good in College* by Randall B. Hamrick, the prospective student was advised "It's almost a farce to suggest that you invest in saddle shoes. They have become a necessary part of you and will continue in this capacity during your higher educational career." In 1949, the Brown Shoe Company (established 1904) sold thirty-seven styles of saddle shoe, and the shoes began to appear off campus in post-war dance halls worn by jitterbugging girls with bobby socks.

By the 1990s, the production of saddle shoes had all but ceased but a couple of fans of the shoe, Allen and Margaret "Muffy" Marshall, were determined to resurrect the style. They hit upon a warehouse with 600 pairs of originals from a defunct manufacturer, Karl Shoes, in 1996 and began selling them on-line. Muffy's is now a well-known purveyor of the traditional saddle shoe and has gained a number of fans as a result of the popularity of swing culture. More recently the saddle shoe has resurfaced in Japan with a resurgence of interest in Ivy-League styling and shoe designer Rupert Sanderson launched the "Saddled O" range for men and women in 2009, saying he "had a feeling people were tiring of trainers and the idea of a shoe with genuine sports provenance felt right."

As the interest in heritage styles continued, G. H. Bass called on fashion designer Rachel Antonoff, renowned for her 1950s-inspired "girlie" aesthetic, to feminize the saddle shoe. For the 2012 collection entitled *Bass Loves Rachel Antonoff* she drew inspiration from Bass' archive of vintage designs and included the "Alice" perforated Oxford with a bow and the "Lulu" leather high-heeled saddle.

below:
New look
Rupert Sanderson's "Saddled O" saddle shoes, launched in 2009 in anticipation of the demise of the trainer.

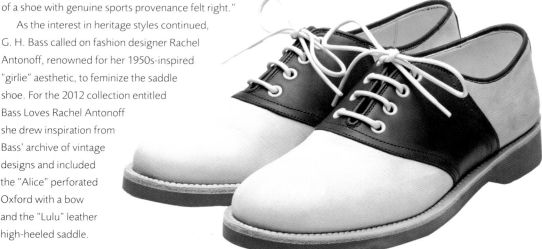

TANGO SHOE

In 1913, the revue *Hullo, Tango!* opened in London and ran for over 400 performances. Tango-mania had hit both Europe and the United States, and the scandalous dance imported from the back streets of Buenos Aires, Argentina, had an insidious whiff of foreign allure, not least because it permitted full-body contact and a seductive entwining of the legs, akin to making love. The strict constraints of the previous century seemed to be in the process of being overturned as women cast off their tight-laced corsets and shortened their skirts, inspired by the exotic designs of couturier Paul Poiret. The tea dance became a popular daily excursion where men and

> "Nobody can dance one of the modern dances in an uncomfortable shoe."
>
> *New York Times*, 1914

women met unchaperoned in local hotels to watch exhibition dances and learn the steps—the tango teas held at the Savoy, London, and the Waldorf were renowned. Young Argentine dance teachers became the subject of disapproval by the press, including the *New York Times*, which ran headlines such as "Tango Pirates Infest Broadway." The "tango pirate" was a swarthy gigolo who preyed on middle-aged women at tango palaces "where the very air of these places is heavy with unleashed passions."

Fashion designers and footwear manufacturers rushed to create related products for women who were learning the new dance craze. Shoes needed a rethink—as the *New York Times* wrote in 1914: "Anyone can dance an old-fashioned waltz in a shoe that sags at the heel, pinches through the arch, and binds through the instep. But nobody can dance one of the modern dances in an uncomfortable shoe." The tango shoe was a case in point, popularized by exhibition dancer Irene Castle who de-sexed the

right:
Richard Tyler (Fall/Winter 1996)
The high-cut back of the tango shoe gave stability to the dancer while the straps displayed the feet.

below:
Dancing queen
A Richard Tyler-designed tango shoe in brown lamé kid with a small nickel buckle and stacked heel.

tango to make it more acceptable to a 1900s audience and was considered something of a fashion plate.

Tango shoes were cut high at the back, had a low Louis heel that was practical for dancing, and were laced up the ankle with a criss-crossed ribbon, some with a multistrap or barrette front. The *Shoe Retailer* in 1913 wrote of the main problem created by the tango shoe vogue— the fashion for lacing: "In lacing this shoe and in fastening the ribbon around and half-way up the calf of the leg, in the manner shown in many of the illustrations of this novel form of shoe fastening, is that it will be impossible to keep the lacing from coming loose and sliding down the leg." Materials were luxurious brocaded silks and exotic skins with decorative details such as rhinestones embedded into the heels by bespoke shoemakers or *bottiers*, many of the most famous based in Paris such as Pinet and Yantorny.

Not only shoes but fashion in general changed because of the cultural obsession with the tango. Hats were designed with feathers that rose vertically rather than sweeping from the side so as to be out of the partner's way, and draped tulip skirts allowed the legs to move freely. Anything that could have the epithet "tango" applied did so: Tango stockings, hats, and dresses—even a color, tango orange— were invented to supply the demand.

The tango shoe remained fashionable into the 1920s until overtaken by other forms of dance shoe that matched the latest dance craze. Today, two elements of the tango shoe—the high-cut back and the straps—appear in footwear design. The actual dance shoe is still produced in both traditional and updated forms, most notably by Alicia Muñiz of Comme Il Faut and Victorio, both based in the "tango" district of Buenos Aires.

below:
Irene and Vernon Castle
Ballroom dancers of the early twentieth century who introduced the tango to the general public.

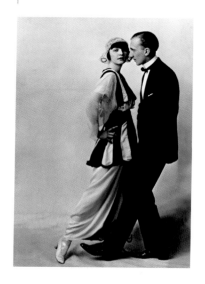

Tango Shoe **171**

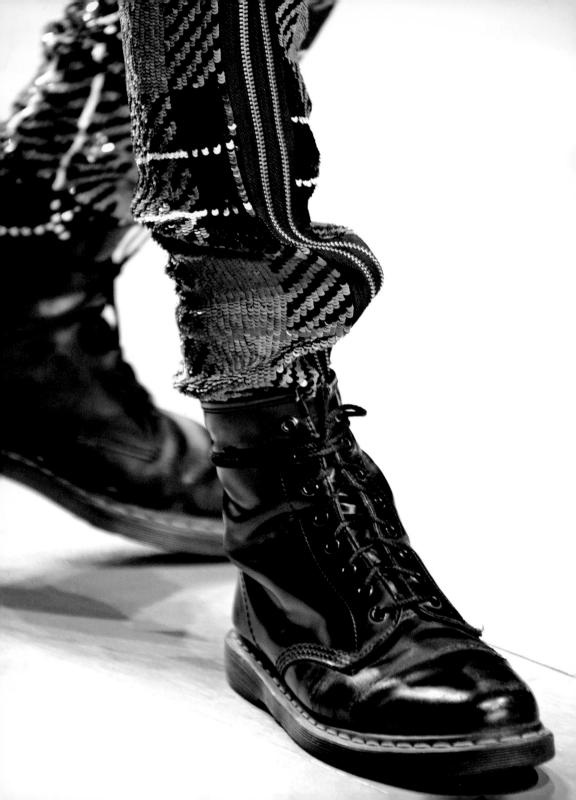

DR. MARTEN

"It was totally cool [being] this close to having your skull crushed by a skinhead wearing a pair of Doc Martens."

Grunge Kid in "Good Sports," Party of Five, 1994

Dr. Martens or Docs are boots that developed out of the carnage of war and went on to become global classics worn by both punks and policemen, and figures as diverse as the Pope and Madonna. Dr. Klaus Maertens of Munich, a medic in the German army during the Second World War, had spent his leave skiing in the Bavarian Alps. He broke his foot and found it impossible to recuperate in standard-issue army boots because the hard leather and hobnail soles only exacerbated his injury. Maertens improved his own army boot by adding cushioned soles that absorbed the impact of his foot on the ground, and after the war in 1947, he used leather found in looted cobblers to develop his ideas. The prototype Maerten boot caused nary a ripple in the footwear trade until he teamed up with Dr. Herbert Funck in Seeshaupt and began manufacturing cushioned soles using discarded rubber from abandoned airplanes left on the airfields that had formerly been used as bases for the Luftwaffe. In the early 1950s, Bill Griggs bought the patent from the German company to manufacture footwear in his Cobbs Lane factory in Wollaston, UK, and began to attach the sole, now called the AirWair, to work boots; he also anglicized the name to Dr. Martens, crucial at a time of huge anti-German sentiment. The result was the "1460" (named after its launch date), a stout eight-laced working boot with distinctive yellow stitches and heel loop that went on to be worn by workers all over the country.

The first instance of the boot being worn for fashion rather than function occurred in the 1960s when they appeared on the feet of skinheads, a street gang who had developed out of "hard mods." Hard mods were an offshoot of the early 1960s mod movement and loyal members of street gangs, each with their own territory that was fiercely patrolled against incursions from rival "firms." Hard

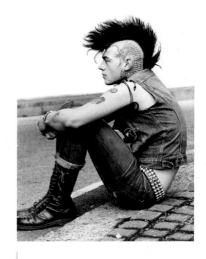

above:

Tribal style

The Dr. Marten boot has been adopted by many street gangs including punks, as seen here in 1982.

left:

Ashish Fall/Winter 2011

Many fashion designers use the Dr. Marten boot to toughen up a collection, from Yamamoto to Ashish.

right:

Yamamoto Fall/Winter 2007
The anti-fit asymmetry of Yohji
Yamamoto's work needs a serious
boot to ground it—a high heel just
wouldn't work.

below:

Silver stomper
As the Dr. Marten boot increased
in popularity to become a fashion
accessory in the 1980s, new colors
were introduced.

mods wore the rolled-up jeans and pork-pie hats of West Indian
immigrants, a.k.a. "rude boys," plus the Fred Perry polo shirts of
mods, and this look began to appear on the terraces of England's
football grounds. Here the implicit link was made between fighting
factions, allegiance to a team, masculine fashion, and intimidating
violence. The boot appeared in rock when in 1969 Pete Townshend,
lead guitarist of The Who, appeared on stage in a boilersuit and a
pair of Docs. He said: "I was sick of dressing up as a Christmas tree
in flowing robes that got in the way of my guitar playing so I thought
I'd move on to utility wear." (In 1975, when the movie based on
The Who's rock-opera *Tommy* was released, it featured Elton John
as the Pinball Wizard dressed in a pair of giant Dr. Marten boots.)
Townsend saw that Docs had a working-class cred that seemed
fresh after the dapper peacock fashions and laid-back hippie vibe
of the late 1960s, realizing that fashionable masculinity was in flux,
toughening up as recession began to bite.

As the peace-and-love optimism of psychedelic counter-culture
began to fade, skinheads adopted the boot as a subcultural group in
absolute opposition to the hippie. Skinheads gained a reputation as
aggressive, confrontational, and violent, especially after right-wing
groups began to infiltrate the skinhead movement as the decade
wore on. Hair was buzzed off—hence the name—and suspenders
were worn with jeans rolled up to showcase the Dr. Marten boot. The
boot had another name too, the "bovver boot," since the wearers
were there to create "bother" or trouble by beating up other gangs,
gay men, and ethnic minorities. The boot became a weapon wielded
by a young white working-class thug—teenage skinhead Gavin
Watson described how he "was twelve when I bought my first eight-
hole Docs. And the rule was that you had to christen them by kicking
someone with them. It didn't matter who, and if you got some blood
on them that was even better." The look became more and more
visible on the streets of the UK and was popularized after the uproar
surrounding the science-fiction film *A Clockwork Orange*
(1971), in which charismatic delinquent Alex DeLarge
wears a ten-eyelet pair while involved in an orgy
of violence with his fellow droogs. An incredibly
successful series of pulp-fiction books by writer
James Moffat who wrote under the pseudonym
Richard Allen also gave Docs teenage appeal. His

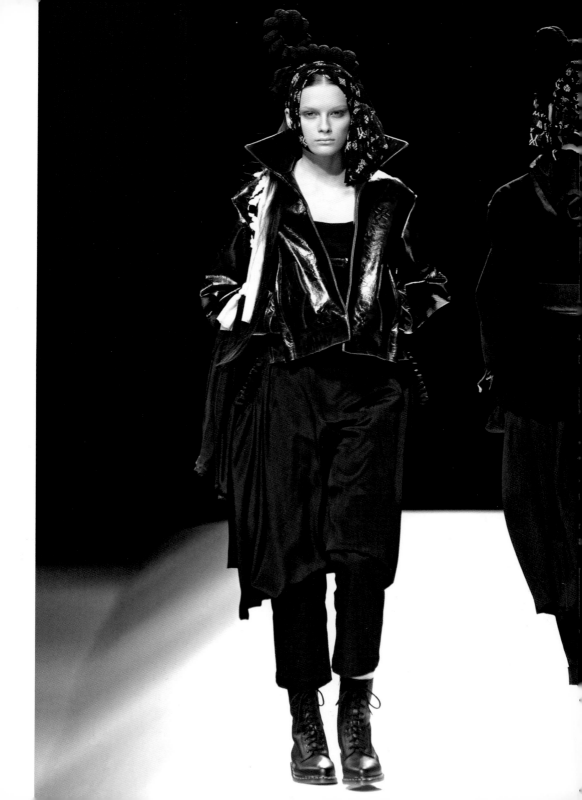

Skinhead series published in the 1970s by the New English Library described the life of one Joe Hawkins, a docker's son who rebelled against the destruction of his own working-class community as a result of global recession and unemployment. Allen described how "without his boots, [Joe] was part of the common herd—like his dad, a working man devoid of identity. Joe was proud of his boots. Most of his mates wore new boots for a high price in a High Street shop. But not Joe's. His were genuine army disposal boots; thick-soled, studded, heavy to wear, and heavy if slammed against the ribs."

The Dr. Marten sixteen-eyelet cherry-red boot was almost fetishistic in its militaristic look and was stylistically replayed again and again whenever skinheads held sway, as in the late 1970s with the rise of Oi music, a genre in which Caucasian right-wing

> "I was wondering if the best was behind me, had the high point... happened?"
>
> Patrick Cox

sentiments were expressed in the lyrics of punk-derived bands such as Skrewdriver. This was the moment when the skinhead found his way to the United States and the boot began to infiltrate subcultural style across the Atlantic, most notably with the rise of grunge in the early 1990s. There was a semiotic retaliation though, beginning in the 1980s when the skinhead and his boots were appropriated and subverted within gay culture. This most hyper-masculine of looks was worn by men whose very sexuality the skinhead despised—but now, few could tell them apart.

The 1980s continued to be a decade in which both men and women experimented with gender stereotypes, some subverting designer looks in ways their creators hadn't intended. A prime example of this is the vogue for body-con instigated by designers Azzedine Alaia, dubbed the "King of Cling," and Hervé Léger known for his skintight spandex "bandage" dresses. Alaia's black jersey contoured mini-dresses, leggings, and cropped jackets were worn on the runway by supermodels Naomi Campbell and Eva Herzigova to create an ultra-glamorous image. However, this deluxe sexually charged look changed

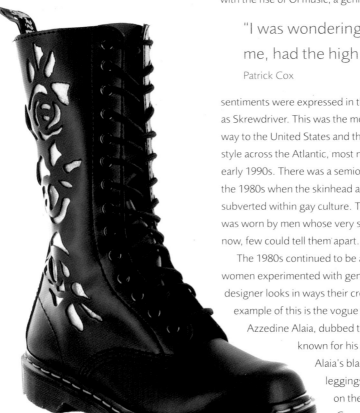

below:

Rad trad

A fourteen-eyelet black leather Dr. Marten boot that belies its traditional looks with side cut-outs.

dramatically when it hit the high street and women combined Gallic chic with elements of Japanese avant-garde fashion. Women took the cling-fit of Alaia and Léger and accessorized it with the now arty Docs, changing the look from vamp to street urchin, and by doing so, playfully rejecting the traditional notion that beautiful women had tiny feet. This had also been noted by designers Wayne and Geraldine Hemingway of the label Red or Dead and shoe designer Patrick Cox. When Cox was a student at Cordwainers College, London, he saw a construction worker getting rid of the debris from his Dr. Marten boot by banging the steel-capped toe against a wall—it had left the steel toe-cap exposed. Cox contrived to customize the Dr. Marten by stripping away the leather, exposing the toecap, and polishing it—an early form of fashion deconstruction. Concurrently the Hemingways had noticed that "there were all these girls wearing tight black dresses, and we changed the silhouette by putting a bloody big pair of boots at the end. Then everyone wanted them—Jean Paul Gaultier was buying them from our stall in Camden, Demi Moore, every star you could think of—it was unbelievable." The plain Dr. Marten was not just worn, it was painted with Day-Glo color and given colored laces to totally change its aggressive reputation. The Hemingways also launched their own range in collaboration with the Dr. Marten brand in ultra-shiny patent finishes and primary colors—in 1990, the Space Baby Collection featured a transparent vinyl pair.

At the onset of the 1990s, the Dr. Marten boot returned to its rebellious origins when worn by fans of grunge, a new form of gritty rock fresh out of Seattle, Washington. Courtney Love wore a scuffed pair with ripped fishnet stockings, a vintage tea dress, and bright red lipstick, the softness of floral silk toughened by black leather. The popularity of Docs declined as that of the trainer and stiletto rose, but began staging a comeback in the early 2000s, worn by a new generation of teenagers who had never experienced the boot before. Docs began appearing on runways again too; in 2007 Yamamoto added an inside zipper, pointed toe, and buckled straps to the classic sole, yellow stitching, and heel loop. A pared-down version was also created in collaboration with designer Raf Simons in Fall/Winter 2009.

above:

High-heel hybrid
A blue patent leather Dr. Marten high stack-heeled ankle boot with embellished flower detail.

PIRATE BOOT

The pirate is a popular figure in the public imagination in the twenty-first century thanks to the swaggering figure of Johnny Depp as Captain Jack Sparrow in the *Pirates of the Caribbean* movie franchise. Pirates, in reality, were unemployed seamen who wore whatever they had stolen. Pirate Bartholomew Roberts, a.k.a. Black Bart, was a particularly flamboyant dresser in his crimson velvet britches, feathered tricorne hat, and dangling gold earrings—a sign of wealth that was also believed to cure seasickness by the pressure applied to the earlobe. Today many believe that pirate attire comes complete

> "Wear something different for a change, so you don't just look like a clone."
>
> Vivienne Westwood, 2008

with a bandanna and boots, but in reality, only the captain would have been able to afford high leather boots, and the rest of the crew would have worn stacked-heel buckled shoes with a squared toe and large tongue. The swashbuckling, bucket-topped pirate boot is, in fact, a Hollywood invention courtesy of Douglas Fairbanks in *The Black Pirate* (1926) and Erroll Flynn as *Captain Blood* (1935).

In the early 1980s, street style met catwalk chic and fashion became willfully eccentric. The New Romantic movement stressed individuality in fashion choice above all else, and its style leaders, Philip Sallon, Boy George, and Steve Strange, had a postmodern approach to appearance; the downbeat mantle of punk was thrown off in favor of styles from every era dexterously reassembled into outfits of extreme theatricality. Adam Ant, for instance bought his trademark braided "Charge of the Light Brigade" military jacket from the closing-down sale of a theatrical costumiers, Charles Fox. As Boy George put it, "Getting a reaction was the ultimate goal." In 1981, British fashion designer Vivienne Westwood launched her Pirate Collection, a historically influenced look that plundered its buccaneer motifs from eighteenth-century

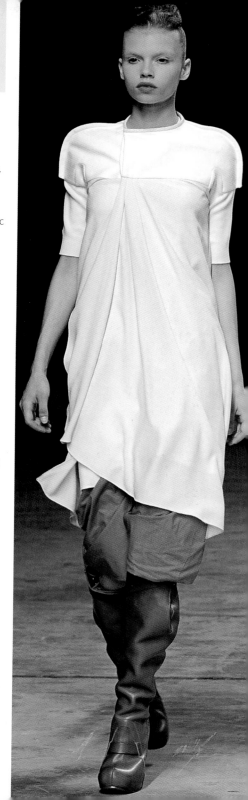

pirates and 1930s Hollywood costume design with the looping squiggle print and color palette derived from the African Gold Coast. Her months of research in the archives of the Victoria and Albert Museum in London led to an exuberant catwalk show of ruffled shirts, stockings and tasseled sashes, slashed jackets, and Napoleonic bicorne hats complete with tricolor rosettes. One member of the audience, Michael Costiff of label World Archive, said: "It was such a gray time in London and the show had so much color with the orange squiggle prints, gold lipstick, and multi-racial models appearing through the smoke to a Burundi soundtrack. It was all so unexpected after punk. We couldn't wait to go shopping." Here Westwood presented her first version of the iconic multibuckled low stack-heeled pirate boot with five natural leather straps and a pale-beige nubuck sole. The adjustable straps allowed the wearer to keep the boots high, tight, and calf-length or allow them to bag low and slouchily around the ankles. The distinctive round-toed boot did not go into large-scale production until many years later when Kate Moss bought a pair from vintage store Rellik, London, in 1999. After the store was deluged with inquiries they became available and are still in production today in a variety of colors and heel shapes, from Cuban to stiletto.

left:

Swashbuckler
Buckled stack-heeled pirate boot by Vivienne Westwood originally launched in 1981 in her seminal Pirate Collection.

right:

Brigand boots
Rick Owens creates a contemporary prow-toed slouchy pirate boot in glossy brown leather (Spring/Summer 2012).

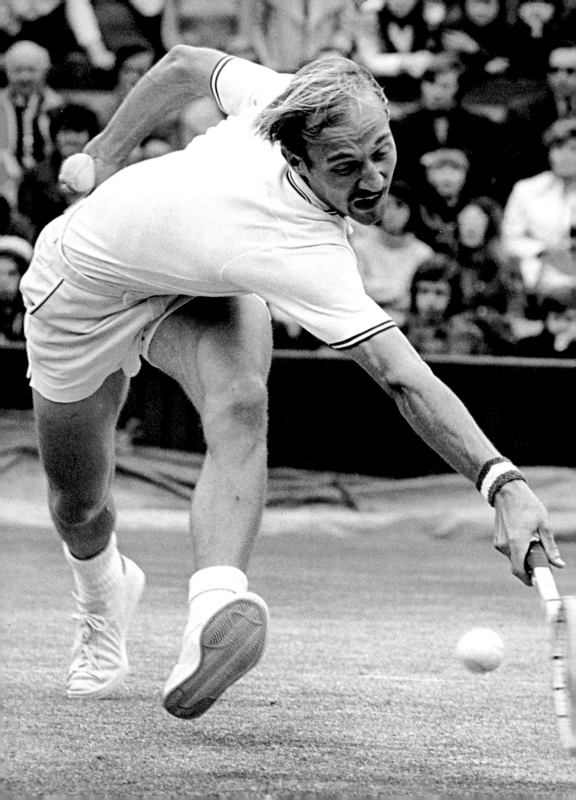

SNEAKER

"We still get around cities the way the Greeks did 5,000 years ago; they put on sandals, we put on sneakers."

Dean Kamen, entrepreneur and inventor

The sneaker is the colossus of shoe design, its UK name—trainer—derived from "training shoe," reflecting its sporting origins. The sneaker developed out of the tennis shoe (see page 138), a rubberized shoe affixed to a canvas upper using vulcanization, a technique invented by Charles Goodyear. Many of the classic sneaker designs were created from 1964–1982 and include the Adidas "Superstar," the Puma "Suede," and the Adidas "SL 72," launched for the 1972 Olympics—today this ubiquitous athletic shoe has been adopted by genres and subcultures from B-boy through to Gangsta Rap. The sneaker began its global domination in the 1970s when the fitness boom took off. By the 1980s, it was being marketed as a lifestyle choice, a visible symbol of social status and identity, and the market was dominated by the big four: Adidas, Puma, Nike, and Reebok. By the 1990s, sneakers were sport-specific masterpieces of innovative engineering with cantilever soles, gel systems, air cushions, and built-in pumps endorsed by stars such as Michael Jordan, Chris Evert, and Bo Jackson. Today sneakers have taken over as the comfort shoe for men, women, and children, and when—ironically—worn with jogging suits, usually have absolutely no connection with playing sport. The history of the sneaker is explored on the following pages through a discussion of key sneakers by important companies.

The Converse "All Star"

Today more MTV that NBA, this iconic basketball shoe is believed to have been owned by 60 percent of all Americans at one time in their lives. The Converse Rubber Corporation was founded in 1908 by Marquis Mills Converse in Maiden, Massachusetts, to manufacture rubber galoshes and work shoes. The work was seasonal so Converse decided it would make more economic sense to employ

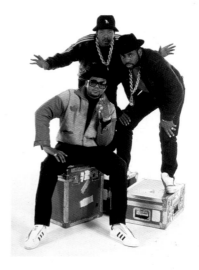

above:

B-boys

Run DMC, one of the most famous bands to adopt Adidas as a trademark, who pioneered the laceless look.

left:

Celebrity endorsement

Tennis star Stan Smith, captain of the US Davis Cup team gave his name to an all-white leather shoe in 1968.

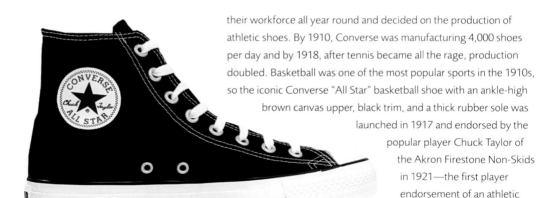

their workforce all year round and decided on the production of athletic shoes. By 1910, Converse was manufacturing 4,000 shoes per day and by 1918, after tennis became all the rage, production doubled. Basketball was one of the most popular sports in the 1910s, so the iconic Converse "All Star" basketball shoe with an ankle-high brown canvas upper, black trim, and a thick rubber sole was launched in 1917 and endorsed by the popular player Chuck Taylor of the Akron Firestone Non-Skids in 1921—the first player endorsement of an athletic shoe in global footwear. Taylor also helped improve the shoe's design, introducing more traction on the soles and improved ankle support, and traveled the country as the shoe's ambassador promoting basketball in schools and colleges by teaching the fundamentals of the sport.

In the 1920s, an all-black canvas took over from natural brown, and all-leather versions in black were also produced. Taylor's signature was added to the "All Star" ankle patch in 1923 and Converse also custom fit basketball boots for the first professional African-American team, the New York Renaissance, or "Rens." In 1936, when basketball was declared an official Olympic sport, the gold-medal-winning American team was all decked out in Converse.

> "I got really annoyed the first time I lost a match against a guy who was wearing them."
>
> Tennis star Stan Smith on the "Stan Smith" Adidas sneaker

The classic black-and-white Converse launched after the Second World War became the shoe worn by college and professional players—the shoe also became a subcultural hit in the 1950s when sported by teenagers with jeans and a leather jacket, a vision of youthful rebellion that has become a classic of rock 'n' roll style when worn by New York New Wave band The Ramones in 1976 and The Strokes in the early 2000s. In 1968, the low-cut Oxford version of the "All Star" was introduced onto the market and

above:

Shoe icon

The classic Converse "All Star" basketball shoe is believed to have been owned by 60 percent of all Americans.

became a favorite of the burgeoning surfing and skateboard culture of California. In 2002, it was estimated that 750 million pairs of Converse All Stars had been sold since the shoe's debut in 1923; in 2002 Kathryn Eisman wrote in *How To Tell a Man by his Shoes*: "These old school kicks were the Air Jordans of their time. But it's been a long time since 'Chucks' ruled the hard court, and these days they stand for anything BUT rigorous athletic effort. Today's All Star Dude cultivates a decidedly laid-back approach to life."

The Adidas "Stan Smith"

The first all-leather tennis shoe on the market, launched in 1968. Adidas was established in 1948 by shoemaker and entrepreneur Adolf Dassler in Herzogenaurach, Germany, who had originally started his business alongside his brother in their mother's laundry room in the 1920s. They expanded the firm in the 1930s after Hitler's rise to power; the dictator believed in the power of sport to mobilize the country's masculinity and turn them into a fully functioning army, so sports-shoe manufacturers had a captive market. After the 1936 Berlin Olympic Games, the Dassler brothers parted company; Adi set up Adidas using the first part of his fore- and surname; Rudi set up the rival brand Puma. After the fall of the Nazi regime, football became the brothers' battleground and both Adidas and Puma shoes were worn on pitches all over Europe.

Adidas harnessed the power of celebrity endorsement and gave away its shoes to the world's best athletes including all participants at the Olympic Games in 1952 and 1956. Puma fought back and in 1970 had Brazilian footballer Pelé in their boots for the World Cup in Mexico at a reputed fee of $25,000 USD upfront and $100,000 for the next four years with royalties of ten percent of any boots sold under his name. The Adidas "Stan Smith" was yet another successful celebrity link-up. The tennis shoe had originally been endorsed by French tennis professional Robert Haillet who had been asked to help in the shoe's development in 1954. Like the basketball shoe, early tennis shoes

below:
Adidas "Superstar"
A basketball shoe manufactured by Adidas in 1969, released as a low-top version of the "Pro Model" basketball shoe.

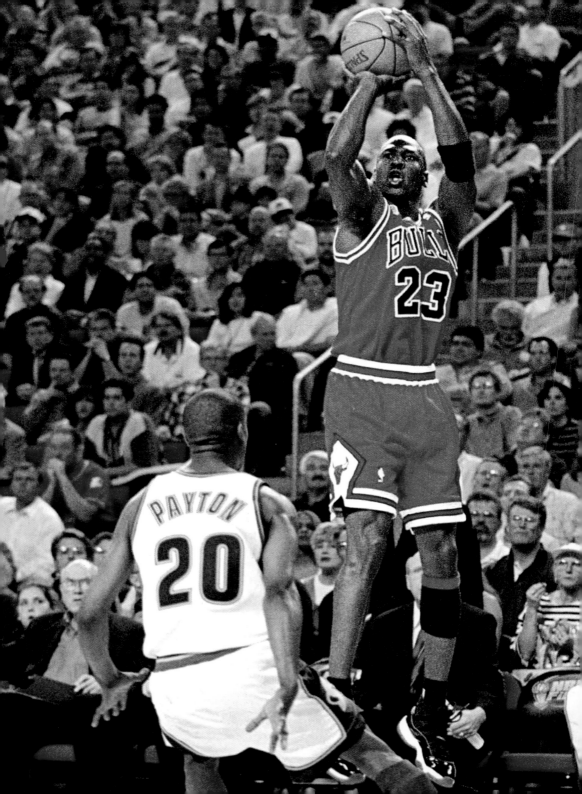

were made of canvas and rubber; the all-leather "Robert Haillet" debuted in 1965 and became the shoe that many tennis professionals preferred because of its firm support and improved grip.

Robert Haillet was pretty much unknown outside of France by then so Dassler sought a new star to rebrand the tennis shoe for the next generation of player and fans, and it had to be the strapping blonde American Stan Smith, captain of America's Davis Cup team and winner of a whole host of tournaments. The crisp all-white shoe took off, making Smith a rich man because of the lucrative royalty deal (at least 40 million pairs have been sold).

The Adidas "Superstar" of 1969 was developed to compete against the Converse. Basketball players were susceptible to knee and ankle injury because of the stop and start moves on the court, and canvas shoes lacked the right support. The Adidas "Superstar" had a firm leather upper with a shell toe to protect the front of the foot and an outsole molded in a thinly grooved herringbone pattern. It was a success—by 1973 almost 85 percent of professional basketball players in the United States were wearing the shoe and it was endorsed by Kareem Abdul-Jabbar (aka Lewis Alcindor) of the LA Lakers. Like the Converse, the Adidas "Superstar" developed its own subcultural fans too, becoming a favorite of New York's B-boys—Run DMC produced an homage to the shoe, "My Adidas."

The Nike "Air Jordan"

Between 1976 and 1984, millions of Americans began taking part in exercise regimes including jogging, running, and aerobics. Concurrently, in the early 1970s, a running shoe was being designed by former track-and-field coach and jogging advocate Bill Bowerman. Bowerman had set up the Oregon-based company Blue Ribbon Sports in 1964 as a distributor for Japanese shoemaker Onitsuka Tiger and its first retail outlet opened in Santa Monica in 1967. Blue Ribbon was renamed Nike in 1971 and the trademark "swoosh" logo designed by Carolyn Davidson was

left:
Retro classic
Michael Jordan wore his "Air Jordan" sneakers on the basketball court, despite the colors being banned.

below:
Nike "Air Jordan"
Designed by Peter Moore and so-named because it had air compressed and stored within the sole.

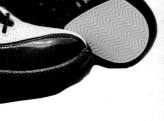

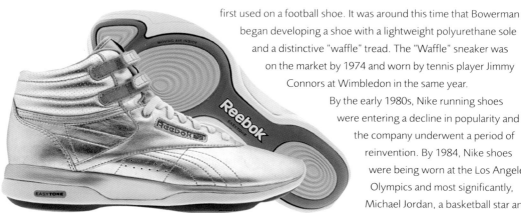

first used on a football shoe. It was around this time that Bowerman began developing a shoe with a lightweight polyurethane sole and a distinctive "waffle" tread. The "Waffle" sneaker was on the market by 1974 and worn by tennis player Jimmy Connors at Wimbledon in the same year.

By the early 1980s, Nike running shoes were entering a decline in popularity and the company underwent a period of reinvention. By 1984, Nike shoes were being worn at the Los Angeles Olympics and most significantly, Michael Jordan, a basketball star and gold-medal winner, was signed up to endorse a new shoe, the Nike "Air" for a reputed $2.5 million USD plus royalties. The Nike "Air Jordan 1," designed by Peter Moore and so-named because it had air compressed and stored within the sole, had the distinctive "swoosh" on the mid-panel, and a wing logo on the upper ankle; other than that it was similar in silhouette to other Nike sneakers of the 1980s such as the "Air Force 1," "Dunk," and "Terminator." The sneaker was a phenomenal success, purely because of its relationship with Jordan and the attendant publicity—the sneaker was given a masculine glamor after Jordan was seen on court in its distinctive red, black, and white colors. The shoe also gained a rebellious reputation— the colors were against the rules and subsequently banned by the National Basketball Association. Jordan kept wearing them, despite being fined $5,000 USD every game; the tab was picked up by Nike—the publicity was very good for business. It also changed the ceiling price of sneakers—it was the most expensive on the market and showed manufacturers that consumers were prepared to pay a premium price if the image was right.

above:

Reebok "Freestyle"

A women's aerobic exercise shoe introduced in 1982 that catapulted Reebok into the mainstream.

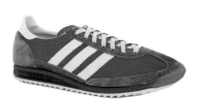

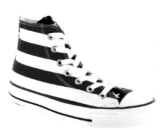

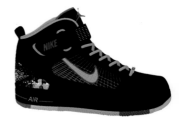

The Reebok "Freestyle"

Bolton, Lancashire, UK, 1890; shoemaker Joseph William Foster was making a living churning out running shoes. After deciding to add spikes to the bottom for the grip needed for cross-country running, he joined together with his sons and created the company J. W. Foster & Sons in 1895. The spiked running shoe was worn by some of Britain's greatest runners, including Harold Abrahams and Eric Liddle, whose gold-medal-winning performances at the 1924 Paris Olympic Games were immortalized on film in *Chariots of Fire* (1981). In the 1960s, the same company, then run by the founder's grandsons, underwent a rebranding and was renamed Reebok, derived from the Afrikaans *rhebok*, a fleet-footed gazelle.

In 1979, the US rights to Reebok running shoes were bought by Boston-based businessman Paul Fireman after he saw a pair at a trade show. Fireman wanted to cash in on the boom in aerobics popularized by Jane Fonda by bringing out a sneaker specifically targeted at women. Women were wearing colorful exercise clothes but only had a choice of basic monochromatic sneakers; in 1982, Reebok launched the "Freestyle" and cornered the market. The shoe was a lace-up design in ultra-soft white leather, with pale-blue lettering for the logo and a Union Jack on one side. A hi-top version with a double-Velcro strap was issued in 1983 in a range of vibrant colors, including vivid pink and cobalt blue, with sales exceeding those of the original. They gained a street name "54.11s," referring to the price of the shoes after sales tax in New York. In 1980, Reebok's global sales were $300,000 USD; by 1983 they were $12.8 million USD; by 1987, sales were $1.4 billion. The Reebok "Freestyle" was worn for fashion as well as fitness—actress Cybill Shepherd, star of the immensely popular television series *Moonlighting* (1985–89), wore a pair in a vivid flame-orange with a strapless black evening dress and matching full-length gloves to the 1985 Emmy Awards.

from left to right:

Old skool

Adidas is known as the "three stripes" company after its trademark logo.

Hi-top

The high sides of the Converse "All Star" are a perfect canvas for special-edition designs.

Enduring legend

New Nike Air designs are still produced today despite Jordan's retirement from basketball in 2003.

Futuristic

Rick Owens' trapezoid-shaped zipper sneaker is a new mold breaker.

Back to the future

The Reebok "Freestyle" has been rediscovered in the 2010s.

Sneaker heels (Spring/Summer 2008)

Pierre Hardy mutates the sneaker into a multicolored killer heel.

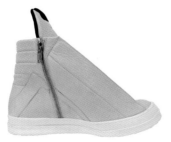
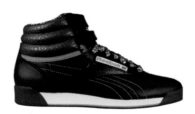
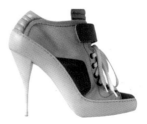

FLOATING HEEL

If the stiletto is phallic, the logic runs that this shoe must be castrated. The floating heel (or no heel) is a gravity-defying form in which a sole cast from metal is suspended above a metal cantilever that lies flat to the floor, eliminating the need for a traditional structural support. It is the ultimate vision of lightness in women's shoes, stemming from the cultural notion that femininity means delicate gossamer-light feet—men's shoes are generally on the sober and heavy side with an emphasis on classic heritage in their branding.

As Victoria Beckham knows, the floating heel presents a red-carpet opportunity that grabs the attention of crowds and cameras

> "My shoes aren't really for everyday wear, so I don't get orders from ordinary people."
>
> Noritaka Tatehana

alike. She chose to wear Antonio Berardi's tight, black-latex thigh boots with a five-and-a-half inch platform and floating heel at the launch of her Signature perfume at Macy's, New York, 2008. In the same way as when Marc Jacobs' "backwards heel" slid onto the runway in Spring/Summer 2008, the fashion (and civilian) world was agape. Berardi explained at the time: "They are perfectly balanced. When the girls come for fittings, they look a bit daunted, but by the end they say it's just like wearing a regular shoe. They are graceful and there is a ballerina nature about them. Having a heel is really just psychological." The boot had stability because it had a larger-than-normal platform sole that stretched back to give support under the arch of the foot. Beckham had to remember to walk on her toes rather than her heels or she would have keeled over.

The floating heel, when worn by Beckham, appeared at the cutting edge of footwear design, yet it had been patented by André Perugia as early as 1920 and

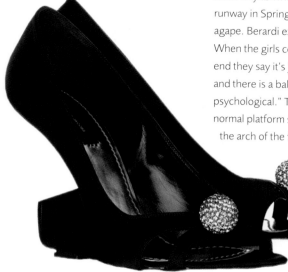

below:

Walking on air

This Marc Jacobs design dubbed the "backwards heel" is a contemporary version of the novelty floating heel that was a fad in the 1950s.

appeared as a prototype in 1937. Perugia was one of the most innovative shoe designers of the twentieth century, displaying his experimental wares at his shop on the Rue de Faubourg Saint-Honoré in Paris from 1921 onward. During the First World War, he had been requisitioned to work in an airplane factory and was educated in engineering techniques that were to radically alter his ideas about shoe construction. As he put it: "A pair of shoes must be perfect like an equation, and adjusted to the millimeter like a motor piece."

Perugia developed many innovative heels as women's skirts grew shorter to display more of the leg, and pushed them to the limits with his invisible heel of 1937. Designs like his heel-less purple calfskin shoe of 1950 that balanced *en pointe* on a polished cork base were conceptual prototypes garnering publicity for his more practical designs sold through labels like Saks Fifth Avenue, I. Miller, and Rayne.

In 1956, another patent was granted for a new version of the floating heel, to Martin Friedmann. The shoe was constructed with a sole and elevated mid-sole cast from one piece of metal so that it was strong enough to take the weight of the body. Shoes of this type were manufactured by Pinet and Preciosa up to the early 1960s, but they remained a fad rather than a mainstream footwear fashion. Beth Levine created another innovative version with her "Kabuki" shoe of 1959, based on the shoes of traditional Japanese Kabuki performers, and it took the form of a black satin pump shoe whose middle part was set on top of a curved gold platform of molded wood. The shoe had an aerodynamic feel that gave the impression it was floating on a magic carpet, and she launched different versions throughout the 1960s. Today this eccentric shoe shape has come in many guises, including a sickle-shaped sole design by Olivier Theyskens for Nina Ricci in 2009; origami-inspired shapes by Kei Kagami in 2009; the "Ein/Tritt" shoe by Catherine Meuter—the first flat-pack shoe—and Noritaka Tatehana's extreme heel-less platforms, including the twenty-eight-inch-high "Circus" platform, are worn by Lady Gaga.

below:

Defying gravity
Noritaka Tatehana creates shoe illusions that fuse art and fashion with their heel-less designs—as worn by Lady Gaga.

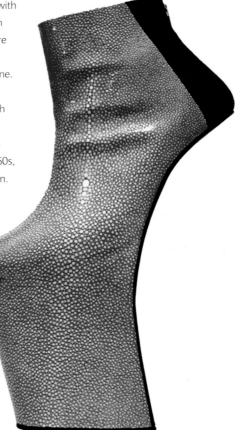

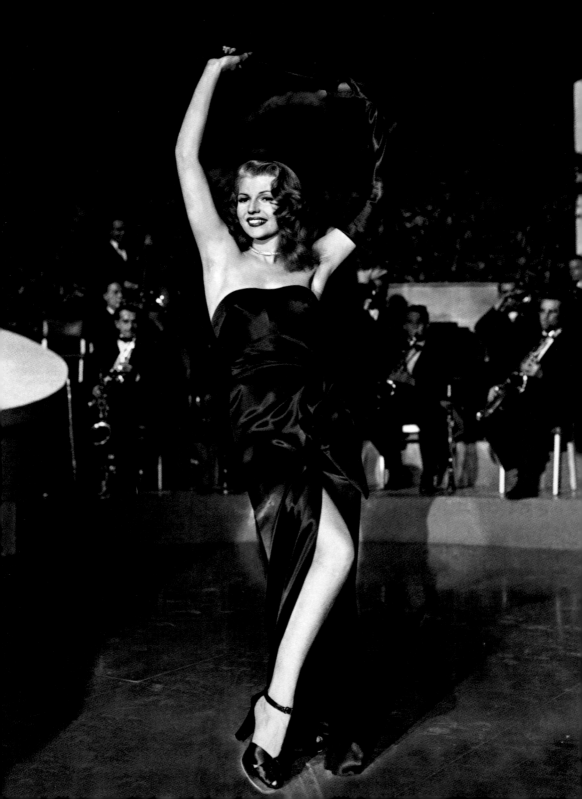

ANKLE STRAP

"And the new strap is like lingerie. It's nylon and caresses the foot around the ankle."

Sergio Rossi

In the nineteenth century, a ribbon or tie was attached to the slipper-sandal and wrapped round the ankle, but it wasn't until the twentieth century that it became a structured element in shoe design. The ankle-strap shoe has, quite simply, a leather strap buckled around the ankle. The strap can be of two types: A bracelet passing through a loop at the back of the shoe or two straps that cross in the front or the back of the foot; both types are fastened with a buckle.

In the 1920s, straps became one of the most important design features in women's shoes and innovations included the T-strap, which by 1921 was attached to an ankle strap coming from an extended quarter that went up the back of the shoe. By the 1930s, ankle straps were used on evening shoes designed by André Perugia and Alfred Argence among others, and the style continued in popularity throughout the war years when attached to a platform or wedge.

On April 26, 1948 *Life* magazine heralded the return of the ankle strap (although it hadn't really been away), describing shoes as "vivid, elegant, and designed to show the ankle at its very best." As skirts became longer and fuller, the magazine went on, "women can no longer draw attention to their legs by just having them." Shoes had to draw the eye "for the twelve inches of leg left on view" and intricate ankle straps became fashionable—Newton Elkin, who was well known for his front-buckled ankle-strap shoes using peek-a-boo vinyl panels, created a shoe that had four buttoned bars ending with an ankle strap that reached up the leg in 1948. In 1949, Beth Levine launched her first shoe collection consisting of one model of shoe, the best-selling "Femme Fatale," named after the vampish heroines of Hollywood's film noir. The shoe had a wrap-around ankle strap and a V-cut closed-toe vamp and could be bought in a palette of suitably

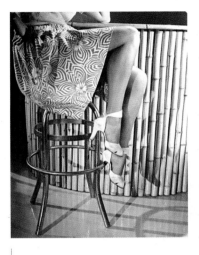

above:

Perfect pins
Betty Grable shows off the legs insured by Lloyds of London for $1 million USD in ankle-strap shoes.

left:

Black satin
Rita Hayworth wears David Evins' ankle-strap shoes for the famous striptease scene in *Gilda* (1946).

sexy colors and materials, including bright-red suede studded with rhinestone flowers or kidskin with pearls. It was one of many versions of ankle-strap shoes that became synonymous with 1950s Hollywood such as David Evins' black ankle-strap shoes designed for Rita Hayworth in the film noir *Gilda* (1946) and worn during the famous "striptease" scene. The ankle-strap round-toed shoe or "baby doll" as it was sometimes known became synonymous with the 1950s pin-up appearing in the work of illustrator Antonio Vargas and on the feet of Betty Grable and Shelley Winters. In her autobiography *Shelley, Sometimes Known as Shirley* (1980), the star tells the now infamous tale of how she and Marilyn Monroe used to liberate shoes from the studio to wear on dates and on seeing a pair of shoes with an ankle-strap that tied into a bow she said: "They really were the sexiest shoes I've ever seen." After they helped Shelley in her seduction of Marlon Brando, she dubbed them "F***-me" shoes.

> "Women's fashion is a subtle form of bondage. It's men's way of binding them."
> David Duchovny

The shoe became synonymous with sex, appearing as a prop of erotica in fashion, the movies, and sado-masochistic pornography, especially when ankle straps were attached to high spike heels. The strapped-up naked foot had a frisson that hinted at girls in bondage. Perhaps that's why in its various incarnations ever since (save the comedic heights of the glam rock ankle-strap platform), the ankle-strap when attached to a shoe with a heel has been perceived as the ultimate in sexy footwear. In the 1970s, for instance, the 1950s ankle-strap stiletto shoe was revived and, when designed by Stephane Kélian in metallic leather and snakeskin, appeared in the pages of French *Vogue* and the advertising of deluxe lingerie firm Janet Reger, creating what writer Angela Carter dubbed "the fantasy courtesan" look. In 1984, actress Britt Ekland singled out the shoe as a key weapon in the wardrobe of the femme fatale in her style guide, *Sensual Beauty and How to Achieve It*, and in

below:

Mixed messages

Galliano matches the traditions of tweed with extreme bondage in his dominatrix-inspired ankle-strap shoe.

1996, the unnamed narrator of *Footsucker*, a novel of foot and shoe fetishism by Geoff Nicholson, says "I'm a great fan of the ankle strap, and even more so of the double ankle strap, I'm absolutely sure this must have something to do with bondage."

Ankle straps have been on trend throughout the 1990s and 2000s: René Caovilla designed a wired suede ankle strap *c.* 1990; for Fall/Winter 2005 Lanvin launched a satin and crystal-studded court shoe with ankle strap and a stainless steel heel; Sergio Rossi designed an ankle-strap gold-sequined satin gladiator sandal for Spring/Summer 2010; and in 2009 author Cooper Lawrence wrote evocatively of her ankle-strap wedding shoes by Manolo Blahnik: "Those shoes were art. The moment I laid eyes on their heart-stopping splendor, I understood the power, sexiness, and utter opulence that men who flaunt expensive race-cars or women who lavish themselves in sensational jewels must feel. The shoes were five inches of silver Etain napa leather-covered spike heels with a glittering bejeweled ankle strap. A second, entirely decorative, jewel-encrusted strap hung down as an ankle bracelet. It was by far the finest pair of shoes designer Manolo Blahnik had created. Although they cost almost as much as my gown, I did not hesitate to buy them."

However, the author was somewhat downcast a few weeks after her wedding after seeing a photograph of "a casually dressed Kimora Lee Simmons coming out of a restaurant. I was less delighted when I saw that she—on an ordinary day—was wearing my wedding shoes... with jeans, no less, as if they were ordinary shoes and not the serious works of art I deemed them to be. It was yet another reminder of how stars are different from the rest of us." The heavily embellished ankle-strap shoe with a huge platform became the daywear shoe of many celebrities such as Sarah Jessica Parker, Victoria Beckham, and Jada Pinkett-Smith in the 2010s, who wore styles such as Christian Louboutin's "No. 299 150 Suede Ankle Strap Pump" with a six-inch heel or his "Boulima Ankle Strap Heels." They were dubbed stripper shoes because of their resemblance to the Plexiglas platforms worn by lap dancers.

above:

Louboutin ankle-strap pumps

Six-inch heels with ankle strap, and backstay. The extreme pitch of the shoe exposes the signature red flash.

BIKER BOOT

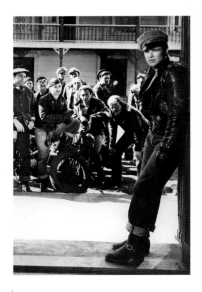

The Wild One (1953)
Brando's boots are probably by
Chippewa, recognizable by the stacked
Woodsman's heels, the double leather
half soles, and the long instep straps.

Originally created in thick black leather to prevent foot injuries suffered by motorbike riders in the 1930s, the stovepipe-leg biker boot entered the vocabulary of street style when worn by Marlon Brando as juvenile delinquent Johnny in *The Wild One* (1953). His countercultural uniform of rolled Levi's 501s, Perfecto leather jacket, and heavy leather biker boot became the look of the rebel and has been associated with a range of street styles ever since.

Motorcycle boots were derived from logging boots—boots that had to withstand one of the toughest forms of manual labor. The first manufacturers of biker boots such as Wesco of Oregon (est. 1918 by

> "The buzz this season is all about biker boots (with or without heels)."
>
> Shane Watson, *The Sunday Times*, September 20, 2009

John Henry Shoemaker), Chippewa (1901), and Dayton (1946) had started off catering to loggers by trekking to remote timber camps to measure the workers' feet and provide custom-made boots. Boots had to last, as John Shoemaker put it bluntly: "A shoe is no better than the leather it is made of—and all the leather on the market is not worth a 'whoop' where there is no shoemaking skill." Charlie Wohlford of Dayton was a bootmaker who had a reputation for being able to repair boots so they ended up better constructed than the originals. Tough Dayton boots were worn by loggers, construction workers, and roughnecks working in the oil fields.

During the Depression years, when logging was hit by the ensuing economic crisis, Chippewa developed a buckled black-leather boot with a stovepipe leg that could be easily pulled on and off—it became known as the "Engineer," since it was originally marketed at land surveyors in Sears catalogs. When the craze for motorbiking took hold, the "Engineer" became a biker's boot worn by biker gangs all over the world as a mark of allegiance to their tribe. In 1965, the "Dayton Black Beauty" double-soled motorbike boot came on the market and continues to be one of the firm's most popular models

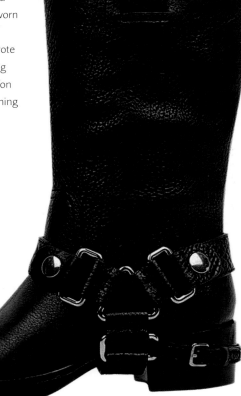

today. The Dayton double-soled "Classic Engineer" boot with Goodyear welted construction, reckoned to be the toughest ever made, debuted in 1978, and biker or engineer boots began to enter fashion in the early 1980s where they have remained ever since.

New versions have found their way onto the runway, designed by Miu Miu, Jimmy Choo, and Jil Sander and on the high street by UK labels Office and Oasis. Even Ugg (see page 128) have launched a pair—the "Kensington" biker boot in distressed pebble-grain leather with an oiled finish and lightweight rubber sole. For men, they can still conjure a rugged style redolent of outlaw masculinity. For women, they act as an edgy alternative to the knee boot and were embraced by the grunge scene in the early 1990s when worn with a floaty dress *à la* Courtney Love, and during the reign of boho fashion in the early 2000s. In 2006, *The Sunday Times* wrote of a new version of boho with "heavy metal attitude," describing the look as "wearing a studded leather jacket with a flimsy chiffon number, stomping about town in biker boots and wearing anything with a skull on it."

In 2012, in a nod to the predicted grunge revival, Chanel launched a black calfskin quilted biker boot, together with an extreme four-buckle metal-plated version, engraved with the double-C logo and a one-and-a-half inch stacked heel.

right:
Miu Miu biker
This modern take on the traditional biker differs little from the 1950s originals—there's little point in tampering with a classic.

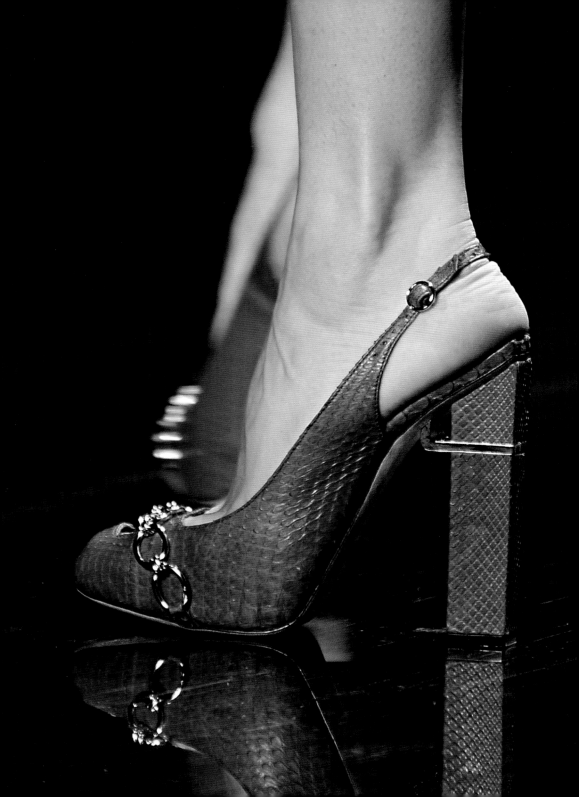

SLINGBACK

> "A slingback in black, gold, silver, or tan is an investment that you'll wear for summers (and winters) to come."
>
> Jess Cartner-Morley, the *Guardian*, June 11, 2005

The slingback shoe has no solid back but takes the form of a strap that crosses behind the heel, a style that has persisted in shoe design up to the present day because it suits most kinds of heel from kitten through to platform. The slingback strap makes the shoe fit securely on the foot with either a buckle or elastic band on the heel strap. It is an innovation that appeared on beach sandals around 1931 and was introduced into shoes in the late 1930s; *Vogue* magazine featured slingback heels in 1936 alongside dresses by Jacques Heim and Edward Molyneux.

When slingbacks were first introduced, as with the peep-toe (see page 210), they were considered daring because a large portion of the foot was revealed, together with the reinforced heel of the stocking. More often than not, slingback shoes were for eveningwear because skirts hid the stocking heels, or as summer shoes toward the end of the decade when bare legs became more acceptable. By the 1940s, slingback shoes with an ankle chain denoted the kind of girl who was prepared to walk on the wild side and in 1942, Laird & Schoeber advertised a range of slingback platforms made out of "the aristocrat of snakeskin" in dramatic high colors including batik red, jungle gold, and parakeet green. The shortage of materials during the war years made the slingback a popular design as manufacturers could render it in materials other than leather and many an American airplane was painted with the forces' pin-up Betty Grable or a fantasy painting by Alberto Vargas of a girl posed in little more than a pair of slingbacks.

In Europe, the slingback was attached to the wedge and after the war, a peep-toe was added; in 1944, Di Mauro made the "Liberation," a halter-neck flag-covered shoe in pigskin and suede to commemorate the Allies' victory. The halter-neck was a variation on the slingback introduced in the 1940s—a strap that was placed

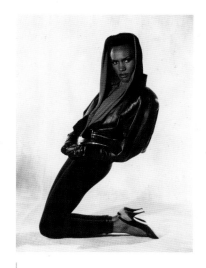

above:

Bond girl

Grace Jones wears slingbacks in her role as May Day in the James Bond film *A View To A Kill* (1984).

left:

Dior Fall/Winter 2008

The slingback of this high stack-heeled purple shoe creates an elegantly streamlined effect.

slightly higher up at the back of the shoe. By the end of the 1940s, high-heeled slingbacks became standard issue for pin-up girls and any film starlet who wanted to suggest a rather risqué image.

The world's most famous (and comfortable) slingback was designed in 1957 by Massaro of Paris for Coco Chanel, who wanted a comfortable alternative to the stiletto. She employed the Parisien *bottier* Raymond Massaro from the Rue de la Paix, founded in 1894 to supply boots, pumps, and mules for a list of wealthy clients including, over the years, the Duchess of Windsor, Marlene Dietrich, Elizabeth Taylor, and fashionista Daphne Guinness. The Chanel slingback sandal, or *soulier* as she called it, had a small heel, a soft broad strap, and was bicolored in beige with a distinctive black toe. Massaro explained: "The black, slightly square toe shortened the foot. The beige melted into the whole and lengthened the leg. It was a very pure design, accentuated by the fineness of the straps. We rejected the idea of a buckle, which looked a little bit old-fashioned, preferring instead to add a little elastic on the low-cut inner side. This elastic adapted to the shape of the foot, adjusting its every tension and following its movement." The choice of beige was key

> "It's hard not to be sexy in a pair of high heels."
>
> Tom Ford

to Chanel's design; as she put it: "I take refuge in beige because it's natural." Chanel liked the fact that beige suggested the color of the skin of her wealthy clientele as well as optically lengthening the leg. The shoe had a black toe-cap for functional reasons—it meant the shoe didn't get dirty or scuffed while traveling and was inspired by the black leather toe-cap Chanel had noted worn by staff on her friend the Duke of Westminster's yacht.

Massaro's slingback formed part of a whole ensemble that was set to successfully relaunch the House of Chanel after the designer's rather dubious activities during the Second World War. Chanel had remained in Paris after its occupation by German forces in 1940 where she was

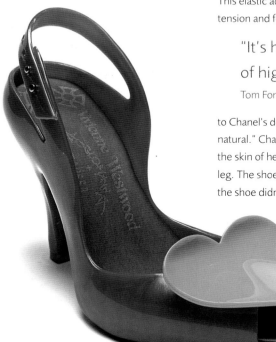

below:
Eco slingback
The "Melissa Lady Dragon" slingback by Vivienne Westwood in easy-to-clean sustainable rubber.

ensconced in the luxurious Ritz Hotel with Hans Gunther von Dincklage, a German military intelligence officer. At the end of hostilities, Chanel's diminished popularity led to an enforced period in Switzerland, after which she returned to Paris and launched a comeback collection with mixed success. The determined designer decided to update her easy-to-wear trademark looks, believing they had a unique selling point that provided a counterpoint to the restrictive silhouette of Dior's New Look. Her classic tweed suit, developed in the 1920s with a collarless cardigan jacket trimmed with braid, patch pockets and gilt buttons, became a symbol of post-war status for thousands of women when worn together with Massaro's slingback shoe.

The shoe is now among one of the twentieth century's most-copied designs, with many footwear manufacturers launching their own versions including Joan & David, an American label started up in 1977 by husband-and-wife team Joan and David Halpern, whose Chanel pump is an homage to the two-tone original. Other innovative slingback designs were developed in the 1950s by Beth Levine; in 1952 the designer launched the "Concerto" halter-back evening sandal in bright-red suede ornamented with jet and sparkling rhinestones that were placed on the breast of the heel, showing the designer's continuing interest in embellishing the underneath as well as upper of her shoe designs. In 1955, Levine designed the "Under Construction" open-toed slingback in black leather; the shoe had a short sole that was placed under the ball of the foot, leaving the rest of the underside of the shoe free. The leather upper wrapped around the rest of the whole shoe, creating a closer fit, and was patterned with gold studs.

The slingback was popular throughout the 1960s with a kitten or low stacked heel, and in the 1970s with stiletto or a wedge. It remains one of the most popular styles for evening shoes today primarily, as writer Mimi Spencer points out, because it is "the most seductive of shoes, chiefly because the strap is ever perilously close to collapse, leaving you—swoon—naked from the ankle down. They're a bit *dishabille*, slingbacks, and thus hopelessly sexy. They also have an illusion going on, leading the eye all the way from hem to toe without any troublesome obstacles."

above:
Kitten heel
A modern Prada slingback in patent leather that seems indistinguishable from its 1960s counterpart.

LOAFER

A loafer is a slip-on, low-cut, laceless shoe, often featuring a tassel on the front or the horse-bit that is the mark of the classic Gucci loafer. Loafers originated as a casual Norwegian shoe, but since the 1980s, have gradually become a formal shoe acceptable enough to be worn with a suit. In the United States, a popular derivation is the Weejun or penny loafer (see page 208); in Europe the loafer became a streamlined shoe of supreme elegance best expressed in the Gucci loafer. The distinctive horse-bit was first introduced into

> "How strange, when your father's wearing women's clothes and platform shoes, that a pair of loafers looks incredible."
>
> Moon Unit Zappa

the brands's merchandise in the 1950s after founding father Guccio Gucci determined to use equestrian details after working at London's Savoy Hotel in the early twentieth century. He realized how much the privileged elite loved their horses and thought that a hint of the beast could give an old-world elegance to a nouveau Italian label set up in 1921. The horse-bit was first used on saddle-stitched handbags and from then was used in different sizes as hardware on accessories as well as a symbol on print design. In 1953, the horse-bit was used for the first time on Gucci's black or brown pigskin loafer for men, worn by John Wayne, Clark Gable, and Fred Astaire, with the female version launched in 1968.

By the 1960s, the almond-toed Gucci loafer was being sold in Bond Street, London, the shopping

below:

European chic

The iconic Gucci loafer is immediately recognizable by its distinctive equestrian-inspired horse-bit chain.

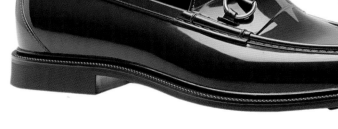

street known for its expensive brands, and it was considered a fashionable alternative to the Oxford (see page 90) or Chelsea boot (see page 140) with its implications of cosmopolitan Italian taste. In 1979, Dustin Hoffman appeared sockless in Gucci loafers in the Oscar-winning movie *Kramer vs Kramer* and the shoe entered another phase in its popularity, becoming embraced by the jet-setters or international businessman. Throughout the 1980s, the loafer was worn by both men and women and symbolized business success and upper-class chic—in *The Official Sloane Ranger Handbook*, style commentators Peter York and Ann Barr described it as "the shoe of the Sloane," a young upper middle-class woman whose status shoes displayed her access to the upper echelons.

Gucci loafers are now a men's shoe classic made in Florence by specialist artisans in stained leather to give a slightly aged patina. Their elegant reputation has meant the Gucci loafer is beginning to appeal to a younger audience; it manages to combine formality successfully with comfort, a difficult thing to do in a business shoe. They are popular in Japan because of the ease with which the shoe can be slipped on and off when entering a room. The Bally loafers are recognized by their tassel; the Tod's loafer or driving shoe by the grips on the extended sole.

The loafer, like the ballet flat and Wellington, has made a huge comeback in women's footwear in the 2010s as a comfortable and fashionable alternative to the high heel. In 2010 Frida Giannini, Gucci's creative director, announced it was back, saying the horse-bit loafer is one of the most iconic items in the Gucci archives: "It's an absolute classic. I play with the design each season, updating the shape, material, and details, but the shoe's essential beauty and functionality remain the same." Tommy Hilfiger launched a high-heeled loafer, a form of dressy day shoe, in 2011.

below:
Upper cut (Spring/Summer 2012)
The front is the only recognizable feature left of the standard tasseled loafer in this Galliano shoe mash-up.

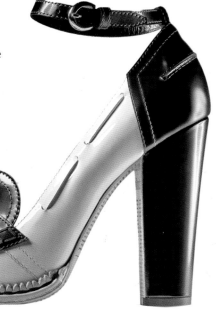

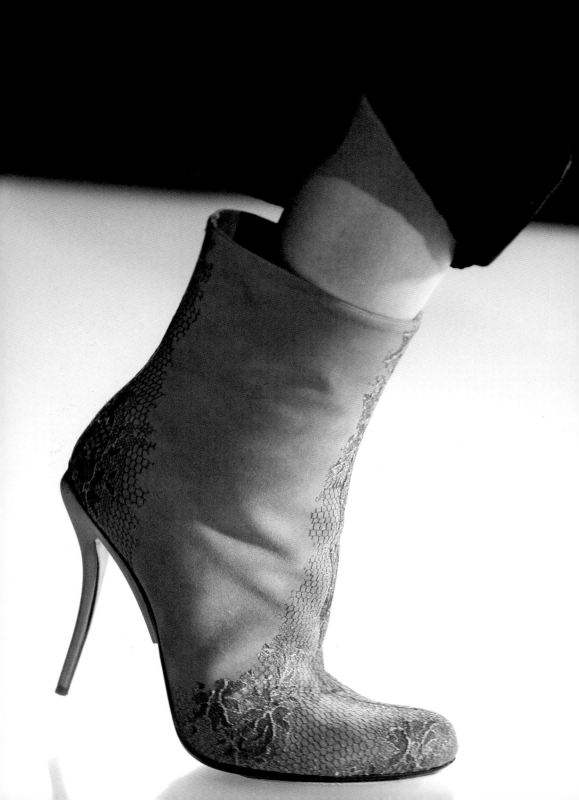

ANKLE BOOT

Anglo Saxons wore a form of shapeless ankle boot over thick, woolen hose, but after the Norman conquest in 1066, boots gradually rose higher and higher. Tight-fitting, front- and side-laced boots or buttoned half-boots (or *bottines*) were worn in the nineteenth century, but as skirts rose, the ankle boot became old-fashioned because it left an unsightly gap between hem and ankle. Ankle boots have remained a constant in men's fashion though, primarily because they are habitually worn under trousers and avoid the unsightly bump given to the silhouette by knee boots.

Shoes worn with galoshes took over in the 1920s in women's footwear fashion, and throughout most of the inter-war period the half-boot was not regarded as fashionable footwear—it was purely a practical form. André Perugia was one of the first shoe designers to begin to experiment with the ankle boot, or "bootee" as it was known in the 1930s, emphasizing its look rather than its function. This coincided with the influence of the Surrealist movement on fashion, an art movement that had made its first appearance in the poetry of Paul Eluard and Louis Aragon in the 1920s as well as the infamous paintings and performance art of Salvador Dalí. Surrealism celebrated the bizarre and strange, displaying the workings of the unconscious in its abstract imagery. Paris was the center of surrealism and fashion so the two worlds were bound to collide—as they did in the work of Italian couturier Elsa Schiaparelli, who created clothes and accessories with chic-shock appeal for her legions of elegant clients. Fashionistas on the way to the Ritz Hotel would linger outside her boutique on the Place Vendôme, entranced by bizarre window displays that included Dalí's bright-red sofa in the shape of film star Mae West's lips. Footwear had already entered her body of work— but in a typically Surrealist fashion. "Schiap," as she was known to

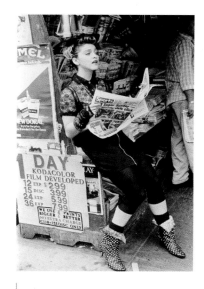

above:
Desperately Seeking Susan (1985)
Madonna on set wearing a pair of roll-down kitten-heeled ankle boots in black suede, studded with diamanté.

left:
Minimalist ankle boot
A clean-and-clear design by Armani for Fall/Winter 2011 with decorative accents created by snakeskin inlay.

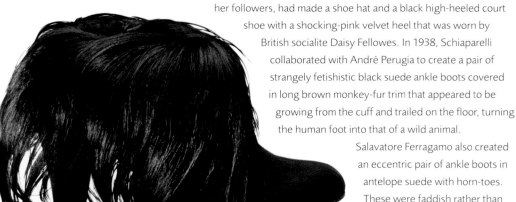

her followers, had made a shoe hat and a black high-heeled court shoe with a shocking-pink velvet heel that was worn by British socialite Daisy Fellowes. In 1938, Schiaparelli collaborated with André Perugia to create a pair of strangely fetishistic black suede ankle boots covered in long brown monkey-fur trim that appeared to be growing from the cuff and trailed on the floor, turning the human foot into that of a wild animal.

Salavatore Ferragamo also created an eccentric pair of ankle boots in antelope suede with horn-toes. These were faddish rather than fashionable, to which Carmel Snow, Editor of *Harper's Bazaar* attested when she gave a talk to the Shoe Fashion Guild in 1939, saying: "I feel sure that the question of the bootie is in your minds. We will show the boot, of course, we couldn't possibly omit it. But whether it will be generally accepted... I think is extremely doubtful. For over a year, M. Perugia in Paris has been showing me his *bottines*. He tells me that his smartest clients order them but I have not seen any smart woman in Paris wearing them. If the French woman does not take to them easily, I don't see why the American will. The best thing we have are our ankles and these boots cut the line of the ankle." That was, in fact, the problem with the ankle boot—it drew attention to heavy legs and could only be successfully worn, women believed, when skirts were long, such as in the 1950s when zipped-up ankle boots were worn for warmth in winter, or when drainpipe jeans were worn by young women in the early 1960s—in 1966, Ferragamo created the "Pull-Over" for Brigitte Bardot, a soft blue velvet pull-on ankle boot with a faux button fastening on the side. The miniskirt's expanse of leg precluded the use of the ankle boot throughout most of the 1960s, and the calf-length Courrèges flat or knee-high kinky and go-go boots held sway.

The wide, flared trousers of the 1970s made the style defunct, until the ankle boot had success in a subcultural form. After the demise of punk in 1978, a new street style emerged in London's clubs, a dramatically theatrical look that took inspiration from the dressing-up box of history, and the style was worn by avant-garde

above:

Surrealist ankle boot
Perugia's infamous and animalistic monkey-fur ankle boot of 1938 created for Elsa Schiaparelli.

creatives involved in the worlds of fashion, art, design, and music, including milliner Stephen Jones and fashion designer David Holah of the legendary label Body Map. By 1979, after a short stint at Club Gossip's Bowie Night where the host and DJ was the stylish Rusty Egan, the epicenter of this new movement relocated to an unprepossessing wine bar named Blitz in London's West End. The pierrots, nuns, and fops in pancake make-up who gathered in their homemade finery rejected the tribal aggression of punk, whose working-class heroics seemed old hat. The in-crowd were dubbed the Blitz Kids and on the door of Blitz was the inimitable Steve Strange, renowned for turning away Mick Jagger—the cloakroom attendant was one Boy George. The so-called sartorial "gender-bending" (a term first used in UK newspaper the *Sun* in 1983) caught the eye of the press, who reveled in the idea of boys looking like girls and vice versa, and they were variously dubbed Posers, Peacock People, and eventually the name that stuck, New Romantics. In catwalk terms, the most obvious manifestation of the New Romantic look was Vivienne Westwood's rakish and flamboyant Pirate Collection of Fall/Winter 1981, a runway fusing of all of the

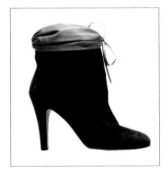

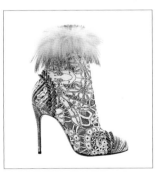

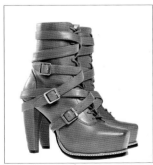

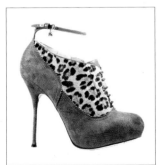

clockwise from top left:

Givenchy, 1979
A high-heeled black suede ankle boot with a red nappa cuff and bow.

Louboutin Fall/Winter 2011
Glitzy trimmed ankle boot with stiletto heel and trademark red sole.

Galliano Fall/Winter 2011
Shoe-boot with ankle strap, leopard-print apron, and high stiletto heel.

Mark Charles
The chunky "Camy Tan" ankle boot has a concealed platform and multibuckle detail.

historical leanings of the movement that included the ankle-length pirate boot (see page 178), and was a critical success.

The Blitz Kids look went global. For teenagers who wanted to buy into this new street style, a boot became available—the Blitz boot, a cross between a winklepicker—a 1950s toe shape that had enjoyed an unexpected revival with punk—and a strapped, studded, and buckled fetish shoe. This innovative ankle boot—usually worn in black suede or leather although bright blue, red, and white were also popular—had a front zip covered by three buckled straps and a low stacked heel; a shoe version swiftly followed. The Blitz boot kept its subcultural credentials when adopted by Goths, a post-punk tribe who congregated at the Batcave Club in Soho in the early 1980s and listened to morbid music by Bauhaus, Siouxsie and the Banshees, The Cure, and later, Sisters of Mercy and The Mission.

> "Not diamonds but heels are a girl's best friend."
> William Rossi

The early Goth look was basic black from eyeliner and fingernails through to drainpipe trousers and Blitz boots, but by the 2000s the scene had become more recognizably historical, taking inspiration from the macabre Victorian England of Bram Stoker's *Dracula* (1897) and horror films such as *Interview with the Vampire* (1994). The Blitz boot also gained a gigantic platform sole and a shiny patent-leather surface, giving any teenaged tattooed and pierced Goth an imposing presence. When a Gothic revival took place in fashion in the 2000s in the work of Alexander McQueen and Gareth Pugh, the Blitz boot had a brief revival among stylists hoping to be snapped by the *Sartorialist*—but it was just one of those passing fashion fads.

The 1980s was an era in which the ankle boot proliferated in a variety of styles—trousers were tapered at the ankles so it gave the short boot a fantastic focus, and leggings covered up and camouflaged the legs. The pixie, the unisex tukka, and the rolled-down ankle boot were worn; in the film *Desperately Seeking Susan* (1985), Rosanna Arquette plays Roberta,

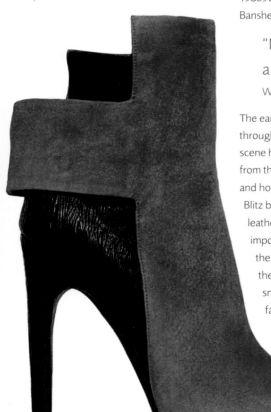

below:

Optical illusion

Aperlai channels Cubism with its blue-and-black illusion ankle boot of 2011.

a suburban housewife who takes on the identity of Susan, played by Madonna. Her sartorial transformation is complete when she puts on a pair of red roll-down ankle boots. In another iconic scene, Madonna trades in her gold lurex pyramid-emblazoned jacket in a vintage store for a pair of magnificent roll-down kitten-heeled diamante-studded ankle boots in black suede.

The early 2000s witnessed another innovation in ankle-boot design—the shoe-boot or "shoot," footwear that could be described as either a high-cut shoe or a low-cut ankle boot. It was the accessory *du jour* in 2007 and remains a popular shape; the shoe-boot ends just below the ankle bone, with the top of the upper higher at the back than the front, and to compensate for the visual cutting-off effect of the leg, it has a stratospheric heel plus platform. The designer most associated with the rise of the shoe-boot is Alexander McQueen, known for brave and uncompromising designs that present a formidable image of a modern femme fatale in collections such as The Hunger of Spring/Summer 1996. The heel of the shoe-boot in McQueen's hands looks less than that of a tottering fashion victim and more a warrior intent on destruction. After his death in 2010, the fashion house continued to launch new versions of the style including the 2011 slingback "Neon Flash Shoe-Boot" in black suede with shocking-pink heels and strap. The shoe-boot has become fashionable, since the silhouette of the trouser shape has been slim enough to accommodate it; perhaps most unusually, the shoe-boot has been worn with the shortest of skirts, primarily because of its ultra-clever flattering design. It's also a trend that has allowed those with gym-honed pins to be at the height of fashion in an era of extreme body consciousness.

In 2012, the ankle boot continued its dominance, with both fashion designers and mainstream brands showing a version; Dior launched an elegant open-toe Victorian-inspired platform ankle boot in nude lace with a corseted heel covered in nude satin; in complete contrast, Schuh's brash "Hamp Zip Glitter" ankle boot had a diagonal zipper and 1980s-inspired cone heel.

above:

Baroque and roll
The cuff of Sergio Rossi's ankle boot forms a dramatic swirling flourish.

WEEJUN

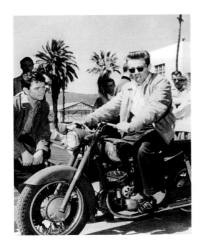

above:

Arbiter of cool
Actor James Dean sits nonchalantly astride a motorcycle with a cigarette in his mouth and Weejuns on his feet (1955).

The Weejun is an American classic with simple, uncluttered lines launched in 1936 by the Maine-based G. H. Bass shoe company, which originated as a boot- and moccasin-maker catering to loggers and woodsmen in 1876. In the 1930s, George Henry Bass spotted an imported flat moccasin-topped slip-on shoe worn by Norwegian farmers. He adapted the shoe for American casual wear with a hand-sewn front, leather soles and heels, and added a leather band with a diamond cut-out across the front of the shoe—in homage to its origin, he named them "Weejun" as in "Norwegian." In the 1940s, Weejun wearers slipped dimes—the price of a pay-phone call—into the front of the cut-out, later replaced by a more aesthetically pleasing shiny penny—an act of early fashion customization that gave the shoe the nickname "penny loafer." The Weejun gained a cool reputation after being spotted on the feet of rebellious young actor James Dean and later John F. Kennedy.

The Bass Weejun also became an essential component of the Ivy League look of America's East Coast upper-middle-class elite. At Harvard and Yale Universities, a style evolved via the clothing stores of Brooks Brothers and J. Press that was casually elegant: Single-breasted suits of soft construction with natural shoulder lines, button-down shirts, chinos, windcheater jackets, and Weejuns were worn by privileged WASPs on campus until neatly subverted by African-American jazz musicians, including Thelonius Monk and Miles Davis, who wore a Madras jacket, chinos, and Bass Weejuns on stage. A number of hip West Coast actors also appropriated the look between 1955 and 1965 and transformed it from straight-laced campus chic into the height of American cool. Dustin Hoffman as college student Benjamin Braddock in *The Graduate* (1967), Robert Redford in *Barefoot in the Park* (1967), Steve McQueen, and Paul Newman all converted the Ivy League look into a vision of laid-back masculinity that conquered the menswear world and still resonates today.

In the late 1970s, a Japanese study of Ivy League campus style, *Take Ivy* (1965) featuring photographs by Teruyoshi Hayashida, achieved cult status. Its arcane images with bizarre captions showing students strolling the leafy quads in checked Bermudas, blazers, and Weejuns led to a renewed interest in this most American of looks, consolidated with the publication of *The Official Preppy Handbook* in 1980. Michael Jackson wore black Weejuns with white socks in an era that rediscovered a whole host of American classics including Levi's 501 jeans and Ray-Ban Wayfarer glasses, and a youthful, colorful, more flamboyant version of Ivy League known as "preppy" (after the pre-college prep schools) dominated the menswear lines of Ralph Lauren, J.Crew, and Tommy Hilfiger. The Bass Weejun remains a popular classic; a slimline version of the original Weejun, the "Dover" was introduced in 2009, and in 2011, the company collaborated with Tommy Hilfiger on Originals With a Twist, a line of classic Weejuns in wool plaid, pony skin, suede, and mirror-polished leather in a palette of bottle green, navy, ocher, and classic burgundy.

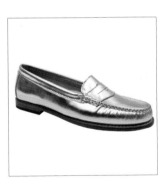
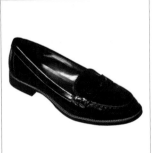
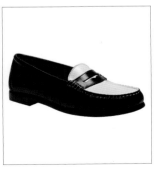
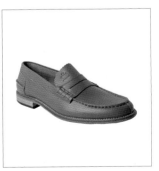

clockwise from top left:

Bass Wayfarer
Gold leather with band across the front in which a penny was originally stuck.

Ivy League
The penny loafer has become a feature of classic "preppy" style.

Mod loafer
The classic Barracuta "Miller" loafer with embossed branded apron and hand-stitched upper.

Black-and-white Bass
Timeless monochrome Wayfarer for Spring/Summer 2011 with penny strap and cushioned footbed.

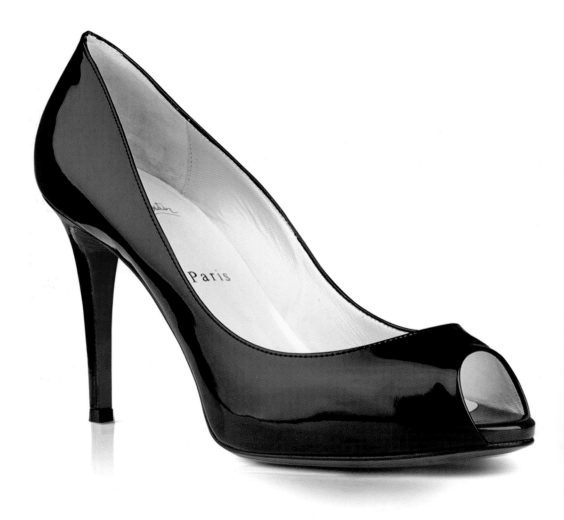

PEEP-TOE

"The toe—it's peeking out just waiting
to be kissed!"

Christian Louboutin, on his "Troulala" peep-toe pumps, opposite

The peep-toe shoe was invented in 1938 with a risqué name
redolent of the peep-show machine, a form of erotic entertainment
showing a saucy photographic narrative found in penny arcades and
fairgrounds. The peep-toe shoe was considered just as racy; it was a
shoe with a section in the front cut away to reveal just the tips of the
toes and was attached to a variety of styles, usually with high heels
and a low-cut upper.

Toes had been shown before but only on the beach in open-toed
summer sandals that were designed to keep the feet cool. There
was something subversively seductive about the peep-toe, it may
have showed much less of the foot, but the cut-out was clearly not
there for reasons of function—this was a sexy shoe that was all about
display. The peep-toe shoe was flirtatious and displayed the toes
purely for the delectation of the observer, calling to the unconscious
desires of foot-lovers everywhere. The suggestive quality of the
shoe was made even more so by the fact that in order for the shoe
to look elegant, it had to be worn with bare legs, otherwise the
reinforced toe of the stocking would be on view.

A frenzy was raised at the thought of women showing off naked
legs in the city. In 1939, Edna Woolman Chase, editor-in-chief of
American *Vogue* begged the Shoe Fashion Guild to stop the rise
of the peep-toe shoe, saying: "From the very beginning I have felt
that it was a distinctly bad style," and adding "I beg you to stop this
promotion of the open-toed, open-backed shoes for street wear.
Open-toed shoes may be worn for dress occasions, not for walking in
the city. They are inappropriate, unsightly, and dirty. Your impractical
footwear is ruining our feet. I won't be a bit surprised if, some day,
women just walk right out on you and shellac their soles and put bells

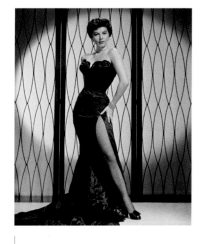

above:

Screen siren
By the time Ava Gardner was
photographed in peep-toes in 1952,
the shoe was a sexy on-screen style.

left:

Ooh La La!
The Louboutin "Troulala" offers
up the big toe in a design of
phallic suggestiveness.

on their toes and say 'to hell with shoes!'." She added in 1954: "One has only to look at the feet of the nation's women to appreciate my remarkable lack of success."

The consternation raised by the exposure of the toes reflected the general censorship of the female body in fashion, particularly the costume design allowed in Hollywood movies. The Hays Code of 1930 forbade "indecent or undue exposure" in movies with a ban on nudity, including a flash of cleavage. Designers like Adrian got around the ban by designing clinging bias-cut gowns that clung to every contour and were worn by stars such as Jean Harlow, often without underwear—the gowns were so tight it showed through. Shoes began to be a way of showing off flesh, and more and more of the uppers began to be cut away; footwear became strappier and backs disappeared completely with the mule and the slingback. Shoes even featured transparent vinyl panels with decorative etching or studded with faux gemstones. By the end of the decade, newspaper the *Victoria Advocate* featured an article that said "the fad hasn't been universally approved" and suggested that the peep-toe was falling from favor, predicting that a slightly raised closed toe dubbed the Sultan, Turkish, or bulldog was poised for success. It is true that during the Second World War, peep-toe shoes were frowned upon, for in munitions factories they could be dangerous, with toes being open to injury, but the Sultan toe was not a resounding success.

By the 1950s, the peep-toe had come back with a bang and it was worn at night with the sheerest of stockings that now emulated the look of bare legs and feet because of advances in hosiery technology. Ferragamo designed the "Claretta" peep-toe slingback sandal in 1952 with a vamp made of two semicircular sections of brown pontova or synthetic straw divided widthwise by a glossy brown leather strap, and Charles Jourdan launched a range of popular peep-toes that were worn throughout the decade. By the 1960s, the open-toe took over from the understated peep-toe, a clear indication of the more blatant sexual mores of a liberated generation, but it bounced back in the 1970s in the same manner as stockings and suspenders—old-fashioned symbols of seduction that were being rediscovered by a new

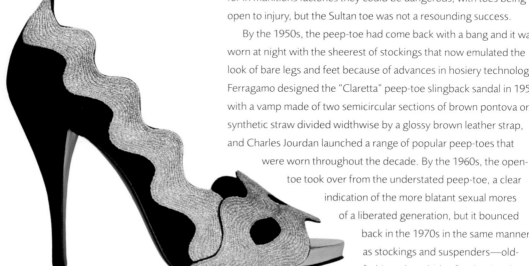

below:

Optical illusion (Fall/Winter 2011)
Pierre Hardy's *trompe l'œil* black-and-nude suede scalloped-edge peep-toe with stiletto heel.

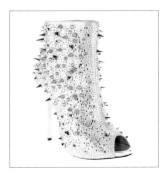

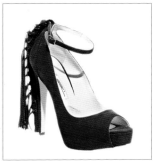

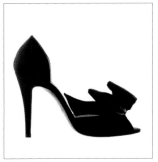

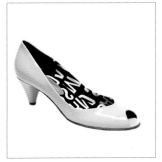

generation. Biba can take much responsibility for the revival of such retrospective styles because many fashion consumers had fallen in love with the way the label's founder Barbara Hulanicki had updated nostalgic styles from the silver screen.

The peep-toe has remained a classic footwear shape ever since, appearing on platforms, wedges, cone heels, and flats and is used most effectively by shoe designer Christian Louboutin in a style such as in the "Yoyo Orlato" of 2005, a black velvet peep-toe shoe with crystal-covered heels. He has loved the peep-toe since the age of seventeen, when the embryonic designer began to visit backstage at the Folies Bergère, observing and sketching the showgirls "partly for their performances, the glitter and sequins, but mostly to watch the way they walked." High heels were being worn by the most glamorous women he had ever seen and these formative experiences led to him creating shoes that throb with sexual tension, making the feet ripe for ravishment. The "Troulala" peep-toe pump of Fall/Winter 2003 is blatant in its sexual invitation—the stiletto-heeled black or red patent pump has a circular shape cut out to reveal the first third of the big toe and no others.

DESERT BOOT

This flexible suede ankle boot with a rubber crepe sole and two-eyelet lacing was innovated by Nathan Clark in 1949. Nathan was the great-grandson of James Clark, the 1825 founder of the famous Clarks shoe dynasty. Clark's desert boot was the first officially manufactured version of the crepe-soled footwear that had emerged from British soldiers stationed in North Africa. When posted overseas they found army-issue footwear unsuitable for the hot climate and sand of Egypt, so had suede boots with rubber crepe soles custom-made in the local bazaars of Cairo. Nathan Clark was familiar with the desert boot after having served as a member of the

below:

New model

The "Oliver" wedge desert boot by Linea, a brand launched in 1997 by the House of Fraser, a UK department store chain established in 1848.

"I could do a high heel with a jumpsuit, or I might do a gown with a desert boot."

Ralph Lauren

Royal Army Service Corps in Burma in the 1940s, and he "thought a version of these boots would make a good all-round shoe."

The prototype of the iconic Clarks "Desert Boot" was shown at the Chicago Shoe Fair in 1949 and proved overwhelmingly popular—its comfortable, casual look stood out among a sea of austere Oxfords and grown-up perforated brogues. By the mid-1950s, the desert boot was adopted by aficionados of jazz and gained a rather bohemian, intellectual reputation as a result. Despite its military origins, the boot appeared on the feet of British beatniks at the first CND (Campaign for Nuclear Disarmament) marches from the British Atomic Weapons Establishment of Aldermaston to Trafalgar Square that took place from 1958 onward. This branded it as a shoe of protest, especially when worn with long hair, jeans, and a duffle coat. The desert boot's countercultural reputation continued into the 1960s, when it was adopted by mods to protect their ankles while riding scooters, and inventor Nathan Clark remembered seeing newsreel footage of the May 1968 riots in Paris and noting with satisfaction that "all the students manning the barricades were wearing desert boots." The desert boot also invaded American college campuses after having been worn by Bob Dylan and the rebel-actor Steve McQueen—Clarks picked up on this unique selling point and used it in its American advertising with the tagline, "the off-beat casual for up-beat intellectuals," adding "it is the worldwide choice of creative intellectuals who prefer rugged masculine casualness to brittle sophistication."

By the 1970s the desert boot was no longer the footwear of the style pioneer—that was the place of the glam rock platform—and, like the car coat, it seemed a middle-aged style that had lost its mojo. Paul Weller, lead singer of The Jam, spearheaded a mod revival in the late 1970s and gave them momentary cool, but it was the Britpop movement of the 1990s that truly reinstated the desert boot; it was rediscovered, branded a British classic, and worn by Johnny Marr of The Smiths and Liam and Noel Gallagher of Oasis. Women have worn desert boots since their inception, but in 2009, on the sixtieth anniversary of the company, Clarks introduced a wholly female version—the "Yarra Desert Wedge," a real step away from its origins as the army's homespun sand shoe.

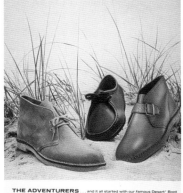

THE ADVENTURERS . . . and it all started with our famous Desert' Boot

Clarks OF ENGLAND

right top:

True original
The original Clarks desert boot, an outdoor shoe for hot climes that gained a boho reputation in the 1950s.

right:

Mainstream crossover
In the 2010s, many brands including Carvela added heels to the boot, converting it into smart city footwear.

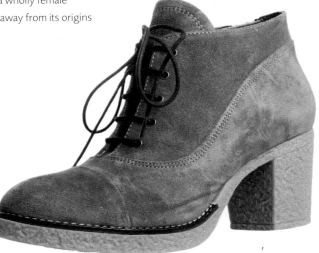

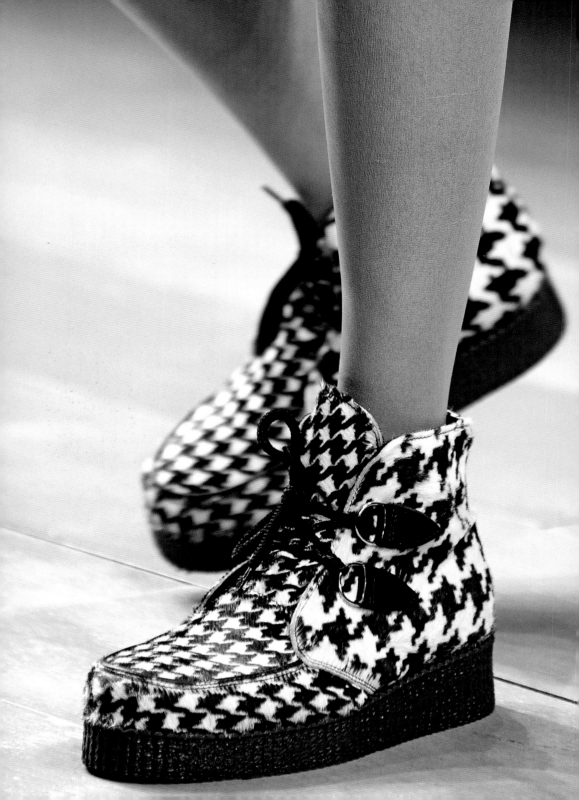

BROTHEL CREEPER

"[Docs] still cut the fashion mustard,
but brothel creepers have taken over."

Giles Hattersley, *The Sunday Times*, October 30, 2011

In North Africa and the Middle East during the Second World War, British soldiers found the standard army-issue footwear unsuited to the blisteringly hot foreign climes. They cleverly coerced shoemakers in the local markets to custom-make what became known as the desert boot, a roughly made lace-up suede boot with a rubber crepe sole that was perfect for walking on the hot sands of the desert (see page 214). Some servicemen also discovered Cairo's red-light district, and their distinctive suede shoes were dubbed "brothel creepers" presumably because they could enter and leave disreputable establishments silently because of the crepe on the soles.

In 1949, back in Northamptonshire, the heart of the UK's footwear industry, George Cox, a company that had been around since 1906, took the crepe sole of the desert boot and exaggerated it to extreme proportions. The result was a stylized shoe with a thick wedge sole of natural plantation crepe with the welt stitched to the insole through the upper and the lining. Cox's brothel creeper had flamboyantly colored suede or leather uppers, buckles, and monk straps or D-ring placements through which to thread the laces. The brothel creeper's oversized styling devices managed to swerve any overtly feminine connotations and it gained fame as the footwear of choice for one of the first post-war youth subcultures: the teddy boy. Teddy boys hailed from some of the poorest districts of London including Elephant and Castle, an area that had been severely damaged during the bombing of the Blitz. Down amid the bombsites, as documented by young photographer Ken Russell, young men of the second Elizabethan age began to assert their individuality through so-called Edwardian dress: drape suits with narrow-lapelled, long knee-length jackets with a moleskin or satin collar, bootlace tie, and skinny drainpipe trousers. Hair was a focal point, squared off at the

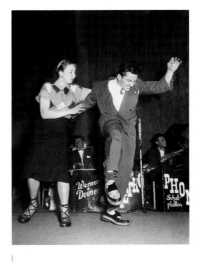

above:

Juvenile style

At the Jitterbug Championships held in Germany in 1952, the male contestant wears rubber-soled brothel creepers.

left:

Cartoon catwalk

Brothel creeper boots for women in oversized houndstooth check by Ashish (Fall/Winter 2011).

back into a Boston neckline, the top grown long and styled into a greasy pompadour coif. For teenagers with no real control over their education, work, or economics, power came through personal appearance, with clothes being used as the way to stand out from the crowd. The brothel creeper was an appropriately startling style of footwear whose heaviness at the foot balanced out the proportions of the hairstyle and was emphasized by the lean trouser silhouette. Its crepe sole also suited the physicality of jiving, an energetic dance associated with the emergence of American rock 'n' roll as played by Bill Haley and the Comets, and pianist and wild man, Jerry Lee Lewis.

The teddy boy soon gained notoriety as a territorial gang-related juvenile delinquent obsessed with rock 'n' roll, one of the first examples of the teenage rebel in Europe, following the pattern set by James Dean in *Rebel Without a Cause* (1955), and the brothel creeper retained a resonance that made it a staple of youth cults to come. However, by the early 1960s, the teddy boy look had been usurped by the fresh, cosmopolitan feel that was entering fashion. Teds had garnered the reputation of being aggressively patriotic and their presence at the Notting Hill race riots of 1958 made them seem redundant when a new teen tribe, the mods, was embracing black culture. In the early 1970s, the teddy-boy look reappeared in a pop-art form, a brightly colored cartoon version that stood as an alternative to the Glam Rock movement and was worn by avant-garde artists Duggie Fields, fashion designer Antony Price, and Andy Mackay of Roxy Music. Being a teddy boy was a way for men to dress up while retaining their masculinity in a sea of lurex and lipgloss as sported by stars David Bowie and Brian Connolly of Sweet. Original and reproduction drape suits and brothel creepers could be found at Let It Rock in London's King's Road, a shop that opened in 1971 and was run by entrepreneur Malcolm McLaren and his partner, teacher-turned-fashion-designer Vivienne Westwood. The interior was pure 1950s kitsch with Formica display cabinets, a jukebox blaring out Billy Fury, and yards of fake leopard skin. At first, Let It Rock catered to both the old and new audience of teddy boys, but the premises soon morphed into Too Fast to Live Too Young To Die in 1973 for another outlaw group, the bikers, Sex in 1974, and then Seditionaries in 1976, where it became the meeting

right:

Burberry Fall/Winter 2011

The dropped shoulder and exploded sleeve of the coat is matched by the exaggerated wedge brothel creepers.

below:

Going Underground

British brand Underground create both traditional and extreme designs to cater to today's street stylistas.

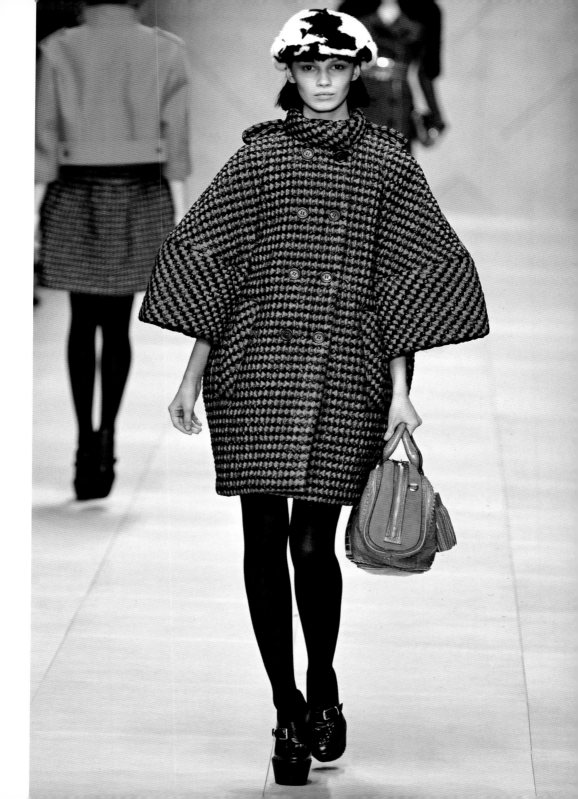

above:

The shoe of rebellion

The classic brothel creeper, beloved by subcultures from teddy boy to punk.

point of punk aficionados. The brothel creeper stayed on the shelves, since it stood for the rebellious rock 'n' roll attitude that McLaren and Westwood were tapping into to style up his protégées the Sex Pistols. Westwood cleverly used garments that embodied a history of rebellious significance such as the 1950s black leather jacket, drainpipe jeans, winklepickers, and George Cox's infamous suede and crepe sole creeper. The shoe was worn by Joe Strummer of The Clash, Johnny Rotten, and the iconic Sid Vicious in the video for his version of Frank Sinatra's "My Way" (1978). The success of the shoe made other companies follow suit including T.U.K. of San Diego, Shelly's Shoes—a company founded in the 1940s who had found fame in the 1980s styling mod-revival shoes for The Jam—and Underground, whose triple-soled version was worn by successive style tribes from the 1980s on including Psychobilly, Goth, and Emo.

In the 1980s, the brothel creeper crossed over into runway fashion when reinterpreted by Wayne and Geraldine Hemingway, whose label Red or Dead launched in 1982. The couple originally sold Dr. Marten boots on a stall in London's Camden Market after recognizing a change in the fashion silhouette—avant-garde designers such as Jean Paul Gaultier and Body Map were showing tight bandage dresses worn with leggings and heavy footwear. In 1986, the couple introduced their own "big" shoe, a thick, bumper wedge that was attached to shoes with overly round toes and in 1987 the "Watch Shoe," another modern take on the brothel creeper. The black leather upper had a buckle strap that took the rather surreal form of a watch strap, complete with face, from which to tell the time—it was a massive success after it was worn by Luke and Matt Goss of Bros who had a huge teenage following in 1987. Bros fans literally queued around the block of the Neal Street shop and contributed to the Red or Dead's runaway success.

The traditional crepe-soled brothel creeper had a widespread revival too, and it was won by both sexes as a subversive take on androgynous dressing. Many women adopted this style for the first time including journalist Deborah Levy, who remembered:

"Walking down the street in my very first pair made me feel like I was wearing a tattoo that marked me out for a meaningful life. Not quite winklepickers, their leopard-skin tongue (V-shaped) was surrounded by two inches of thick black crepe sole. To slip my naked foot into them was to literally walk on air. They were the metropolis, my ticket out of suburbia, my exit sign from everything women were supposed to become." By wearing such a robustly rock 'n' roll shoe, women created a powerful post-punk and post-feminist fashion that refused to equate dressing up with being a fashion victim.

The brothel creeper slipped back into subculture in the 1990s and early 2000s, and was associated with both the Emo and Visual Kei movements. An eccentric hybrid of skater shoe and creeper entered the market in 2003: the "Osiris Ali," designed by Swedish pro-skater Ali Boulala, which had a double-stitched leather upper and a thick rubber sole with a triple-stitched toe-cap and padded heel cuff, and was designed for streetwear rather than skateboarding. In 2008, Rupert Sanderson created a flamboyant mix of brothel creeper and high heel. The "Jupiter" and "Thunderbolt" models came in a variety of psychedelically printed pony skin, suede, and leathers, and were worn by Kate Moss and Alexa Chung. Other designers began to discover the shoe and for Spring/Summer 2010, Prada launched a hybrid of patent-leather brogue upper and brothel creeper that was a curious mix of two classic men's shoes, one conservative and the other countercultural. Its towering triple-decker layers were picked out in tan, white, orange, and gray to create a futuristic postmodern shape that even incorporated a layer referencing the rope sole of the espadrille (see page 52). It was the first of many updated and embellished creepers including Miu Miu's patent-leather lace-ups, Asos' "Mackie" platform brogue in silver and blue metallic with a thick rubber sole, and Topshop's "Kingston" tan brogue with a turquoise crepe sole. British designer Ashish teamed up with Underground and released a pair of houndstooth creepers, and black creepers that came with correction fluid for DIY customization. The shoe, once the most countercultural of shapes was having another mainstream moment, precisely because the shape seemed to fit after years of killer heels.

below:

Graffiti creepers (2011)
These leather-studded creepers by Ashish come with a bottle of correction fluid and an instruction booklet of graffiti tips.

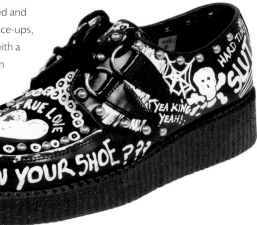

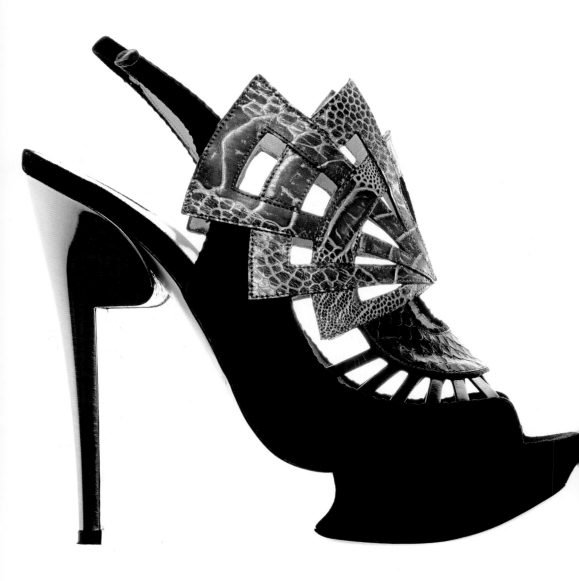

STILETTO

"Stiletto, I look at it more as an attitude as opposed to a high-heeled shoe."

Lita Ford

The stiletto heel is a badge of audacious femininity. It's sleek, sharp, and sexy with an aura of elegant menace—as slender, tapered, and dangerous as the eponymous Sicilian fighting knife after which it was named. The heel's post-war birth was accurately forecast in 1948 when the British trade magazine *Footwear* declared, "the heavy, bulky shoe is definitely OUT." Shoe manufacturers realized that they needed to respond rapidly to the new decade of post-war affluence by making a shoe that could stimulate demand after wartime stagnation and the ubiquity of the wedge. The race was on: who could create an elegant, modernist shoe, one fitting for a new age and fashion expectations of women that had been dormant for so long?

Clothing styles in the late 1940s and early 1950s began to re-emphasize the traditional female figure that had been lost with the masculinized wide-shouldered shape of the 1940s. Christian Dior's New Look incorporated tailoring techniques that emphasized the bust, waist, and hips and needed an accompanying shoe that complemented the silhouette. Footwear manufacturers debated "whether heels should reach a new extremity of height or a new low; which is the most flattering line for the ankle and interprets best the revival of flourishing femininity?" Roger Vivier was on hand and became pivotal in the development of the tapered heel. Known as the Fabergé of Footwear, Vivier created tailored shoes for Dior that were pure haute couture; elegantly exclusive and beloved by stars such as Grace Kelly and the Empress of Iran who ordered 100 pairs per year. At the age of seventeen, Vivier had worked on the floor of a shoe factory, giving him the advantage, he said, of "being able to discover the basics empirically, forms that are as old as the world itself, which I subsequently combined and presented in my own way." Together with his study of sculpture at the Ecole

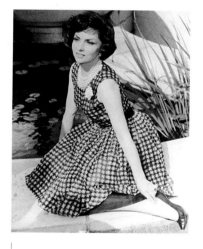

above:

Made in Italy
Film star Gina Lollobrigida embodies *la dolce vita* with her New-Look silhouette and stiletto heels in 1959.

left:

Balancing act
Nicholas Kirkwood's "Python Web Suede" sandal with cut-out open toe, python web vamp, and killer heel.

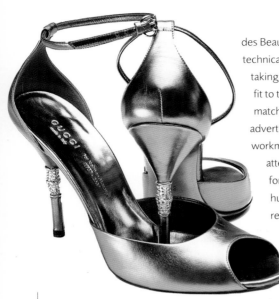

Birthday shoes

Bronze peep-toe, ankle-strap shoes
by Gucci with rhinestone-embedded
stiletto heels, designed for the
brand's ninetieth anniversary.

des Beaux Arts, Vivier had a combination of both aesthetic and
technical skills that allowed experimentation in heel design. By
taking the basic pump and cutting curves into the vamps so as to
fit to the foot more closely, Vivier created a shoe tailoring that
matched that used in Dior's couture designs and was reflected in
advertising that stressed the shoe designer's "perfection of fit and
workmanship." Heels were sculpted into a variety of increasingly
attenuated shapes, but Vivier was clear on never sacrificing
form for comfort, saying: "I have revised my designs five
hundred times to test whether an idea is right and whether it
respects the arch of the foot." In 1953, an advert for Vivier's
shoes in American *Vogue* asked the viewer to look beyond
the design to understand the ergonomics of the finished
product, showing the shoe in conjunction with
precision tools. The text ran: "Now study the heel!
It announces an entirely new principle—the heel
moved forward, where it carries the body's weight better."

Vivier's heels became increasingly attenuated, and by 1952, he
had created the classic stiletto shoe—a pump shape with a pointed
toe and a four-inch tapered heel. In July of that year, American *Vogue*
was using the term "stiletto" and designers Charles Jourdan, Herbert
Delman, Salvatore Ferragamo, and André Perugia experimented
with thinner heels. Vivier's shoes were the height of luxury, akin
to boudoir slippers and afforded by the few. They were certainly
not meant to be durable—fashion historian Mary Trasko writes of
one woman "who once purchased a pair of Vivier's rapturously
embroidered, very steep stiletto pumps. She returned the following
day with the beadwork slightly torn, complaining that the shoes were
uncomfortable. After examining the soles, the manager responded—
'But Madame, you walked in these shoes.'"

Those who attempted to walk in the new heel found it did present
a few problems. In 1953, *Picture Post* warned of the disadvantages
of the innovative heel "which has just reached London, at last, from
Paris." In "The Hazards of the Stiletto Heel," an English model tried a
pair out on the streets of London and was photographed getting her
heel caught in a drain cover, twisting her ankle, and tripping over in
a rather ungainly fashion. Her shoe heels still appear to be relatively
thick, though, and this was one of the fundamental problems in
the development of the stiletto; how could the heel be kept high,

thin, and weight bearing? Vivier's early designs relied on wood, the traditional material used for heel construction, and the thinner the heel the more likely it was to snap at an inopportune moment. French designer Charles Jordan (not to be confused with Jourdan) had the foresight to use a metal rod in the heel of his shoes, and in the UK Mehmet Kurdash at Gina shoes was using Hollis wooden heels with an aluminum spigot that reached from the heel tip to the body of the shoe, and then encased the whole heel in leather as early as 1954.

In 1956, a breakthrough occurred when a new heel was exhibited at an Italian trade fair with a metal spigot in a plastic heel shell that prevented breakage. With this design, heels could be ultra-thin but perfectly reliable, less prone to snapping, and a five-inch heel became industry standard by the end of the 1950s. Injection molding meant that the cheap and durable plastic heels could be produced in vast numbers by 1957. Italy became the established center of directional shoe design, and from the mid-1950s onward, fashionable footwear had to have a "Made in Italy" label. Even Gina, a success in its own right, used Italian references to associate its stilettos with the quality Italian footwear. Gina was named after Italian screen legend Gina Lollobrigida and inside every shoe the firm placed a griffe that read "Inspirazione Italiana," despite their being an entirely British design and production outfit. Vivier responded with the reinforced steel *talon aiguille* or "needle heel" in 1955, and Ferragamo's heels hit their most teetering heights between 1958 and 1959. Shoe manufacturers in other countries followed suit including Bally of Switzerland, Russell & Bromley, and Rayne in the UK, and Delman, Kinney Shoes, and Julianelli in New York.

Hollywood stars loved the Italian stiletto such as Marilyn Monroe, who had forty pairs of Ferragamos with a quarter of an inch cut off one heel of each pair so that she wiggled when she walked. The piercing, penetrating nature of the new heel was also beginning to cause a disturbance wherever it roamed, damaging floors and the feet of others, sparking outrage and moral panic. In 1962, for instance, the British National Coal Board announced the "end of the stiletto vendetta" to advertise its new Armourtile flooring with the capacity to resist "the trail of destruction left in the fashionable wake of women. One ton of female—the average impact of the stiletto heel is the lacerating, splintering,

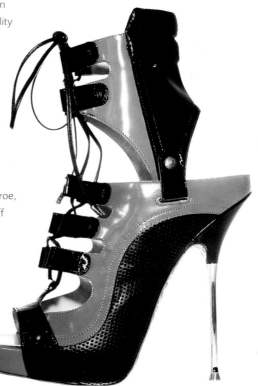

below:
To the point
Galliano gladiator shoe-boot in nude and black with an exaggerated needle heel.

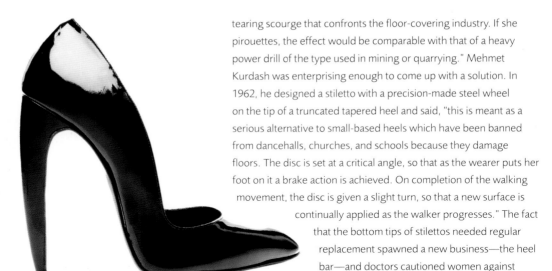

Moltissimo (Fall/Winter 2011)
An implicit threat seems to lurk in the weaponlike profile of this shoe by Walter Steiger.

tearing scourge that confronts the floor-covering industry. If she pirouettes, the effect would be comparable with that of a heavy power drill of the type used in mining or quarrying." Mehmet Kurdash was enterprising enough to come up with a solution. In 1962, he designed a stiletto with a precision-made steel wheel on the tip of a truncated tapered heel and said, "this is meant as a serious alternative to small-based heels which have been banned from dancehalls, churches, and schools because they damage floors. The disc is set at a critical angle, so that as the wearer puts her foot on it a brake action is achieved. On completion of the walking movement, the disc is given a slight turn, so that a new surface is continually applied as the walker progresses." The fact that the bottom tips of stilettos needed regular replacement spawned a new business—the heel bar—and doctors cautioned women against damaging their feet, backs, and posture.

By the late 1950s, the stiletto was being worn by stars who had a reputation for being rather risqué, famed for their lurid lives off screen—women such as Marilyn Monroe, Ava Gardner, and Diana Dors, who were clearly transgressing the codes of respectable domestic femininity. For many women, these shining stars showed them a new identity that was glamorous with a hint of danger, far removed from that of their mothers. Through consuming commodities such as the stiletto, women could stand out from an older generation. By 1959, the stiletto had reached its most extreme height—six inches of sharpened steel with a plastic-coated tip. The impracticality of the aggressively modern heel was a clear sign of open resistance by young women, who were challenging traditional roles by wearing such a sexy shoe by day as well as night—this was a shoe for girls who walked on the wild side. At the end of the decade, the lines were beginning to be drawn on the meaning of the stiletto—an argument that still rumbles on today. Did the needle heel subjugate women? Or were wearers openly revisiting their roles as domestic drudges? The stiletto's role as a rite of passage from girlitude to womanhood was clear, thus it could be seen to represent an emergence into a world of feminine power, albeit a conservative one based around fashionable consumption. But at the same time, needle heels were uncomfortable, physically restricting, and bad for the feet.

By the mid-1960s, the stiletto had had its day, being replaced by the new flats that suited the liberated, androgynous image of young women. The stiletto went underground, emerging by the late 1970s stronger, leaner, and faster than ever before. Terry de Havilland revived the heel for fashion designer Zandra Rhodes and it began to grace the pages of French *Vogue* and the disco floor of Studio 54 in New York. Punk women made the heel a symbol of defiance, inventing a powerful femininity that was to resurface as "girl power" in the 1990s, and the mod revival of the early 1980s caused a renaissance of the white stiletto shoe—in 1987, UK shoe manufacturer Dolcis sold 260,000 pairs and their popularity spawned the stereotype of the "bimbo," who danced around her handbag at the local club.

In the 2000s, the stiletto became a high-fashion must-have once again as well as a badge of status, authority, and sex appeal. The term "stiletto feminist" was coined by American lifestyle magazine *George*, founded by the late John F. Kennedy, Jr. in 2000, to describe a woman who "embraces easy expressions of sexuality that enhance, rather than detract from, women's freedom." The renaissance of the stiletto appeared to be mirroring women's feelings of sexual freedom and power as seen on screen in the character of Carrie Bradshaw of *Sex and the City* fame. First aired in 1998, the TV series showed four successful and independent career women working and playing hard. In one episode styled by Patricia Field, Carrie prizes her pink suede stilettos so highly that while being mugged she cries "You can take my Fendi baguette; you can take my watch, but don't take my Manolos. I got them half price in a sample sale!" Designed by Manolo Blahnik, Jimmy Choo, Sergio Rossi, Gina, Cesare Paciotti, and Christian Louboutin, the stiletto lives on, now no longer a killer heel but a symbol of celebrity culture. It can be an object of pure sexuality in the hands of Walter Steiger when designed to be vertiginously high in leopard-print (Fall/Winter 2009), bejeweled frippery by Jimmy Choo, or seriously avant-garde by Nicholas Kirkwood. It can even embody the animal-rights ethics of Stella McCartney, whose vegetarian stilettos removed eco-fashion from the worthy to the erotic.

below:

Color pop (Fall/Winter 2011)
In 1990, the Gucci Group bought out Sergio Rossi, and Edmund Castillo took over as design director in 2006.

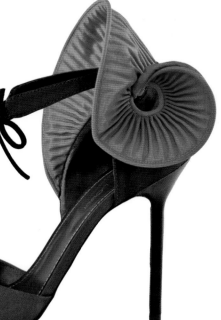

SPRINGOLATOR MULE

The mule moved out of the boudoir in the 1950s when taken up as the uniform of the Sweater Girl, whose sexy style comprised a tight pencil skirt and sweater fitted snugly to show off a pneumatic embonpoint created by a whirlpool-stitched, cone-cupped bra. The shoe of choice to accompany this look was the mule as worn by bombshell Marilyn Monroe in *The Seven Year Itch* (1955), Mamie van Doren in *High School Confidential* (1958), and Jayne Mansfield who was consistently photographed both on and off screen in a pair of spike-heeled mules. Once the spike heel was attached to the backless mule there were a few design deficiencies, since the steep

> "Almost every woman is not only conscious of her feet, but sex conscious about them."
>
> André Perugia

incline of the shoe and the almost completely cutaway upper meant they were impossible to keep on, particularly when one was wearing stockings. The mule also made loud slapping sounds when it hit the floor and could unexpectedly flip off.

The solution was the springolator, invented by Maxwell Sachs in 1954, an elastic and leather insert that ran under the ball of the foot. Beth Levine was the first footwear designer to use this device on a mule—it kept the sole under tension and pushed up from below to keep the feet in firm contact with the mule's strap when walking. Levine's black silk-crepe springolator mule was called the "Magnet" because it gripped to the foot as if magnetized and was described by *Glamour* magazine as "the next thing to no shoe at all." At one shoe convention, Levine sprinted across the lobby in springolators to show buyers that they really worked, and throughout the 1950s and 1960s, mule manufacturers were galvanized into using it. Frederick's of Hollywood launched the "Springolator

Bareback" mule in zebra print and transparent Lucite studded with rhinestones and it was bought by pin-up Bettie Page and film star Cyd Charisse. By the end of the 1950s, the springolator mule was undoubtedly the sexiest shoe on the block, worn in bedrooms, bars, and bordellos. Pulp writer Al Dewlen in *The Bone Pickers* (1958) described a typical springolator wearer as "blatant and wenchy," because when walking "as each springolator touched down the resulting small shocks put motion in her breasts."

The added expense of inserting the springolator into shoes meant they fell from fashion by the late 1960s; the innovation was also less necessary as it became permissible for women to wear backless shoes with bare legs and feet so the shoes were easier to keep on. Terry de Havilland revived the style in the 1980s after having seen it used in his father's shoe factory, liking the way it allowed women to walk "without having to claw up their toes" in high backless shoes. His Glitter and Twisted range of 2003 featured the "Sugar Plum Leyla" in silver, green, and fuchsia-pink brocade with a tassel hanging from the back and the "Zap Pow" of 2006, inspired by Pop artist Roy Lichtenstein, and the Fiorelli were all contemporary versions of 1950s springolator mules. In high fashion, the springolator sashayed down the runway in Dior's Spring/Summer 2001 Trailer Park collection alongside cropped minis with visible zips and burnt orange-and-black fishnets with visible holes in an ironic defiance of good taste, but despite these incarnations, the shoe has never retained its mainstream position. Its overtly sexual appeal remains however, not least because it is popular with exotic dancers.

below:

Legendary legs

Cyd Charisse, owner of reputedly the most beautiful legs in Hollywood, shows them off in springolator mules.

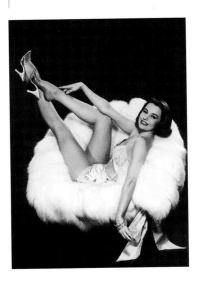

KITTEN HEEL

right:

Fierce kittens

Christian Louboutin refines the kitten heel down to two vicious spikes, belying its cute reputation.

below:

French kittens

Lanvin's gray and candy-pink ankle-strap kitten heels are an exercise in graphic lines.

The kitten heel or *petit stiletto* was originally a teenage "starter" heel invented in the 1950s for the budding stiletto wearer, because the sexually provocative connotations of the full-blown stiletto were considered inappropriate for an adolescent. The heel must be less than two inches to qualify as a true kitten, with a nuanced curve setting the heel slightly in from the edge of the shoe. Audrey Hepburn wore kitten heels in both *Sabrina* (1954) and *Funny Face* (1957), movies in which she appeared as an innocent young woman in a romantic affair with a much older man—the choice of shoes was a styling device to emphasize the age gap.

> "I still have my feet on the ground,
> I just wear better shoes."
>
> Oprah Winfrey

In 1957, Sébastien Massaro designed a simple slingback beige kid pump for Chanel with a black patent leather toe-cap and a low, thick heel for the couture enthusiast who found the high stiletto heel a little too much. Shoe manufacturers took Massaro's shape and added a kitten heel in the early 1960s—it became a teenage classic and was worn by Jean Shrimpton in many of the classic fashion photographs taken by David Bailey for British *Vogue* in that decade.

In the early 1960s, kitten heels gained a pointed winklepicker toe and were popularized by Brigitte Bardot; by the minimalist 1990s, Kate Moss was spotted at Cannes in 1997 with Johnny Depp on her arm and strappy kitten heels on her feet. Today the kitten heel is considered a grown-up shoe, and a strategic shape for women who want to remain heel-shod while not towering over shorter consorts—they are a particular favorite of the politician's wife, for instance. Carla Bruni-Sarkozy wears

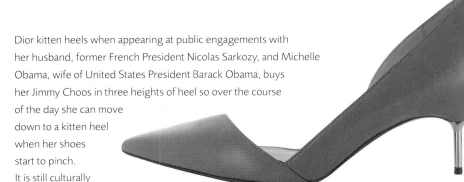

Dior kitten heels when appearing at public engagements with her husband, former French President Nicolas Sarkozy, and Michelle Obama, wife of United States President Barack Obama, buys her Jimmy Choos in three heights of heel so over the course of the day she can move down to a kitten heel when her shoes start to pinch. It is still culturally unacceptable for the wife of a powerful man to be taller than him. As psychologist Rita Freedman explains: "Size and strength influence social power. To stand above confers an inherent power advantage. Big females and little males are socially mismatched." Thus, although they were equal in height, for their engagement photos in 1981, Prince Charles stood one step above Lady Diana Spencer to create the illusion of being the dominant male and she wore kitten heels.

Designer L.K. Bennett who opened her first shop in 1990 after studying at Cordwainers College, London, and working for Robert Clergerie, has been dubbed "Queen of the Kitten Heel." She believes they work as a practical form of footwear because they are "glamorous but at a comfortable height." In 2011, after a decade of skyscraper heels, fashion journalists began to announce the return of the kitten heel (although it had never really gone away). Louboutin launched the "Newton" kitten heel in red or beige suede; Valentino a studded leopard-print; Lanvin, an ankle-strap design in bubblegum pink, and Stuart Vevers designed crystal bedecked versions for Loewe.

In 2012, the UK's Home Secretary Theresa May, a politician and well-known lover of kitten heels, hit the headlines when her heel got stuck in a crack between the paving stones outside 10 Downing Street, London, in full view of the paparazzi. She removed her shoe, pulled it free, and trotted gamely on.

below:

Audrey in kittens

Hepburn's style as Holly Golightly in *Breakfast at Tiffany's* (1961) has become a template for modern chic.

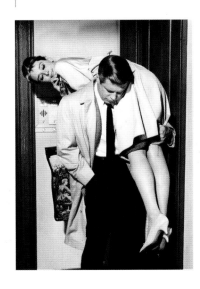

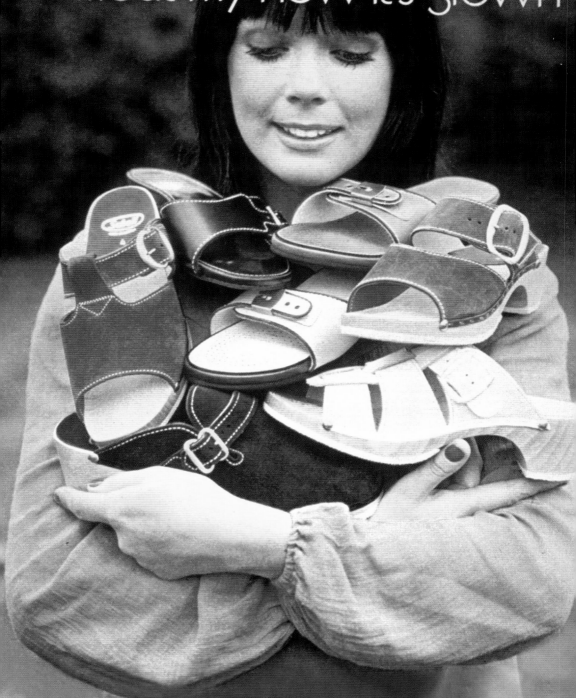

...but my how it's grown

EXERCISE SANDAL

> "I'm struggling with the etiquette on when, where, and how
> a girl makes the switch from fitness shoe to shoe-for-show."
>
> Polly Vernon, *The Guardian*, May 16, 2010

Feet are the body's shock absorbers because they are first point of contact with the ground, and exercise sandals are designed to cushion the initial impact. This is a foot-friendly shoe and, according to its advocates, has the ability to improve health and well-being as opposed to a high-heeled shoe that can damage the back and feet and tighten and shorten the ligaments in the legs. Dr Scholl's sandals were the first in the genre, launched in 1958 with a contoured cedarwood sole and a leather upper in the form of a buckled strap. Scholl was originally founded in 1906 by William Mathias Scholl in Chicago, Illinois, after he had worked for shoe retailer Ruppert's in Chicago. Scholl discovered that many customers had problems with their feet and realized there was money to be made from footcare. Scholl sold shoes by day and at night took evening classes in podiatry at the Illinois Medical School, graduating in 1904 as a fully fledged podiatrist. Scholl's first patented invention was Foot-Eazer, a form of arch support, in 1904, the first of many foot-related inventions sold through the Scholl company, including cushion insoles, anti-corn pads, and contemporary foot gels. The first Scholl retail outlet opened in London in 1913.

The wooden Scholl exercise sandal was developed by his son, William, when in Germany after the Second World War he had seen a vernacular folksy wooden shoe. He adapted the design for the American market by adding a brightly colored leather buckled strap to the natural wood of the sandal, but most crucially, a raised toe crest and contoured sole to encourage the feet to grip and flex when walking. It was marketed in 1959 as the "Original Exercise Sandal" with the unique selling point of toning up the muscles of the leg. As luck would have it, more and more focus was being attached to that specific area of the body as skirts grew ever shorter. Fashion designer

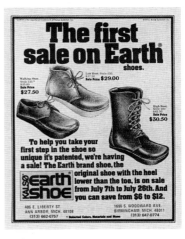

above:

Right on

The Earth Shoe, originally developed in 1957, became associated with environmental protest.

left:

Haute hippie

Dr. Scholl's exercise sandals had the right credentials for hippie chic, as this 1970s magazine advertisement shows.

John Bate's invention of the miniskirt made women rush for the Scholl in the hope that it would give them a pair of perfect pins. The sandal was a massive success, especially after being seen on the feet of the decade's style icons, models Jean Shrimpton and Twiggy. By the 1970s, this orthopedic shoe had made its way into fashion and was worn by many women for style rather than function.

Two other classics in exercise footwear are the Earth Shoe and MBT. The former was invented by Anne Kalso, a native of the Faroe Islands and a lifelong practitioner of yoga. In 1957, after studying in Santos, Brazil, Kalso became fascinated by the perfect posture of indigenous Brazilians and began observing the footprints left by their bare feet on the beach. She realized that when walking on wet sand, the heels naturally dug in deeper than the toes, mirroring a well-known yoga position, the Tadasana or "mountain" pose. On her return to Denmark, Kalso began to develop the Kalso shoe, a process that would take ten years, during which she thoroughly tested prototype shoes on extreme hundred-mile hikes. The Kalso shoe was straightforward—it reinvented walking by shifting the weight of the body through the metatarsals, away from the ball of the foot to the heel, by making the heel lower than the raised toes. The wearer was forced to walk with the heel down first in the manner of walking on sand, a method of mobility that was said by the inventor to realign the body to its correct natural posture. The first Kalso shoes were sold in Copenhagen in 1957 and the word went out from enthusiastic wearers that it helped with breathing, posture, and cured backache and painful feet.

April 1970 would mark the much-heralded opening of the first United States distribution point for Kalso's shoes, which were marketed under license by Raymond and Eleanor Jacobs. The couple had a brainwave when it came to publicizing the shoe Stateside. The opening of their New York retail outlet coincided with the world's first Earth Day, a day instigated by Senator Gaylord Nelson to put the environment into the political limelight. A full five months before Earth Day, on Sunday November 30, 1969, the *New York Times* reported on the increasing rise of grass-roots activity: "Rising concern about the environmental crisis is sweeping the nation's campuses with an intensity

right:

Granny chic

Actress Maggie Gyllenhaal wears the German orthopedic Worishofer sandal at the outset of the "granny chic" trend in 2010.

below:

Ugly beautiful

The Worishofer, a perforated leather sandal with a low cork wedge, became a "faux irony" fad alongside the Croc in the 2010s.

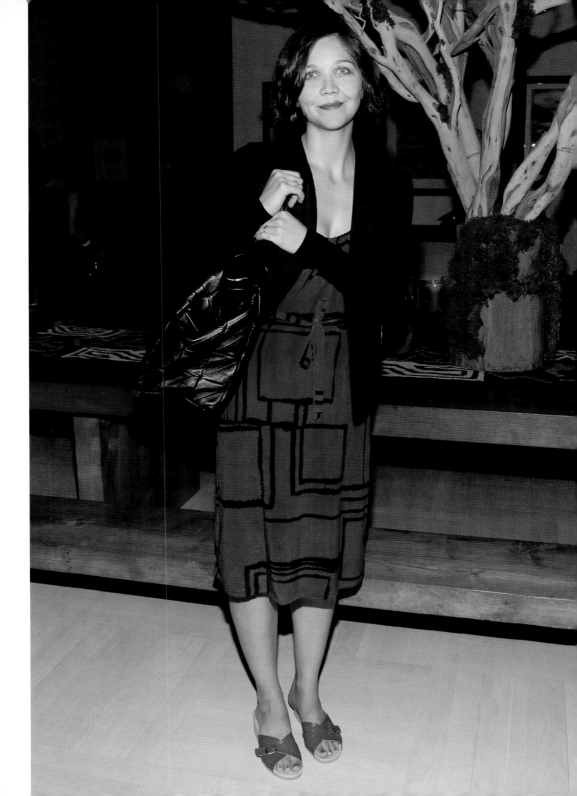

above:

Metallic strap

The classic Dr. Scholl's exercise sandal, with adjustable leather strap featuring a suede-lined padded backing for comfort and fit.

that may be on its way to eclipsing student discontent over the war in Vietnam... a national day of observance of environmental problems... is being planned for next spring... when a nationwide environmental 'teach-in'... coordinated from the office of Senator Gaylord Nelson is planned." Twenty million people are said to have participated and some of those crowds of environmental protesters were milling around Jacobs' shoe store. To capture such a willing audience, the couple capitalized on the wholesome back-to-nature hippie credentials of the shoe with "negative heel technology." Its name was instantly changed to Earth Shoe, the start of a multimillion dollar success. The shoe became available in a variety of styles from the initial shoe through to sandals, clogs, and fleece-lined ankle-boots, with sales peaking in 1974. The bubble burst in 1977 when the company filed for bankruptcy and the Earth Shoe disappeared, its flanged, boxy shape reviled as all that was bad about 1970s shoe design when dubbed the "Cornish pasty," because of its resemblance to a traditional British form of meat pie. The shoe with a social conscience was back on the radar in the 2000s however, as its anti-fashion stance appears refreshing in an age of anti-capitalist protest and increasing concern for the welfare of the world. After an avid fanbase for vintage pairs grew in the late 1990s, the Earth Shoe was relaunched with some success by Earth Inc. in 2001.

The MBT—an acronym for Masai Barefoot Technology—was innovated by Swiss engineer Karl Müller in 1990, who suffered from years of chronic back and leg pain. His inspiration came from the practice of the agile Masai people of Africa of walking great distances over rough terrain in their bare feet; they appeared to suffer none of the back and foot problems of the developed world. Muller believed the solution was to completely change the way he walked by developing a shoe with a sole that would force more natural movement—essentially a rolling front-to-back action. He took the negative heel technology of the Earth Shoe a step forward by using a thick, curved sole that forced the foot to move naturally while cushioning the joints. When walking in MBTs, the ground no longer feels flat and stable, so the body has to compensate. Muller explains, "The key to the function of MBTs is the curved sole construction. Its integrated balancing area requires an active and controlled rolling movement and can help the body to improve balance and posture while standing and walking." The calorie-busting propensity of the shoe was another marketing tactic that worked in the body-conscious 2000s—walking in an MBT burned more calories while helping tone up the bottom and thighs.

In the 2000s, the exercise sandal has made an astounding rebirth in the form of the FitFlop. Beauty therapist and entrepreneur Marcia Kilgore developed the FitFlop in 2007 as an exercise sandal that gave legs a workout when walking as a result of the patented Microwobbleboard positioned in the mid-sole, which acts as a shock absorber. The thick, curved sole of the FitFlop floats the foot over the board making walking more of a toning exercise for the legs and bottom and improving blood flow to the feet. Marketed as "the shoe with a built-in gym," the FitFlop tuned into the body consciousness of the time, and the success of the brand was also helped by the design, which managed to combine function with glamor. The FitFlop had fashion focus with its sequined strap; other designs included a gladiator FitFlop; metallic snowboots; knee-high Inuks and a limited-edition Liberty-print version of the original exercise sandal. It became an alternative to the extreme high heel, a type of shoe that left Kilgore unimpressed: "A smart shoe that doesn't terrorize your body is absolutely the most fashionable. Low energy levels, an aching back... what's beautiful about that? I love men, but I'm not going to be uncomfortable for them."

The buyer should beware though, for the exercise benefits of the exercise sandal or shoe may be negligible. In 2011, Reebok was forced by the Federal Trade Commission of America to pay $25 million USD to customers who bought their Easytone trainer—shoes that apparently made the wearer fit without them having to do any exercise. "The FTC wants national advertisers to understand that they must exercise some responsibility and ensure that their claims for fitness gear are supported by sound science," said David Vladeck, Director of the FTC's Bureau of Consumer Protection.

below:
Getting physical
The FitFlop sandal is biomechanically engineered to help tone and tighten your leg muscles when you walk.

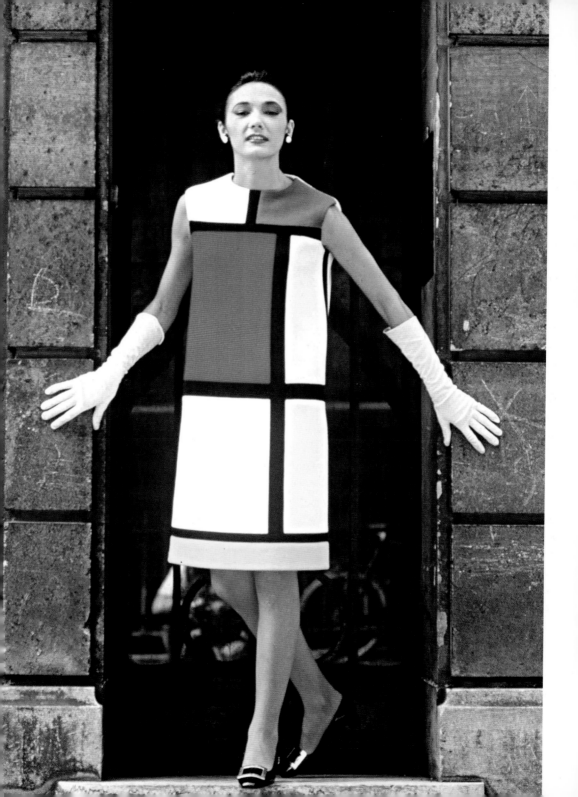

PILGRIM PUMP

"To wear dreams on one's feet is to begin to give reality to one's dreams."

Roger Vivier

In the early 1960s, both shoes and fashion began to morph into a brand new shape. As cultural historian Elizabeth Wilson wrote in her *Memoirs of an Anti-Heroine* (1986): "The fifties had been so sinful, so old. In my twenty-first birthday photograph my dark lips, vaselined lids, tightly waved hair, stiff black dress, and pearl necklace age me poignantly; by the time I reach thirty I'm dressed like a Kate Greenaway child in white stockings, flat shoes, and high waisted dresses, with my cropped hair I look about twelve years old."

Skirts were getting shorter following the raised hemlines of Mary Quant's designs shown at her King's Road boutique in London, Bazaar, from 1955 onward, and following her cues, the womanly curves of the 1950s were supplanted by a cool look of youthful androgyny, perhaps best exemplified by the pre-adolescent body of top model Twiggy. Sartorial references to adulthood such as hats, gloves, and high heels were energetically rejected and girlishness pervaded mainstream fashion—all schoolgirl pinafores and button-bar Mary Janes from Anello & Davide. On March 3, 1961, *Time* magazine begged the question "Is the winklepicker on the way out?" The article ran, "in Manhattan shoe salons last week, style setters and trend diviners were claiming that the pointed-toe look was slowly becoming old shoe. Offering blessed relief to women, who for five years have painfully squeezed their feet into narrow, stiletto-heeled, pointed-toe shoes, is the radically different 'chisel toe' look—long flattened square-toed shoes."

The chisel toe operated as fashion often does, from the position of polar opposition. It seemed almost as if the pointed toe had reached the absolute limits of its exaggerated dimensions and fashion's logic could only accept a shoe that was radically different. Shoe toes became blunt and square or elegantly chiseled and could be seen

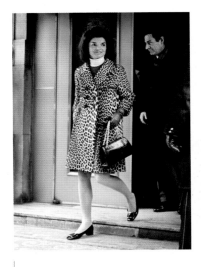

above:

Rive gauche shoe

Jackie Kennedy looking stylish in Roger Vivier's original shiny Corfam "Pilgrim Pump" in the 1960s.

left:

Fashionably flat

Yves Saint Laurent commissioned Roger Vivier to create a simple, flat shoe to accompany his graphic 1960s clothes, such as the Mondrian dress.

on the feet of the post-war dandy—the mod—in the form of the Chelsea boot (see page 140). An elongated squared-off toe had, of course, existed in footwear before, most notably in the second half of the seventeenth century—being dubbed "square toes" or "square" dates from the eighteenth century when such shoes had become desperately outmoded.

Fast forward to the early 1960s and Roger Vivier, closely followed by Edward Rayne and Capezio, showed modified blunt toes in their collections and had gained fans as prestigious as Queen Elizabeth II, Marlene Dietrich, and Jackie Kennedy. In 1963, Vivier launched his own boutique at 24 rue Francois 1st, where his latest experimental shoe shapes were sold, including the most copied design of the 1960s, the "Pilgrim Pump."

> "He is very middle-of-the-road French, very Pied-Noir, very provincial."
>
> Karl Lagerfeld on Yves Saint Laurent, 1984

This iconic example of footwear design had been born out of the mindset of Parisian couturier Yves Saint Laurent who had developed an obsession with the work of Dutch De Stijl artist Piet Mondrian. Mondrian was a pioneer of abstraction whose primary-colored paintings with an interlocking gridwork of horizontal and vertical lines had anticipated the monochromatic minimalism of the Op movement that was proving popular in the 1960s. On August 2, 1965, YSL showed a series of wool-jersey shift dresses that became physical canvases using an aesthetic lifted from the great Dutch painter. Prior to the launch, Saint Laurent asked Vivier to design shoes to accompany the graphic outfits and he came up with a flat pump with a square tapered toe and low stacked heel with a body made out of a new form of artificial leather called Corfam. By deliberately choosing such a slick, shiny plastic rather than the more expensive leather, Vivier was placing the shoe firmly in a new decade, when manmade material was being marketed as luxurious and space-age rather than cheap and nasty.

The focal point of the shoe was a large silver buckle that covered the front of the foot, a modern interpretation of the buckles worn

below:

Pumped-up pilgrim

The modern incarnation of the Vivier "Pilgrim Pump" has a platform and high stiletto heel.

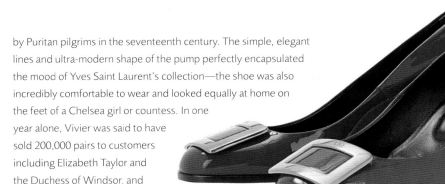

by Puritan pilgrims in the seventeenth century. The simple, elegant lines and ultra-modern shape of the pump perfectly encapsulated the mood of Yves Saint Laurent's collection—the shoe was also incredibly comfortable to wear and looked equally at home on the feet of a Chelsea girl or countess. In one year alone, Vivier was said to have sold 200,000 pairs to customers including Elizabeth Taylor and the Duchess of Windsor, and this nonchalant take on French chic was given a further push with the elegant ennui displayed by Catherine Deneuve in the film *Belle de Jour* (1967), directed by Spanish Surrealist Luis Buñuel. Deneuve's YSL suits and Vivier "Pilgrim Pumps" oozed an icy sophistication that was all the more compelling when worn on her erotic journey of sexual self-discovery as Séverine Serizy, a bored bourgeois housewife-turned-prostitute. The "Pilgrim Pump" went on to become the most imitated shoe of the decade. As skirts shortened and the leg grew ever more visible, the low-heeled Pilgrim Pump also helped reduce the overt eroticism of the 1960s look, turning it away from seduction into something more youthful and sporty.

above:

Pilgrim heel
Red leather Cuban-heeled "Pilgrim Pump" by Vivier, a chic city classic derived from the 1960s original.

The shoe also suited the increased popularity of trousers for women, one of the reasons why it made such a comeback in the 1980s when women wanted an appropriate look for the executive arena that was becoming increasingly open to them. In the 1960s, many pumps were made in shiny patent leather, and the red, white, and blue of the Union Jack, now a symbol of Swinging London, was a particularly popular color combination—Bruno Magli created a pair out of red "wet look" vinyl during this decade and Courrèges went one step further by substituting the metal buckle with large bells in 1969. Authentic Vivier pumps were expensive so teenagers sourced their pumps from cheaper manufacturers of chisel-toed flat shoes, such as Craddock-Terry of Virginia, United States.

The Pilgrim Pump has now aged with the first generation that wore it and is considered the most stuffy of shoes—if a woman wants to wear flats, she will turn to a ballet pump or loafer rather than a black patent Pilgrim. Yet the Chanel suit, an equally bourgeois mode of apparel, was successfully relaunched to young fashionistas—so why not Vivier's so-elegant shoe?

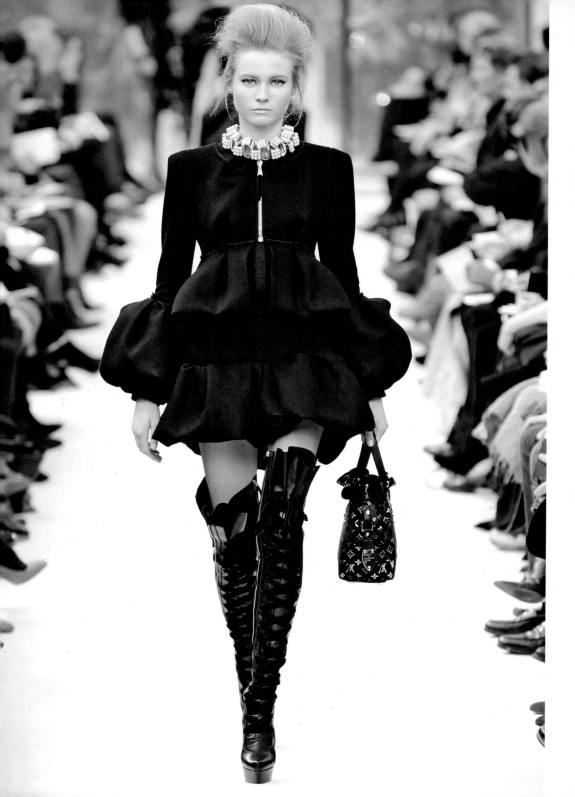

KINKY BOOT

"There are twenty million women wearing kinky boots, kinky boots... /Footwear manufacturers are gathering the fruits... "

John Steed, "Kinky Boots," 1964

January 1962, and British fashion photographer David Bailey landed his first overseas assignment, a feature for British *Vogue* commissioned by fashion editor Lady Clare Rendlesham entitled "New York: Young Idea Goes West." Taking the trip alongside him was nineteen-year-old model, muse, and girlfriend Jean Shrimpton, whose only luggage was a plastic bag, but that wasn't what caused eyebrows to raise. It was Shrimpton's outfit—distinctly provocative, or, in the parlance of the times, downright kinky. She wore black leather from head to toe: a black leather coat, black leather shift dress, and custom-made black boots that laced up the front, in a style that was traditionally associated with the underground world of fetishist sado-masochism (and allegedly specially commissioned by Bailey to wind Rendlesham up after she had forbidden him to wear his trademark black leather jacket).

Shrimpton wasn't the first to make fetish-wear fashion; two years earlier, Yves Saint Laurent had launched the Fall/Winter Beat Collection for Christian Dior with a runway show that paid homage to the beatniks of the Left Bank, Paris. He showed black turtleneck cashmere sweaters, glossy black crocodile-skin jackets lined ostentatiously with mink, and black fur jackets with knitted sleeves. YSL's sexy all-black collection caused a frenzy at the time and alienated Dior's couture customers, but it reflected the changes that were happening in fashion and the fetish element of black leather that was slowly entering into the mainstream. The fashionable kinky look was given a further boost by the publicity surrounding the actress Honor Blackman, who starred in the cult TV series *The Avengers* (1961–69) as Cathy Gale, a leather-suited and booted anthropologist and judo expert. Her wardrobe, designed by Frederick Starke, included black leather hip-length long-sleeved tops with matching

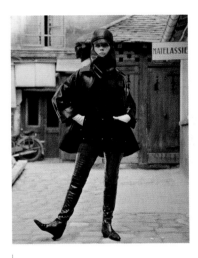

above:
London, 1963
Model Enid Boulting in Yves Saint Laurent's leather jacket, helmet, and thigh-high crocodile boots.

left:
Catwalk kinky (Fall/Winter 2009)
Louis Vuitton kinky boots straight from *The Story of O* with high platforms, lacing, and pleated tops.

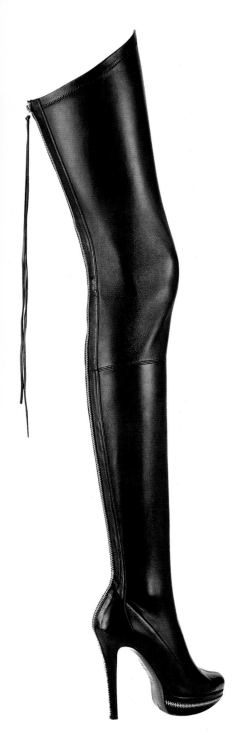

knee-length breeches over black-leather boots, a black-leather coat lined with civet, and an imitation leather floor-length evening gown and cloak that would have had the Marquis de Sade salivating. The subcultural sexual codes embodied in her black-leather outfits were certainly not lost on journalists, who dubbed her "the leather fetishist's pin-up" and commented that "she can look after herself—and the viewer's sado-masochistic fantasies." Blackman's knee-length boots with a low stack heel were designed by Frederick Starke and made by the family firm of Clarks, best known for their desert boot.

Kinky boots such as Starke's usually only appeared in the pages of "specialist" magazines such as *Exotique* magazine published by Leonard Burtman (1955–59), *Bizarre*, run by fetish photographer John Willie (1946–56), and *Fantastique* produced by the Sheba Publishing Company, a magazine for die-hard shoe and boot

> "I'm not a sadist... But comfort is not part of my creative process."
> Christian Louboutin

enthusiasts that served up an exotic array of fetish footwear including extreme platform pumps with ankle-straps and knee-high black leather boots with contrasting white front lacing. In a backlash against Puritanism in a liberated decade that had accepted the sophisticated mores of *Playboy*, kinky boots were blatantly strutting their stuff on British TV. In an issue of the *TV Times* in 1963, journalist John Gough wrote: "Honor Blackman manages to cause a sensation even at showbusiness parties. I saw it happen recently. She had come straight from the studios wearing one of her Mrs. Cathy Gale outfits from *The Avengers*, black leather waistcoat over a black sweater, tight, black leather trousers, and high black leather boots. Aware of the heads turning in her direction, but neither embarrassed by them nor encouraging them, she said, 'I'm told leather drives men up the wall. I like wearing it because it feels nice. Off screen? No, of course I wouldn't go shopping in an outfit like this. Apart from anything else, I find boots are too hot except in wintry weather. At home I usually wear a sweater, shirt, and slacks.' Somebody asked her husband's view of her leather gear. 'He thinks it's fun,' she said, 'He's very well balanced.'" Fashion was prepared to flirt with fetishism, and kinky knee-length boots, black leather coats, and even catsuits began to be seen on TV screens, even at family viewing times. And the naughty origins of the look were acknowledged when black leather boots were christened "kinky," a term that literally meant "not straight" or slightly naughty, rather than a full-on sexual perversion. So blasé were the British public over the kinky boot that in 1964, Blackman and her co-star Patrick MacNee as bowler-hatted Old Etonian John Steed had a top-five hit with the song "Kinky Boots."

Kinky boots of the 1960s were pull-on, calf- or knee-length with pointed toes and stack heels, and made by established designers such as Roger Vivier, who fashioned them from black suede with a center black patent stripe and white kid lining, or footwear chains such as Dolcis and Freeman, Hardy and Willis. As the boot's design became less obviously fetish, the tag disappeared, especially when colors other than black entered into the mix, and the boot with the sexual kink went back underground, overtaken by the spirited go-go (see page 246). Today the term is only used to describe thigh-length dominatrix boots. Red and black patent are the most popular colors with their lascivious hint of the forbidden, and heels are extremely high, lengthening the leg, thus creating a powerful vision of femininity. Firms such as Fantasy Heels sell open-back lace-up thigh boots with a five-inch stiletto heel and the "Heat 3010" thigh boot with electroplated heel and chrome toe-cap with a side zipper and spiked heel. In 2005, the movie *Kinky Boots* premiered, based on the true story of an ailing boot factory in Northampton—Price & Sons Shoes—who were forced into manufacturing fetish boots for transvestites to help the firm stay afloat.

left:

Extreme kinky boots

Black leather thigh-length dominatrix boots are converted into footwear couture by Christian Louboutin.

right:

Vintage kinky boots

1920s button-fetish combos by French bottier Maniatis were the precursor to the 1960s kinky boot.

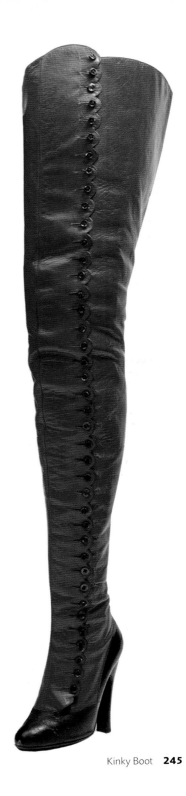

GO-GO BOOT

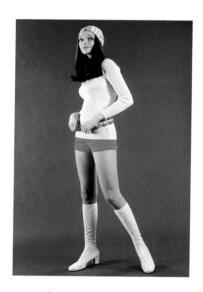

above:

Disco boot
The 1960s go-go boot derived its name from the boots worn by disco dancers at the Whiskey à Go-Go in LA.

In Paris, in 1947, at a club called the Whisky à Go-Go, the discotheque was born. Régine Zyldeberg, "Queen of the Night," laid down a dancefloor surrounded by multicolored lights, threw out the jukebox, and installed two turntables on which she played records alternately so there would be no lulls in the music. The first American version opened in Chicago, Illinois, in 1954, but the concept really caught on in the 1960s when the second Whiskey à Go-Go opened on Sunset Strip, West Hollywood, in 1964. The club showcased a female DJ, Rhonda Lane, who spun vinyl from a suspended cage in which she danced

> "Boots are a more feminine solution—
> and more rational and logical."
>
> André Courrèges

to the music, and thus "go-go" dancing was born. More female dancers were recruited for the club and were given a uniform that consisted of a fringed mini dress and white knee boots, an American version of the flat chisel-toed leather boot that had been introduced by Parisian yé-yé designer André Courrèges in the 1960s when shorter hem lengths had given emphasis to the leg.

For his Moon Girl collection of 1964, Courrèges had faced the future, creating clothes for modern cosmonauts. Models stalked the runway in silver minis, sequined trousers, and dresses with porthole cut-outs filled in with transparent vinyl. The footwear accompanying this space-age look consisted of perfect pairs of pull-on/pull-off flat-heeled glace kid leather boots with a stylish faux bow to the front. Courrèges explained: "It is not logical to walk all day on three-inch heels. Heels are as absurd as the bound feet of ancient Orientals."

The American go-go boot had a pointed or chisel toe, a flat sole or very low heel, and zipped up at either the back or the side. The flatness of the boot was what made it modern—this was clearly not

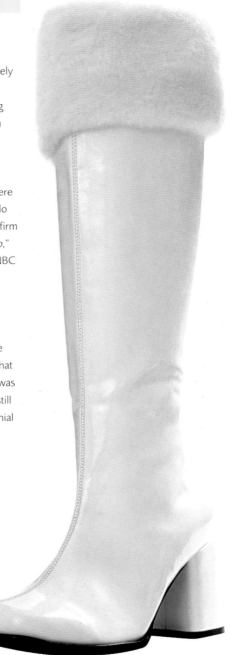

a rugged boot for walking the hills and dales outdoors, it was purely designed for energetic dancing.

After the Whiskey scene was immortalized in the song "Going to à Go-Go" by Smokey Robinson and the Miracles in 1966, from then on, any white leather flat-heeled boot that stopped at calf height was known as a go-go boot. As the decade progressed, they slowly crept up the calf to become knee-length with an elasticized top by the early 1970s. Cheap white-vinyl versions were manufactured all over the world by firms with names such as Golo Boots, College Girl, and Battani, and were sold by the American firm Hi Brow, who marketed them "as worn by the girls on *Hullabaloo*," a television series devoted to pop music that was broadcast by NBC from 1965 to 1966.

The racy image of the mini-skirted dolly bird in white go-go boots invaded fashion imagery and advertising in the late 1960s and became a shorthand for a modern take on old-fashioned "glamour." By the early 1970s, a fake go-go boot was sold on the high street made up of a fake white "wet-look" knee-high sock that could be worn with a pair of white shoes to create a boot—this was unsurprisingly a rather short-lived fad. Today the go-go boot is still worn by female performers such as cheerleaders and is a perennial favorite for dressing up in 1960s or early 1970s style.

right:
Going to à Go-Go
White wet-look go-go boot with a faux-fur cuff, chisel toe, and stacked heel.

MOON BOOT

Space-age styling really took off in the 1960s. André Courrèges, Paco Rabanne, and Pierre Cardin laid down the gauntlet to London's Carnaby Street, a street that together with the King's Road had been dominating the fashion headlines as the epicenter of all things "swinging." Couture needed to rebrand itself; it was considered stuffy and outdated. The solution was a Gallic vision of the future in which female cosmonauts wore silver wigs, white shifts, and huge aluminum neck-pieces.

In 1969, the first men landed on the moon in their distinctive spacesuits—outfits that bore little relation to the futuristic fantasies

> "There is a massive energy on fur—it is all about fur."
>
> Tom Berry of Technica on the 2012 Moon Boot trends

of the Parisian catwalk, and a young Italian designer, Giancarlo Zanatta of Montebelluna, Italy, was inspired. He was based in a place of great significance to footwear because Montebelluna had established the reputation as being the center of production of ski boots in the late nineteenth century, when many of the companies that began to industrially produce them were established, including Tecnica (1890), Dolomite (1897), and Alpina (1908). During the 1960s, many of the firms began to modify the ski boot; a metal lever was introduced as a fastening device instead of laces to give the boot better waterproofing, and an innovative injection-molded plastic boot was a global success. Many firms began to diversify into different products, including the après-ski boot. Zanatta created the most famous—he took the look of the American astronauts' boots and created a fashionable alternative for the snow in brightly colored nylon and polyurethane foam with a rubber outsole and cellular rubber

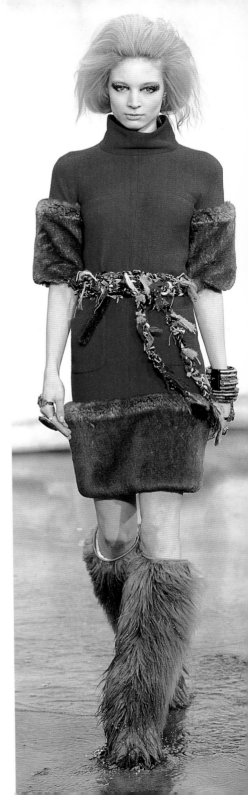

midsole. There was no distinction between left and right and the boot was closed around the top with a lacing. When manufactured by the Tecnica Group in 1970 the Moon Boot was born, and trademarked by 1978.

The soft-shell calf-high boot looked a little in silhouette like a Wellington (see page 124), Inuit, or Valenki (see page 116) boot and itself had many imitators, but that didn't stop Tecnica selling 22 million pairs. In 2000, the Louvre in Paris included the Moon Boot in an exhibition of 100 significant symbols of twentieth-century design. The Moon Boot's insulation and fashionability made it a favorite for après-ski—in 1985, one fashion journalist wrote: "Let's not overlook the significance of after-ski boots. The lodge, after all, is where the heavy-duty socializing takes place and you wouldn't want to be caught in your slippers. Fera Moon Boots with Velcro buckles are the thing. With their fleece lining and rubber bottom with a treaded sole the boots are equally popular with both sexes." The Moon Boot also had a derivative by this time—the yeti boot made of goat hair or rabbit fur. It hit the disco floors of the 1970s and then bizarrely reappeared on the feet of *Baywatch*'s swimsuit-clad Pamela Anderson in the 1990s. In 2010, Chanel launched a deluxe faux-fur pair with a transparent plastic heel to mimic the look of an icicle.

left:

"Drop Boot" (Fall/Winter 2011)
Moon Boot nylon ankle boot, with round toe, rubber sole, and fastened with three loop laces and a Velcro strap.

right:

High-fashion yeti
In 2010, Chanel launched a deluxe faux-fur yeti boot with a transparent heel to mimic the look of an icicle.

CONE HEEL

right:

Lightning flash

Former model Maud Frizon invented the cone heel, so called because of its resemblance to an ice-cream cone.

below:

Linear cone

Oscar de la Renta reduces the cone heel to a simple linear silhouette in this monochrome ankle-strap sandal.

The cone heel is a shoe named after its heel. The heel is literally the shape of an ice-cream cone, starting wide at the top and tapering toward the bottom, giving it a sturdier and more futuristic feel than the stiletto. This innovative heel was invented by French footwear designer Maud Frizon, who started her fashion career as a model working for the houses of Patou, Nina Ricci, and Courrèges. In the 1960s, there was no such role as a fashion stylist, so models were expected to do their own hair and make-up and come equipped with classic accessories to help style the couturier's clothes. If shoes were supplied they tended

> "Oh yes, I love to do shoes. I'm not a fetishist but I love to do shoes."
>
> Karl Lagerfeld

to be rather unimaginative, so Frizon decided to start creating her own more up-tempo designs. They were such a success that in 1969 she opened her own-name boutique in St-Germain-des-Prés, presenting her first show of hand-cut and finished shoes in 1970. Frizon made her name with unexpected juxtapositions of materials such as canvas and crocodile skin or matte suede working against the shiniest of satins, but her greatest innovation was the cone heel, a shape that began appearing in her shoe designs toward the end of the 1970s. On March 28, 1978, the *New York Magazine* urged its readers to "note the new cone heel by Maud Frizon" and featured a cuffed ankle boot in baby-soft raspberry suede and a beige suede boot with French rabbit trim.

Although Frizon's new heel featured in the runway collections of Thierry Mugler and Azzedine Alaia, it was not until the mid-1980s that it really caught on in mainstream fashion, hitting its stride with the power-dressing trend that dominated the second half of the decade. With the rise of women entering male bastions of power and the dominance of Margaret Thatcher, the first female prime minister of the United Kingdom, fashion journalists and style gurus began analyzing the working woman's wardrobe. In 1980, John T. Molloy had written *Women Dress for Success*, one of the first books to advise how best to present oneself in the office environment. He advised that "the best shoe for the businesswoman is the plain pump, in a dark color with a closed toe and heel. The heel should be about an inch and a half high." Molloy clearly thought high heels inappropriate—women were unable to project an image of authority in such a sexy shoe. Many disagreed however, and the stiletto in an extreme form by Givenchy, YSL, or their many copies was worn with vividly colored padded-shouldered suits and backcombed hair.

Molloy's sober businesswoman in plain pumps and the sexy power dresser in spike heels were polar opposites—frumpy versus glamazon—and for women who wanted to perch somewhere in the middle, the cone heel was perfect. It had the height but also a width of heel that made it easier to walk in and was less reminiscent of the ball-busting dominatrix. Cone heels appeared on Bruno Magli's peep-toed pumps, Andrea Pfister's slingbacks, and Frizon's cavalier boots. Pfister wittily played with the heel's name by making it look like a *trompe l'œil* multicolored ice-cream that appeared to drip down the back of the shoe. In the 2010s, the cone heel reappeared, most notably at the House of Lanvin but this time in a towering, rather than comfortable form—its wearable proportions were ignored to fit with the maximalism of early twenty-first century fashion.

below:
1980s cone
Model Christy Turlington wears a Donna Karan outfit with Maud Frizon silver high-heel sandals (1986).

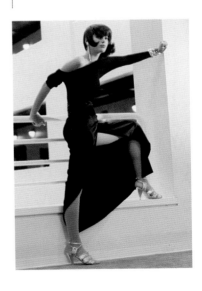

INDEX

Page numbers in *italics* refer to caption

300 (2006) 35

A

A. F. Vandevorst *66*
Abdul-Jabar, Kareem 185
Abrahams, Harold 187
Acme 154
Acne *75, 87, 103*
Adam Ant 60, 178
Adidas 181, *187*
   "Stan Smith" 182, 183–185
Adrian 151, 212
Aguerre, Fernando and Santiago 38
Akris *142*
Alaia, Azzedine 35, 176, 177, 250
Albert, Prince Consort 110
Albert slipper *107, 109,* 110–111, *111*
d'Alencon, Emilienne 96
Allen, Richard 174–176
Alpina 248
Amies, Hardy 71
And God Created Women (1956) 101
Anderson, Pamela 130
Anello and Davide 142, 239
Aniston, Jennifer 7, 21
ankle boots 202–207
ankle straps 190–193
Anne of Bohemia 80
Annie Hall (1977) 161
Antigua Casa Crespo 53
Antonoff, Rachel 169
Aperlai *69, 206*
Aragon, Louis 203
Arentz, Gertrude 107
Argence, Alfred 191
Arletty 63
Armani *203*
Armstrong, Louis 159, *159*
Armstrong, Rebecca 39
Arquette, Rosanna 206–207
Art Deco 43
Ashish *154, 173, 217, 221, 221*
Asos 221
Aspinwall, Two Gun Nan 81
Assous, Andre 55
Astaire, Fred *104,* 110, 161, 200
AtomAge 165
Attila Giusti Leombruni 25
Atwood, Brian *213*
Aurore, L'97
Aussie Dogs 130
Autry, Gene 154
Avengers, The 243

B

Bailey, David 230, 243
Baker, Josephine 19, 20
Baker, Nicholson 138
Balenciaga 8, 35
ballet flats 12, 98–103, 201, 241
Bally 225
Balmain 35
Barbarella (1968) 57
Bardot, Brigitte 13, *27, 32,* 57, *58,*
   101, *101,* 204, 230

Barefoot in the Park (1967) 208
Barr, Ann *The Official Sloane Ranger*
   Handbook 201
Basie, Count 159
Bass, George Henry 208
Bates, John 102, 234
Battani 247
Bauhaus 206
Bayley, Stephen 61
Baywatch 130, 249
Bearpaw 130
Beatle boots 113, 142
de Beauvoir, Simone 101
Beckham, Victoria 60, *69, 69,* 165, 188
Bell, Quentin 6, 9, 19–20
Belle de Jour (1967) 241
Ben Hur (1959) *31,* 35
Bennett, L. K. 55, *55,* 231
Berardi, Antonio 188
Berluti 92
Berry, Tom 248
Biba 74, 213
biker boots 194–195
Bill Haley and the Comets 218
Bird, Isabella 80
Birkenstock sandal 7, 21, 43
Bizarre 164, 244
Black Pirate, The (1926) 178
Blackman, Honor 243–244, 245
Blahnik, Manolo 7, 21, 29, 54, 95, 97
   ankle straps 193
   Mary Janes 135, *135*
   pumps 149, 151
   stiletto heels 227
Blitz boots 206
Bloch, Jacob 100
Blondie 60
Blue Mountains Ugg 129
Blue Skies (1946) *104*
Blundstone boots 141
Body Map 205, 220
Boedecker, George Jr 50
Bon Jovi 157
Boot and Shoe Recorder 118
Bottega Veneta 35
Boucher, François *Daphnis and*
   Chloe 66
Boulala, Ali 221
Boulting, Enid *243*
Bow, Clara *47*
Bowerman, Bill 185, 186
Bowie, Angie 74
Bowie, David 64, 218
Boy George 119, 178, 205
Brand, Russell 114
Brando, Marlon 192, 194, *194*
Breakfast at Tiffany's (1961) 231
brogues 84–87, 214
Brooks Brothers 208
Bros 220
brothel creepers 8, 216–221
Brown Shoe Company 133, 169
Brown, Cocoa 58
Brown, Duckie 87
Brown, George Warren 133–134
Brubach, Holly 15
Bruce Boyer, G. 159
Brummell, Beau 114, 125
Bruni-Sarkozy, Carla 137, 230–231

buckles 42–43, 91, 96
Buffalo 74–75
Buñuel, Luis 241
Burberry 127, *127*
Burch, Tory *39,* 55, *81,* 85, 103
Burtman, Leonard 244
Bush, George W. 51
button boots 123, 144–147

C

Cagney, Jimmy 161
Cambridge, Duchess of 55
Campbell, Naomi *63,* 68, 176
Candies 50, 65
Caovilla, René 97, 193
Capezio 240
Capezio, Robert 12
Capezio, Salvatore 100, 101
Captain Blood (1935) 178
Cardin, Pierre 57, 248
Carroll, Lewis *Alice in Wonderland* 133
Carter, Angela 192
Cartner-Morley, Jess 69, 197
Carvela 51, 215
Carven 75
Castañer 55
Castañer, Lorenzo and Isabel 54
Castillo, Edmund 227
Castle, Irene 170–171, *171*
Castle, Vernon *171*
Cavalli, Roberto 60, 157
Chanel 29, *47,* 50, 68, *103,* 195, 230,
   241, 249
Chanel, Coco 113, 134, 198–199
Chariots of Fire (1981) 187
Charisse, Cyd 229, *229*
Charles Fox 178
Charles, Prince of Wales 10, 110, 231
Charlie Dunn's 157
Chase, Edna Woolman 211–212
Chaucer, Geoffrey *Canterbury Tales* 79
Chelsea boots 113, 123, 140–143,
   201, 240
Chernikova, Olga *118,* 119
Cherokee 65
Chevellard, Matthew 85, 111
Chic 160
Chinese feet binding 8, 63, 107
Chippewa 194
chisel toes 45, 239–240
Chloe 103, *127*
chopines 8, 63, 71
Chung, Alexa 221
Church's 87, 91–92
Churchill, Sir Winston *107*
Clare, Alberta 81
Clark, Nathan 214–215
Clark, Ossie 54
Clarks 214, 215, 244
Clash 220
Cleo B *75*
Cleopatra (1934) 20
Clergerie, Robert 231
Clinton, Bill 114
Clockwork Orange, A (1971) 174
clogs 9, 43, 46–51, 71, 75, 111,
   126, 137
   Ugg clogs *131*

Coach 55
Cobblers to the World 74
Coffeyvilles 153–154
Colbert, Claudette 20
Cole Haan *111,* 159–160
Cole, Cheryl 10
College Girl 247
Coltellacci, Giulio 57–58
Comme des Garçons 87, 103, 135
Comme Il Faut 171
cone heels 250–251
Connery, Sean 37i
Connolly, Brian 218
Connors, Jimmy 186
Converse "All Star" 181–183, 185, *187*
Cordero, Calleen 50, *51*
Costiff, Michael 179
Courrèges, André 102, 134, 204, 241,
   246, 248, 250
court shoes 148–151
Cover Girl (1944) *149*
Coward, Noël *107,* 110
cowboy boots 9–10, 152–157
Cowell, Simon 137
Cowie, John 37
Cox, Patrick 75, 114, 176, 177
Craddock-Terry 241
Croc 50–51, *234*
Cromwell shoes 164
Croslite 51
Crowe, Russell 32, 114
Cruickshank, George 125
Cruise, Tom 156
Cuban heels 9, 10, 93, 97, 112–115, 142
   cowboy boots 153, *154*
   spectator shoes *160*
Cubine, John 153
Cubism 43
Cult 206

D

Dali, Salvador 53, 203
Damned, The (1969) 83
Daniel Green 110
Darin, Bobby 136
Dassler, Adolf 183, 185
Davidson, Carolyn 185
Davis, Miles 208
Dayton 194–195
de Havilland, Terry 13, 29, 63, 74, 75, 227
   springolator mules *228,* 229
de la Renta, Oscar 250
Dean, James 208, *208,* 218
Deckers Outdoor Corporation 130
Deee-Lite 66
Del Toro 111
Della Valle, Diego 25
Delmain, Herbert 224
Delman 225
Delman, Herman 64
DeMille, Cecil B. 156
Deneuve, Catherine *239,* 241
Depp, Johnny 178, 230
desert boots 214–215, 217
Desperately Seeking Susan (1985)
   203, 206–207
Dewlen, Al *The Bone Pickers* 229
di Fabrizio, Pasquale 137

Di Mauro 197
Diana, Princess 10, 102, 103, 231
Dietrich, Marlene 150, 198, 240
Dior Homme *113*, 114
Dior, Christian 35, 97, *97*, 134, *197*, 199, *207*, 223, 224, 229, 243
Disney, Walt 133
Doc Martens 172–177, 220
Dogg, Snoop 160
Dolce & Gabbana 35, *72*, *149*
Dolcis 119, 227, 245
Dolomite 248
dominatrix shoes *35*, *65*, *192*
Donen, Stanley *99*, 101
Dors, Diana 226
Douglas, Michael 137
Dr Scholls 43, 233–234, *236*
Duchovny, David 192
Dudley, William A 161
Dunlop 138, *138*
Duran Duran 54
Dylan, Bob *141*, 142, 215

E

Earth Inc. 236
Earth Shoes 233, 234–236
Eastman 25
Eco-Waste Coalition 39
Edward Green 86
Edwards, Bernard 160
Egan, Rusty 205
Eisman, Kathryn *How to Tell a Man by his Shoes* 183
Ekland, Britt *57*, 74
    Sensual Beauty and How to Achieve It 192
Elias, Eileen 145
Elizabeth II 240
Elkin, Newton 191
Ellington, Duke 159
Eluard, Paul 203
Empress of Iran 223
Emu 130
Epart 53
espadrilles 52–55, 137
Evert, Chris 181
Evins, David 8, 20, 63, *149*, 150–151, *191*, 192
exercise sandals 232–237
Exotique 244
Exposition des Arts Décoratifs, Paris 43

F

F-Troupe *87*, *87*
Fairbanks, Douglas 178
Fantastique 244
Fantasy Heels 245
Favreau 118
Federal Trade Commission 237
Fellowes, Daisy 204
Ferragamo, Salvatore 7, 8, 10, 40, 63, *64*
    ankle boots 204
    Audrey Hepburn *100*, 101–102
    cowboy boots 156
    peep-toes 212
    sandals *19*, *20*, 21
    slap soles 88–89
    stiletto heels 224, 225
    wedges 71–72
fetish footwear 12, 35, 162–165
    kinky boots 242–245
    staggerers 123, *164*, *164*
    thigh-high boots 57–61
Fields, Duggie 218
Fieramosca, Franco 102
Finsk 75

Fiorucci 126
Fireman, Paul 187
FitFlops 38, 237
Fitz-Gibbon, Bernice 13
flip-flops 36–39
floating heels 188–189
Florsheim 12, 86, 87
Fluevog, John 43, 66, 68, 97
Flynn, Erroll 178
Foam Creations 51
Fonda, Jane *57*, 187
Footwear 223
Ford, Lita 223
Ford, Tom 198
Forever 21 35
Fortune 92
Foster, William 187
Fragonard, Jean Honoré 66
    The Swing 28
Frank Wright 142
Frederick's 228–229
Freed of London Ltd 100
Freedman, Rita 231
Freeman, Hadley 129
Freeman, Hardy and Willis 245
French Sole 102–103
Freud, Sigmund 12, 163
Frick, Robert 51
Friedmann, Martin 189
Frizon, Maud 8, *151*, 250, 251, *251*
Frye boots 136–137
Frye, John A. 136
Funck, Dr Herbert 172
Funny Face (1957) *99*, 101, 230
Fury, Billy 218

G

G. H. Bass 169, 208
Gable, Clark 200
Gainsbourg, Serge 57
gaiter boots 104
Gallagher, Noel 215
Galliano, John *28*, *66*, *192*, 201, *205*, 225
galoshes 120–121, 203
Galsworthy, John 79
Gamba 100
Gandolfi 103
Gardner, Ava 150, *168*, *211*, 226
Garland, Judy 20, 63, *64*, 151
Garwood, Lawrence 35
Gaucher, Jean-Marc 103
Gaultier, Jean Paul *177*, 220
Geiger, Kurt 7, 21, *51*
Gentleman's Jodhpur 65
George 227
George Cox 217, 220
Gere, Richard 60
Giannini, Frida 201
Gianuto Rossi 61
Gibson, Charles Dana 146
Giese, Dave 48
Gilda *191*, 192
Gina 13, 225, 227
Ginsberg, Allen *Howl* 101
Gisele 38
Givenchy *21*, 35, *157*, *205*, 251
Gladiator (2000) 32
gladiator sandals 13, 30–35
Glamour 228
go-go boots 8, 204, 246–247
Godey's Lady's Book 80, 108
Golo Boots 247
Goodyear 87, 92, 114, 195
Goodyear, Charles 120, 126, 181
Gordon, Bryony 127
Goss, Luke and Matt 220
Gough, John 244

GQ 92
Grable, Betty *191*, 192, 194
Graduate, The (1967) 208
Grant, Cary 110
Grease 50
Great Gatsby, The (1974) 85
Green, Daniel 110
Greer, Germaine *The Female Eunuch* 48
Grenson 87
Griggs, Bill 173
Grimes, William 68–69
Gucci 85, 200–201, *224*, 227
Guess 157
Guinness, Daphne 198
gumboots 124–127
Guns N' Roses 157
Gyllenhal, Maggie *234*

H

H. Stern 38
Haddon, Vicky 114
Haillet, Robert 183–185
Halpern, Joan and David 199
Hamrick, Randall B. *How to Look Good in College* 169
Hanson, Lyndon, V. 50
Hardy, Pierre 8, *21*, 50, 69, *75*, *103*, 187
    Mary Janes *135*
    peep-toes *212*
    pumps *151*
    stacked heels *136*
Haring, Keith 69
Harlow, Jean 27, 29, 212
Harper's Bazaar 204
Harris, Richard 114
Harry, Debby *57i*, 60
Harry, Prince 110
Hasbeen *50*, 51, *142*
Hattersley, Giles 217
Havaianas *37*, 38, 39, *127*
Hayashida, Teruyoshi 208
Hayes, Isaac 65
Hayworth, Rita *149*, 150, *191*, 192
heels 9
Heim, Jacques 197
Hemingway, Wayne and Geraldine 177, 220
Hendrix, Jimi 136, 156
Henry VIII 133
Hepburn, Audrey 12, *99*, 100, 101, 230, *231*
Hepburn, Katherine 93
Hermès 55, *79i*
Herzigova, Eva 176
Hessian boots 125
Hi Brow 247
high heels 9, 77
High School Confidential (1958) 228
Hilfiger, Tommy 201, 209
Hilton, Paris 130
Hines, Earl 159
Hoby 125
Hoffman, Dustin 201, 208
Holah, David 205
Holmes, Oliver Wendell 107
Hope, Emma 97
House of Fraser *214*
House of Harlow *23*, 25
House of Worth 109
Household Magazine, The 139
Howl's Moving Castle (2004) 146
Hoyle, Mick 87
Hudson 114
Hulanicki, Barbara 74, 213
Hunter Wellingtons 15, *125*, 126, 127, *127*

Hutchinson, Hiram 126
Hyer, Charles 153–154

I

I. Miller 189
Interview with the Vampire (1994) 206
Ishibashi, Shojiro 40
Ivory, June 154

J

J. Artola 35
J. Crew 103, 209
J. Press 208
J. W. Foster & Sons 187
jackboots 82–83, *91*
Jackson, Bo 181
Jackson, Michael 137, *137*, 209
Jacobs, Marc 35, 85, 89, 103, 135, *213*
Jacobs, Raymond and Eleanor 234, 235
Jagger, Bianca 74
Jam 215, 220
Janet Reger 192
Jean-Gaborit 61
Jefferson, Thomas 91
Jimmy Choo 7, 10, 13, 21, *24*, 25, 195
    stiletto heels 227
    Uggs *130*, 131, *131*
    Wellingtons 127, *127*
Joan & David 199
Joan of Arc 58, 81
Jodhpur boots 141
John Lobb 86
John, Elton 64, 65, 137, 174
Johnson, Don 53
Johnson, Samuel 85
Johnston & Murphy 86, 161
Jolie, Angelina 127
Jones, Brian *114*
Jones, Erasmus *The Man of Manners* 42
Jones, Grace 160, *197i*
Jones, Stephen 205
Joplin, Janis 136, 156
Jordan, Michael 181, *185*, 186, *187*
Jourdan, Charles 212, 224, 225
JP Tod 25, *25*
Julianelli *145*, 225
June, Jennifer 153
Justin 154, 157

K

K. Jacques 32
Kagami, Kei 189
Kalso, Anne 234
Kamen, Dean 181
Kamikaze Shoes 74
Karan, Donna 89, *251*
Kate Spade 55
Keaton, Diane 161
Keds 159
Keklikian, Jacques 32
Kélian, Stephane 192
Kelly, Grace 20, *53*, 151, 223
Kennedy, Jackie *79*, 240
Kennedy, John F. 53, *139*, 208, 227
Kenneth Cole 157
Kenzo 103
Kerouac, Jack 101
Kier, Lady Miss 66
Kilgore, Marcia 237
Kings of Leon 142
kinky boots 242–245
Kinky Boots (2005) 245
Kinney Shoes 225
Kirby, John *105*

Kirkwood, Nicholas 13–15, 69, *69*, *75*, *151*, *223*, 227
KISS 64
kitten heels 10, 38, 126, *198*, 230–231
Klaw, Irving 58
Koolaburra 130
Kors, Michael 32i, 156–157
Koslow, Brian 92
Kramer vs Kramer 201
Kraus, Karl 163
Kravitz, Lenny 114
Kumagai, Tokio 135
Kunzle, David *Fashion and Fetishism* 164
Kurdash, Mehmet 225, 226

L

laces 42, 91
Lacroix, Christian *21*, *29*, *72*, 97
Lady Gaga 189, *189*
Lagerfeld, Karl 68, 103, 240, 250
Laird & Schoeber 197
Lama, Tony 154
Lane, Rhonda 246
Lanvin 55, 103, 193, *230*, 231, 251
Larin *103*, *151*
Lauren, Ralph 50, 156, *157*, 209, 214
Lawrence, Cooper 193
Le Bon, Simon 54
Léger, Hervé 176, *177*
Lennon, John 142
Leno, Dan 47–48
Lestage, Nicholas 95
Leto, Jared 51
Levine, Beth 29, *74*, 151, 189, 191, 199, 228
Levis 136, 194, 209
Levy, Deborah 220–221
Lewis, Jerry Lee 218
Lichfield, Patrick *57*
Lichtenstein, Roy 229
Liddle, Eric 187
Life 168, 191
Lilley & Skinner 12, 119
Lim, Phillip 55
Linea *214*
lingerie 28
Liverpool Rubber Company 138
loafers 200–201, 241
Loake 91–92
Lobb, John 159
Lollobrigida, Gina *223*, 225
London Life 164
Longley, Jay R. 38
Lord & Taylor 100
Loren, Sophia 13
Lorenzi 69
Lorenzi, Gianmarco *81*, 213
Louboutin, Christian 8, 13, *29*, 47, 55, 69, *69*, 97
  ankle boots *205*
  ankle straps 193, *193*
  button boots 145, *145*, 146, *147*, *147*
  fetish shoes 165
  kinky boots 244, *245*
  kitten heels *230*, 231
  Mary Janes *134*
  peep-toes 211, *211*, 213, *213*
  pumps 151, *151*
  stiletto heels 227
Louis heels 10, 20, 28, 43, 60, 66, *77*, 94–97, 113, 118
  button boots 147, *147*
  pumps 149–150
  tango shoes 171

Louis Vuitton 35, 55, 60, 83, *95*
  kinky boots *243*
  Mary Janes *135*
Love, Courtney 135, 177, 195
Lucas, George 142
Lucchese Company of Texas 154
Ludwych & Lodger 87
Lundsten, Julia 75
Lydig, Rita de Acosta 96
Lynch, David 165

M

Mackay, Andy 218
MacNee, Patrick 245
Madonna 60, 66, 103, *203*, 207
Maertens, Dr Klaus 172
Magli, Bruno 50, 241, 251
Mansfield, Jayne 228
Marcos, Imelda 10
Margiela, Martin 40–41, *41*
Marie Antoinette 95
Mark Charles *205*
Marr, Johnny 215
Marsalis, Wynton 161
Marshall, Allen and Margaret 169
Martin, Ricky 114
Massaro, Raymond 198, 199
Massaro, Sébastien 230
Master John 65
May, Theresa 231
Mayfield, Curtis 65
MBT 234, 236–237
McCardell, Claire 100
McCarthy, Joseph 119
McCartney, Stella 137, 227
McKinney, Henry Nelson 139
McLaren, Malcolm 218, 219
McQueen, Alexander 13, 32, *35*, *63*, 206, 207
McQueen, Steve 208, 215
Messel, Oliver 72
Meuter, Catherine 189
Miami Vice 53
Michael, George 54
Michonet 109
Middleton, Kate 51, 55, 55i, 69, 165
Midler, Bette 9
Milholland, Inez 81
Miller, Savannah 32–35
Miller, Sienna 75, 103
Milne, A. A. *Winnie the Pooh* 133
Minnetonka 24, 25
Miranda, Carmen *20*, 64
Mission 206
Missoni *37*, 127
Mistinguett 29
Mitsubishi 37
Miu Miu 50, 75, 85, 103, *195*, 195, 221
Mix, Tom 153, 154
Mme. Demorest's What to Wear 109
moccasins 22–25, 111, 137
Molloy, John T. *Women Dress for Success* 251
Moltissimo *226*
Molyneaux, Edward 197
Mondrian, Piet *239*, 240
Monk, Thelonius 208
Monroe, Marilyn 12, 27, *71*, *153*, 192, 225, 226, 228
Montreal Gazette 65
Moon Boots 248–249
Moonlighting 187
Moore, Demi 177
Moore, Peter *185*, 186
Morris, Olivia 87
Morrison, Miranda 38, 39

Morrison, Patt 27, 29
Morton, Digby 71
Morton, Jelly Roll 159
Moss, Kate 13, 15, 24, 32, 75, 102, 103, *125*, 127, *129*, 179, 221, 230
Motley Crüe 157
Mr & Mrs Smith (2005) 127
Muffy's 169
Mugler, Thierry 250
mules 8, 12, 26–29, 102, 111
  fetish shoes 164
  springolator mules 228–229
Müller, Karl 236–237
Muñiz, Alicia 171

N

N. W. Ayer & Son 139
Native Americans 23–24
needle heels 28
négligées 27–28
Nekola, Charlotte *Dream House* 134
Nelson, Gaylord 234, 235
New Look 13, 21, 32, 199, 223
New York Herald 133
New York Times 68, 170, 234–236
Newman, Paul 208
Newton John, Olivia 50
Nicholson, Geoff *Footsucker* 193
Nicholson, Jack 51
Night Porter, The (1974) 83
Nike 41, *41*, 160, 181
  "Air Jordan" 185–186, *187*
Nina Ricci 189, 250
Nocona Boot Company 154
Norris, Henry Lee 126
North British Rubber Company 126
Novak, Kim 165
Nudie 24
Nunn-Bush *159*
Nureyev, Rudolph 57, 100

O

O'Neill, Ron 65
Oasis 195
Oasis (band) 215
Obama, Barack 231
Obama, Michelle 231
Oduwole, Bayode 87
Office 195
Official Preppy Handbook, The 209
Olicker, Richard 99
Olympia, Charlotte *103*
One Million Years B. C. (1966) 24, 35
Otero, La Belle 96, 109
Outcault, Richard Felton 133
Owens, Rick 82, 83, *187*
Oxfords 90–93, 114, 201, 214
  spectator shoes 158–161

P

Pacino, Al 51
Paciotti, Cesare 13, 227
paddock boots 141
Page, Bettie 229
Palter de Liso 64
Paltrow, Gwyneth 7, 21
Parker, Sarah Jessica 13, 14, 35, 193
Patou 250
Pavlova, Anna 100
peep-toes 197, 210–213
Pelé, Edson 183
Penthouse 136
Personal Finance 51

Perugia, André 8, 20, 29, 63, 150, 228
  ankle boots 203, 204, *204*
  ankle straps 191
  floating heels 188–189
  stiletto heels 224
Peter the Great 117
Petit, Roland 100
Petridis, Alexis 141
Pfister, Andrea 7, 21, *21*, 157, 251
Philips, Lindsay 39
Picture Post 224
pilgrim pumps 102, 238–241
Pinet 53, 171, 189
Pinet, Jean-Louis François 96
Pinkett-Smith, Jada 193
pirate boots 178–179
Pirates of the Caribbean 178
platform shoes 8, 10, 62–69
Playboy 244
Pleaser 147, *228*
Plimsoll, Samuel 138
plimsolls 138–139
Poiret, Denise 118
Poiret, Paul 118, 170
Pokit 87
Pompadour, Madame de 27, 29, 95, 95, 107
Porsche *111*
de Pougy, Lianne 96, 109–110
poulaines 17, 44–45
Prada 13, 29, *29*, 32, 66, *74*, *86*, *133*, *198*, 221
Prada, Miuccia 75, 137
Preciosa 189
Pretty Ballerina 103
Pretty Woman (1990) 60
Price & Sons Shoes 245
Price, Antony 218
Prince 113
Pritchett, Oliver 39
Pucci 127
Pugh, Gareth 114, 206
Puma 181, 183
pumps 148–151
  pilgrim pumps 102, 238–241

Q

Quant, Mary 102, 126, 134, 239

R

R. M. Williams 114, *114*
Rabanne, Paco 248
Rag & Bone 93
Rainbow 38
Ramones 182
Ravel 119
Raverat, Gwen *Period Piece* 146
Ray-Bans 209
Rayne 189, 225, 240
Reagan, Nancy 150–151
Reagan, Ronald 54
Rebel Without a Cause (1955) 218
Red Or Dead 177, 220
Redford, Robert *85*, 208
Reebok 103, 181, 237
  "Freestyle" *186*, 187
Reed, Oliver 114
Reef 38
Rellik 179
Rendlesham, Lady Clare 243
Repetto, Rosa 100, 101, 103
Rétif de la Bretonne, Nicolas 12, 163
Rexford, Nancy E. 109
Rhodes, Zandra 227
Richard II 80
Richardson, Samuel *Pamela* 42

Richardson, W. H. *Boot and Shoe Manufacturer's Assistant and Guide* 108
Richie, Nicole 23, 24–25
Ridgeley, Andrew 54
riding boots 78–81
Rihanna 35, 61
Robe, The (1953) 31
Roberts, Bartholomew 178
Roberts, Julia 60
Rockwell, Hannah 53
Rodgers, Nile 160
Rodrigues, Narcisco 135
Rogers, Roy 154
Rolling Stones 142
Romea 89
Rossi, Sergio 13, 61, *69*, 191, 193, *207*
    stiletto heels 227, *227*
Rossi, William A. *The Sex Life of the Foot and Shoe* 20, 206
Rossimoda 97
Rotten, Johnny 220
Rowley, Cynthia 35
Roxy Music 218
Run DMC *181*, 185
Rupert Sanderson *32*, 168, 169, *169*, 221
Ruppert's 231
Russell & Bromley 225
Russell, Ken 217
Russian boots 118–19

S

Sabrina (1954) 230
Sacha 119
Sachs, Maxwell 228
saddle shoes 168–169
Saint-Laurent, Yves *21*, *39*, 54, *54*, 57, 69, 134, 243
    cowboy boots *157*
    pilgrim pumps *239*, 240–241
    stacked heels *136*
    see also YSL
Saks Fifth Avenue 189
Sallon, Philip 178
Salon Kitty (1976) 83
Salon, Joseph 64
Sanchez, Paula 164
sandals 6–7, 9, 17, 18–21
    exercise sandals 232–237
    gladiator sandals 13, 30–35
Sander, Jil 75, 89, *92*, 195
Sandgrens 48
Sarkozy, Nicolas 137, 231
Sartorialist 206
Sartre, Jean-Paul 101
Saval, Ted 64
Schiaparelli, Elsa 134, 203–204
Schneider Boots 82
Scholl, William Mathias 233
Schuh 207
Scott, Ron 65
Sears catalogs 194
Sebastian 61
Seven Year Itch, The (1955) 228
Sevigny, Chloë *51*, *142*
Sex and the City 13, 14, 15, 35, 227
Sex Pistols 220
Shaft (1971) 65
Sheba Publishing Company 244
Shelly's Shoes 77
Shepherd, Cybill 187
Shepherd, E. H. 133
Sherman, Allan 12
Shillan, Bill 65
Shoe Fashion Guild 204, 211
Shoe Retailer 171

shoe-boots 207
Shoemaker, John 194
Shrimpton, Jean 230, 234, 243
Sigerson Morrison 38–39
Sigerson, Kari 38
Simmons, Kimora Lee 193
Simon, Carly 31
Simons, Raf 83, 177
Sinatra, Frank 137, 220
Siouxsie and the Banshees 60, 206
Siouxsie Sioux 60
Sisters of Mercy 206
Skrewdriver 176
slap soles 88–89
Slimane, Hedi *113*, 114
slingbacks 196–199
slippers 9, 24, 27, 96, 106–111
Smith, Brian 130
Smith, Stan *181*, 182, 185
Smiths 215
Smokey Robinson and the Miracles 247
sneakers 138, 139, 180–187
Snow, Carmel 204
Snuggies 111
Solarz, Stephen 10
Some Like It Hot (1950) 104, 105
Sonny and Cher 24, *137*
Spalding 139, 168
Sparkes-Hall, J. 141
Spartacus (1960) 31
spats 104–105
spectator shoes 65, 158–161
Spencer, Mimi 197
Spice Girls 74–75
springolator mules 228–229
St. Clement of Alexandria 20
St. Jerome 20
stacked heels 136–137
Stacy Adams 159, 161
Stallone, Sylvester 137
Stan's of Battersea 45
Stanton, Eric *163*, 164
Star Wars 142
Starke, Frederick 243–244
Stedman, Shane 129, 130
Steiger, Walter *75*, *226*, 227
stiletto heels 9, 10, 13, 45, 64, 74, 134, 139, 177, 222–227, 251
    fetish shoes 164
Stoker, Bram *Dracula* 206
Stoker, Joanne 89, *89*
Stone *138*
Strange, Steve 119, 178, 205
Strokes 182
Strummer, Joe 220
Sui, Anna 135, 157
Sultan toe 212
Sun 205
Sunday Times, The 64, 195
Superfly (1972) 65
Surrealism 203
Sutcliffe, John 165
Sweet 64, 218
SwitchFlop 39

T

T. U. K. 220
tabi 40–41
Taglioni, Marie 99, *99*
Take Ivy (1965) 208–209
tango shoes 170–171
Tatehana, Noritaka 189, *189*
Taylor, Chuck 182
Taylor, Elizabeth 20, 198, 241
Tecnica 248, 249
Temperley *58*
Temple, Shirley 134
Tenniel, Sir John 133

tennis shoes 138–139
Thatcher, Margaret 54, 251
The Spats Factory 105
Theyskens, Olivier 189
Thierry and Sons 108
thigh high boots 56–61
Tigre, Fernando 37, 38
Time 51, 239
Tony Lama 157
Top Gun (1985) 156
Topshop 35, *108*, 139, 221
Townshend, Pete 174
trainers 74–75, 177, 237
Trasko, Mary 224
Travolta, John *113*, *113*, 156
Treacy, Phillip 15
Trickers Ltd 86–87, 110
Troentorp 48
Troy, Seymour 72
Truth or Dare (1991) 66
Turlington, Christy 251
TV Times 244
Tweedie, Ethel 80–81
Twiggy *133*, 134, 234, 239
Tyler, Richard 170

U

UGG 130
Ugg Australia 130, 131
Uggleno 48
Uggs 111, 119, 128–131, 195
Underground *218*, 220, 221
Ungaro, Emanuel 57
Urban Cowboy 156
UturnUtopia 147

V

Vadim, Roger 101
valenkis 116–119, 129
Valentino 231
Van Doren, Mamie 228
Van Noten, Dries 35
Vans 25, 25
Vargas, Alberto 197
Vargas, Antonio 192
Vault-Este 108
Verne, Jules 146
Vernon, Polly 203, 233
Versace 68
Vevers, Stuart 231
Vicious, Sid 220
Victoria Advocate 212
Victorio 171
Viktor & Rolk 47i
Vionnet, Mademoiselle 134
Visconti, Luchino 83
Visser, Margaret 9
Vivier, Roger 8, 15, *42*, *43*, 55, 63–64
    kinky boots 245
    Louis heels 97, *97*
    pilgrim pumps 239, *239*, 240–241
    pumps *150*, 151
    stiletto heels 223–224, 225
Vogue 74, 150, 192, 197, 211, 224, 227, 230, 243
Vreeland, Diana 74

W

Wallace Collection, London 66
Wallace Elliott Company 110
Walpole, Horace 27
Wang, Alexander *91*, 93
Wang, Vera *21*, *29*
Warmbat 130
Washington Post 110
Watanabe, Junya 86

Watson, Shane 194
Watteau, Antoine 66
Waverley Shoes of London 74
Wayne, John 200
wedges 17, 70–75
weejuns 208–209
Weitzman, Stuart 35, 97
Welch, Raquel *24*, 25
Weller, Paul 215
Wellington boots 124–127, 153, 201
Wellington, Duke of 123, 125
Wells, H. G. 146
Wesco 194
West, Jeffrey 114, 114i
West, Kanye 111
West, Mae 203
Westminster, Duke of 198
Westwood, Vivienne 15, *29*, *35*, *42*, 43, 218, 219
    ballet flats *103*
    brogues *87*
    fetish shoes 165
    galoshes *121*
    Mary Janes *135*
    Oxfords *93*
    pirate boots 178–179, *179*, 205–206
    platform shoes *63*, 66–68, 69
    slingbacks 199
    slippers *110*
    thigh-high boots 58–60, 61
Weyco Group 161
Wham! 54
Who 174
Wild Ones, The 194, *194*
William, Prince 69, 110, 165
Williams, Cayte 41
Williamson, Matthew 24, 121i
Willie, John 164, 244
Wilson, Elizabeth *Memoirs of an Anti-Heroine* 239
Winchell, Walter 151
Windsor, Duchess of 20, 198, 241
Windsor, Duke of *85*, 86, 92, 160
Winehouse, Amy 103
Winfrey, Oprah 130, 230
Winger, Debra 156
winklepickers 17, 44–45
Winkworth, Jane 103
Winters, Shelley *Shelley, Sometimes Known as Shirley* 192
Wizard of Oz 151
Wohlford, Charlie 194
Wolfe, Tom "Funky Chic" 65
Worishofers *234*
World Archive 179
Worth, Charles Frederick 96

Y

Yamamoto, Yohji *174*
Yanturni/Yantorny, Pietro 9, 96, 171
Yock, Morris 37
York, Peter T*he Official Sloane Ranger Handbook* 201
YSL 54, *111*, *151*, 240, 241, 243, 251
    see also Saint-Laurent, Yves

Z

Zabot 75
Zaitsev, Vyacheslav 117
Zanatta, Giancarlo 248–249
Zanotti, Giuseppe 89
Zappa, Frank 156
Zappa, Moon Unit 200
Zdar 119
Zola, Emile 28
Zyldeberg, Régine 246

PICTURE CREDITS

KEY

Top = t / bottom = b / center = c / left = l / right = r / top left = tl / top center = tc / top right = tr / bottom left = bl / bottom center = bc / bottom right = br

The Advertising Archives: 159, 215t, 232. **Alamy:** 19 © Pictorial Press Ltd / Alamy, 40 © Travel Pictures / Alamy, 53 © Photos 12 / Alamy. **Art + Commerce:** 62 © Sølve Sundsbø / Art + Commerce. **Brian Atwood:** 213tr. **Ashish:** 154, 221. **G. H. Bass & Co:** 161, 209tl, 209bl. **Bata Shoe Museum, Toronto:** 88. **Manolo Blahnik:** 135bl. **The Bridgeman Art Library:** 76–77 © Wallace Collection, London, UK / The Bridgeman Art Library. **Catwalking:** 18, 33, 34, 49, 73, 78, 83, 132, 143, 148, 155, 172, 175, 179, 196, 202, 216, 219, 242, 249. **Jimmy Choo:** 24. **Cleo B:** 75tr. **Corbis:** 6b © Image Werks / CORBIS, 7t © Wolfgang Kaehler / CORBIS, 7b © Andreas Schlegel / fstop / CORBIS, 14 © Condé Nast Archive / CORBIS, 23, 26 © Leonard de Raemy / Sygma / CORBIS, 30 © Condé Nast Archive / CORBIS, 38 © Bettmann / CORBIS, 47 © John Springer Collection / CORBIS, 48 © Condé Nast Archive / CORBIS, 52 © Lama / epa / CORBIS, 58 © Bettmann / CORBIS, 85 © Hulton-Deutsch Collection/CORBIS, 94 © Hulton-Deutsch Collection / CORBIS, 101 © John Springer Collection / CORBIS, 105 © Hulton-Deutsch Collection / CORBIS, 113 © Bettmann / CORBIS, 122–123, 133 © Bettmann / CORBIS, 137 © Steve Schapiro / CORBIS, 139t © Condé Nast Archive / CORBIS, 145 © Courtesy of Museum of Textil y de la Indumentaria; Ramon Manent / CORBIS, 146 © Bettmann / CORBIS, 149 © Sunset Boulevard / Corbis, 162 © Ocean / CORBIS, 171b © CORBIS, 203 © Andy Schwartz / Sygma / CORBIS, 204 © Philadelphia Museum of Art / CORBIS, 239 © Condé Nast Archive / Corbis, 251 © Condé Nast Archive / CORBIS. **Del Toro Shoes:** 109. **F-Troupe:** 87br. **firstVIEW:** 90. **John Galliano:** 28t, 66, 192, 201, 205br, 225. **Getty Images:** 2 © WireImage / Getty Images, 6t © Alessia Pierdomenico / Bloomberg / Getty Images, 9, 27, 31, 37, 46 © AFP / Getty Images, 56, 57, 63, 70, 79, 91, 98, 99, 100 © AFP / Getty Images, 104 © Time & Life Pictures / Getty Images, 106, 107 © Popperfoto / Getty Images, 115, 124, 125, 128 © WireImage / Getty Images, 129, 131bl, 140, 141, 152, 153, 158 © Redferns / Getty Images, 166–167, 168, 173 © SSPL via Getty Images, 180 © Popperfoto / Getty Images, 181, 191 © Time & Life Pictures / Getty Images, 197, 208, 211, 217 © Gamma-Keystone via Getty Images, 223, 224, 235 © WireImage / Getty Images. **Caroline Groves:** 96 © Dan Lowe. **Pierre Hardy:** 21bc, 69bl, 75bl, 103br, 135tr, 136, 151br, 187br, 212. **House of Harlow 1960:** 22. **Nicholas Kirkwood:** 75tl, 150t, 222. **The Kobal Collection:** 84 © PARAMOUNT / THE KOBAL COLLECTION, 190 © COLUMBIA / THE KOBAL COLLECTION / CRONENWETH, FRANK, 194 © COLUMBIA / THE KOBAL COLLECTION, 229b MGM / THE KOBAL COLLECTION, 231b PARAMOUNT / THE KOBAL COLLECTION. **Larin:** 102bc, 151bl. **Christian Louboutin:** 29bc, 68br, 134, 144, 147, 205tr, 210, 213bl, 231t, 244. **Maison Martin Margiela:** 41tl. **Museo Salvatore Ferragamo:** 20t, 44, 64. **OWENSCORP:** 82, 187bl. **Prada:** 28bl, 74, 86, 198. **Repetto:** 102t. **Rex Features:** 112 © ITV/Rex Features, 184 © Sipa Press/Rex Features, 238 © Sipa Press / Rex Features. **Sergio Rossi:** 227. **Rossimoda Shoe Museum, Foto Dives of Gianfranco Brusegan:** 20bl, 20bc, 20br, 21bl, 21br, 28bc, 28br, 39tl, 39bl, 72, 96bl, 96bc, 96br, 97bl, 97bc, 97br, 111tr, 111bl, 137t, 150bl, 150bc, 150br, 156, 170, 171t, 205tl, 213br. **Rupert Sanderson:** 32, 169. **Scala:** 16–17 © 2010. Photo Scala, Florence—courtesy of the Ministero Beni e Att. Culturali. **The Shoe Collection, Northampton Museums & Art Gallery:** 65, 139b, 164, 165. **Shutterstock:** 87tl. **Walter Steiger:** 226. **Joanne Stoker:** 89. **Temperley:** 59 © Temperley London Autumn Winter 2008/09 show—boots by Brian Atwood for Temperley. **Underground:** 218, 220. **A. F. Vandevorst:** 67. **Victoria and Albert Museum, London:** 243. **Vivienne Westwood:** 29br, 35, 42, 60, 87bl, 93, 102bl, 110, 120, 135tl, 178, 199. **Matthew Williamson:** 121. **Yay Micro:** 116.

ACKNOWLEDGMENTS

To brave and beautiful Charlotte,
also Jane Laing, Mark Fletcher, Ruth Patrick, and all at Quintessence; literary agent Sheila Ableman; Maggie Norden; all at Sassoon Academy; Lionel Marsden; Noel East; Joanna and Clive Ball; Mary, Ryan, and Kaleigh.

Quintessence would like to thank all the designers who generously provided images for this book.